PRISONER
FOR
POLYGAMY

PRISONER
— FOR —
POLYGAMY

The Memoirs and Letters
of Rudger Clawson at the Utah
Territorial Penitentiary,
1884–87

EDITED BY

Stan Larson

UNIVERSITY OF ILLINOIS
Urbana and Chicago

Library of Congress Cataloging-in-Publication Data

Clawson, Rudger.
    Prisoner for Polygamy : the memoirs and letters of Rudger Clawson at the Utah
Territorial Penitentiary, 1884–87 / edited and with an introduction by Stan Larson.
    p. cm.
    Includes bibliographical references and index.
    ISBN 0-252-01861-3
    1. Clawson, Rudger—Correspondence. 2. Bigamy—Utah. 3. Church of Jesus Christ
of Latter-day Saints—Apostles—Correspondence. 4. Mormon Church—Apostles—
Correspondence. 5. Prisoners—Utah—Correspondence. I. Larson, Stan. II. Title.
BX8695.C32A4 1993
289.3'092—dc20
[B]   91–16365
                                                                                    CIP

To
Tim, James, Dan, Debbie, and Melissa

CONTENTS

ACKNOWLEDGMENTS

Sincere gratitude is expressed to Obert C. Tanner (whose grandfather, Ezra T. Clark, was imprisoned with Rudger Clawson in 1887) for his funding in support of the editing of this volume. Gregory C. Thompson of Special Collections at the Marriott Library, University of Utah, where the Rudger Clawson Collection resides, provided constant encouragement during this project. A. J. Simmonds of the Merrill Library at Utah State University was very helpful, as well as the staff members of the Lee Library at Brigham Young University, the library of the Utah State Historical Society, the Utah State Archives, and the University of Arizona at Tucson. The staff at the Historical Department of the Church of Jesus Christ of Latter-day Saints assisted as much as they are allowed, since the church hierarchy has restricted the collections of the three imprisoned apostles—Lorenzo Snow, George Q. Cannon, and Francis M. Lyman—and these documents cannot be examined.

Marian Bond, a granddaughter of Rudger Clawson, found additional manuscripts of Clawson's memoirs in the trunk in her basement and donated them to the Marriott Library. Two of Clawson's grandchildren and Roy Hoopes and Linda Tracy donated to the Marriott Library the cryptic 17 October 1904 letter of Clawson to Pearl Udall. David S. Hoopes, another grandson, donated the 1910 graduation photo of Pearl Udall, with Clawson's inscription on the back. Maria S. Ellsworth and Elma Udall shared with me the letters and family tradition concerning Rudger Clawson's post-Manifesto marriage to Pearl Udall. The two transcriptions of Pitman shorthand in Rudger Clawson's 1887 prison letters were made by LaJean Purcell Carruth of Louisville, Kentucky. Rosa Mae M. Evans granted permission to quote from the list of Mormon polygamists in her master's thesis.

The quality of this volume has been much improved by the corrections and suggestions of Everett L. Cooley, Brigham D. Madsen, Dean L. May, William Mulder, and Richard S. Van Wagoner, but the editor is fully responsible for any errors. Elizabeth Dulany and Becky Standard of the University of Illinois Press nurtured it through the publication process. The editor presents these prison memoirs and letters to the public with the conviction not only that they have value and interest to people in the last decade of the twentieth century, but also that Rudger Clawson, who has been dead for fifty years, would be pleased.

Prisoner for Polygamy

INTRODUCTION

Rudger Clawson (1857–1943) was a prominent member of the Church of Jesus Christ of Latter-day Saints, serving in the positions of missionary, stake president, mission president, apostle, president of the Quorum of Twelve Apostles, and counselor in the First Presidency. Clawson was himself a product of Mormon polygamy, being born in pioneer Utah on 12 March 1857, the son of four-time polygamist Hiram B. Clawson and his second wife, Margaret Gay Judd.[1]

Clawson attended school in the Salt Lake City Nineteenth Ward, the Social Hall, and the University of Deseret. Since both parents were connected with the Salt Lake Theatre, at the age of thirteen he played the part of a robber in "The Robbers of the Rocky Mountains." In the 1870s he was an active member of the Wasatch Literary Association. From 1875 to 1877 he worked, in both Salt Lake City and New York City, as a secretary to Brigham Young's son, John W. Young, who was a railroad contractor. While in New York, he attended and graduated from Scott-Browne's College of Phonography. With this shorthand experience Clawson was the official reporter for 1877 sermons by John Taylor, Erastus Snow, and George Q. Cannon, which were delivered on Sundays at the Salt Lake Tabernacle.[2] Also, after attending the funeral service of President Brigham Young in September 1877, he recorded at the cemetery the dedicatory prayer offered by Wilford Woodruff.

In April 1879 young Rudger Clawson was called as a Mormon missionary to the Southern States Mission, and in July 1879 he witnessed the murder of his missionary companion, Joseph Standing, by a mob near Varnell's Station, Georgia. Clawson brought the body of his slain companion back to Salt Lake City, and then after attending Standing's funeral service in August 1879, he returned to Georgia in

October to attend the trial of the three men accused of Standing's murder, which resulted in their acquittal. Because of the murder of his companion and his composure at the scene, Clawson became a folk hero in Mormonism.

After recovering from his experiences, back in Salt Lake City in 1879 and 1880 Clawson worked as a corresponding secretary for Zion's Co-operative Merchantile Institution, and from 1882 to 1884 he worked as a bookkeeper for his half brother, Spencer Clawson, in the wholesale dry goods business. In 1884 he was convicted of polygamy and became a different kind of hero. To understand why Rudger Clawson had married two women, one must survey the history of polygamy in Mormonism.

Mormon Polygamy

Joseph Smith (1805–44), the founder of Mormonism, appears to have initiated the practice of polygamy when he took his first plural wife, Fannie Alger, in 1835.[3] Counting only the marriages performed during Joseph Smith's lifetime, he had from twenty-seven to forty-eight plural wives.[4] The existence of this practice by Joseph Smith and other members of the church hierarchy was emphatically and repeatedly denied in the 1830s and 1840s, but it was secretly practiced for seventeen years. Finally, in August 1852 Orson Pratt, at the direction of Brigham Young, publicly announced its existence among the Mormons.[5]

Within orthodox Mormon tradition several explanations were offered in support of polygamy, though there appears to be very little development from 1852 to 1890 in the rhetoric of justification.[6] Most of the arguments were used in the initial announcement by Orson Pratt. The main religious justification was that Joseph Smith had received a revelation from God commanding him and other faithful Mormon men to practice polygamy, like the ancient patriarchs in the Old Testament. Pratt argued that this was part of God's cosmological plan for his spirit children, ranging from the preexistence to the present earth life to the future heavenly existence. Pratt also presented a social defense of polygamy, since this type of marriage would do away with the need for adultery, fornication, and prostitution. Pratt was also convinced that men were polygamous by nature, while women were naturally monogamous.[7] As a further justification of Mormon polygamy, a number of church leaders speculated that Jesus was not only married but had married several women. Orson Pratt stated in 1853 that "if all the acts of Jesus were written, we no doubt should learn" that Mary Magdalene and the sisters Mary and Martha were his wives.[8]

That same year Jedediah M. Grant affirmed that the reason Jesus was persecuted was "because he had so many wives."[9] The next year at the 6 October 1854 general conference, Orson Hyde preached that Jesus was married to Mary, Martha, and several others.[10] Ascribing polygamy to Jesus was popular in Mormon culture up to the last decade of the nineteenth century, but it is an unjustifiable interpretation of the New Testament documents.[11]

The anti-Mormon attacks against polygamy came from gentile business leaders, gentile and apostate women, sectarian ministers, federally appointed officials, and newspaper reporters. These attacks focused on four areas: the degradation of Mormon women, the lust and immorality of polygamy, the resultant domestic disharmony of the marital relationship, and the deceit and lies involved in public denial and private practice in Nauvoo and then later the public disclosure in Utah but continued denial in Europe.[12]

For ten years after the 1852 announcement the Mormons in the Utah territory were free from prosecution for polygamy. Then in 1862 Congress passed and President Abraham Lincoln signed the Morrill Antibigamy Act, which made bigamy a criminal offense in U.S. territories, invalidated the Utah territorial laws that had sanctioned polygamy and had incorporated the Mormon church, and limited the real estate of a religious organization in the territories to $50,000. The polygamous Mormons ignored this law, feeling that it was unconstitutional and believing that they would eventually be vindicated by the U.S. Supreme Court. George Reynolds, Brigham Young's private secretary, was chosen by the church leaders to be the test case for this legislation. After being convicted of bigamy, Reynolds was sentenced in 1875 to two years' imprisonment and a $500 fine. The U.S. Supreme Court in January 1879 upheld the constitutionality of his conviction, arguing that although laws "cannot interfere with mere religious belief and opinions, they may with practices."[13] This meant that religious freedom could not be appealed to when it involved a practice contrary to contemporary morals, and it was shattering to the already shaky Mormon confidence in the protection of the Constitution. Reynolds was taken into custody in June 1879 and imprisoned at Lincoln, Nebraska, for a month and then was transferred to the Utah Territorial Penitentiary in Salt Lake City, where he was released in January 1881, five months early for good conduct.

The Edmunds Act of March 1882 passed both houses and was signed by President Chester A. Arthur. It made unlawful cohabitation a misdemeanor, allowed counts of polygamy and unlawful cohabitation to be joined in the same indictment, disfranchised polygamists, disqualified them for jury duty, and replaced election officers with the Utah Commission, a board of five presidential appointees.[14]

Clawson's Marriages, Trials, and Conviction

About 1881 Rudger Clawson got engaged to Lydia Elizabeth Spencer, the daughter of Daniel Spencer and Mary Jane Cutcliffe. Lydia's mother was a widow, and Lydia sewed dresses to make some money for the family. However, Rudger's mother broke off the engagement because she did not want her son to marry "a Poor sewing Girl."[15] Rudger Clawson then became engaged to Florence Ann Dinwoodey, the daughter of wealthy Henry Dinwoodey and Anne Hill, but when Florence asked him about the possibility of practicing polygamy, he responded by saying, "Yes, if conditions arise in the future that make the step appear to be right and proper for me, I will undoubtedly take a plural wife." Their engagement was immediately broken off.[16] Later they got back together and were married on 12 August 1882 at the Salt Lake Endowment House. About seven months later and with his wife pregnant, Clawson announced to her his intention of taking another wife. Florence's reaction was: "That's all right for you. Go ahead, but don't count on me!"[17] Accordingly, Rudger Clawson went ahead and took Lydia as his plural wife, being married on 29 March 1883 at the Endowment House.

By early 1884 efforts were initiated to begin prosecutions under the Edmunds Act. The impaneling of a grand jury took place on 14–15 April 1884 when the suspected Mormons were asked: "Do you believe in the doctrines and tenets of the Mormon Church? Do you believe in the doctrine of plural marriage, as taught by the Mormon Church? Do you believe it is right for a man to have more than one undivorced wife living at the same time?"[18] A positive response would disqualify that individual for jury duty. On 24 April 1884 the grand jury indicted Clawson for polygamy and unlawful cohabitation. As a consequence of this indictment a warrant was issued by Judge John A. Hunter, and Clawson was arrested by U.S. Marshal Elwin A. Ireland. Clawson was brought before U.S. Commissioner William McKay and released later that day on a bail of $3,000 promised by his father, Hiram B. Clawson, and his half brother, Spencer Clawson. On 30 April 1884 Clawson's attorney, Franklin S. Richards, filed a motion to quash the indictment on the ground that the grand jury was not legally drawn. He contended, among other things, that fifteen Mormons from among those summoned were excluded from the grand jury.

On 4 October 1884 Clawson was arraigned before Judge Charles S. Zane[19] and pleaded not guilty to the charges. The impaneling of the jury began on 15 October. David Archibald expressed belief in polygamy and was excused. Louis Oviatt, a Mormon, said he did not believe in the practice of polygamy, but he was still excused from being a juror. The next day the twelve-man jury was finally decided upon, the trial began, and several witnesses were called. On the seventeenth further witnesses were called, including John Taylor, president of the Church of Jesus Christ of Latter-day Saints.[20] Most of the witnesses were evasive and had convenient lapses in their memory.

The final arguments were heard on 20 October 1884, and on the morning of 21 October Judge Zane delivered his charge to the jury. This charge illustrates his fairness, since, based on the evidence presented during the trial, he specifically instructed the jury to return a verdict of not guilty on the count of unlawful cohabitation. The jury took eleven hours in its deliberations, but at 9 P.M. the foreman of the jury admitted that they could not agree on a verdict—with eight for conviction and four for acquittal. The hung jury was discharged by the judge, and he declared it a mistrial.

Perhaps Lydia felt it was safe to come out of hiding in the "underground,"[21] since the trial was over, because later that night she was located by federal deputies and served with a subpoena. A new jury having been drawn, the retrial was held on 24 October 1884. Lydia was in attendance but when called to take the oath, she refused to do so. She was, accordingly, ruled by Judge Zane to be in contempt of court and was put in the custody of the U.S. marshal, who took her to the Utah Territorial Prison. That night Clawson begged Lydia to testify so that she would not have to remain in prison.

The following day, 25 October 1884, Lydia was sworn in and admitted under oath that she was married to Rudger Clawson in 1883, though she could not remember the month.[22] Lydia was the only witness that day, and no further arguments were heard from either the prosecution or the defense. In his charge to the new jury Judge Zane defined unlawful cohabitation as "the living together of a man and woman, as husband and wife, or under such circumstances as induces a reasonable belief of the practice of sexual intercourse."[23] This time the jury took only seventeen minutes and returned a verdict of guilty on both counts of the indictment—polygamy and unlawful cohabitation. Judgment was set for nine days later.

Contemporary evidence indicates that Rudger Clawson expected the sentence to be about one year. On 3 November 1884 Judge Zane sentenced him to an imprisonment of three-and-a-half years and a fine of $500 for polygamy (the law allowed up to five years) and six months and $300 for unlawful cohabitation (the maximum permitted by law), the terms to be served consecutively. Clawson thus became the first Mormon to be convicted and imprisoned for violation of the 1882 Edmunds Act. However, there was no shame in his imprisonment because Clawson considered it as a mission for the church. Years later he affirmed that he "filled mission to the penitentiary—3 years a month and 10 days—some might say, what a disgrace—it was not a disgrace but a distinct honor—went to Penitentiary to defend a principle of Gospel—plural marriage—I don't brag of these things."[24]

During the next eleven years the sentences imposed by the judges varied from five days to five years and the fines ranged from nothing to $1,200.[25] One six-month sentence was cut short when ten days after entering the Mormon prisoner died and became a martyr on behalf of polygamy.[26] Because it was much easier to prove, 83 percent of the successful prosecutions were for unlawful cohabitation. The crime of adultery accounted for 16 percent of the polygamous convicts, but this statistic is subject to a 5 percent margin of error, since "a surprising number of [nonpolygamous Mormon] men served prison sentences for adultery after being convicted on charges brought by the wife."[27] Just over 1 percent of the convictions were for polygamy. There was one instance in which Mormon polygamy was prosecuted under the charge of incest, since the 1887 Edmunds-Tucker Act defined incest as a sexual relationship within but not including the fourth degree of consanguinity, which would include an uncle marrying his niece.[28]

When Clawson entered prison there were about 90 prisoners, of which about 12 were murderers. In mid-May 1885 there were 6 polygamous prisoners and 96 regular convicts.[29] By the end of the year the number of Mormon "cohabs" (as they became known) had risen to 28 and the gentile prisoners to a little over 100. In mid-1886 there were about 150 prisoners, of which about 50 were cohabs. By the beginning of June 1887 the cohabs had risen to 92 and there was one more than that number of gentiles, giving a total prison population of 185.[30] When Clawson was released from prison in December 1887, there were 88 polygamous Mormons and the number of gentiles was about 100. From 1884 to 1895 there were over a thousand convictions of polygamous Mormons for bigamy, polygamy, unlawful cohabitation, adultery, and incest. Since cohabs were often indicted on two counts or were imprisoned more than once, the number of different Mormon men convicted was around 900.[31] It is ironic that on 6 October 1890, the day Wilford Woodruff's Manifesto against new polygamy was ratified by church members, four Mormon polygamists entered prison, and during the ensuing five years there were 123 additional convictions and imprisonments.

Clawson's Prison Life

These memoirs provide insights into what life was like for a Mormon imprisoned for practicing polygamy.[32] The Utah Territorial Penitentiary had been under the direct supervision of the U.S. marshal since 1871, so Rudger Clawson was escorted to the prison by Marshal Ireland on 3 November 1884. Clawson arrived at 7 P.M. and weighed in at 160 pounds. New inmates had to undergo some form of initiation ceremony or hazing, which had become an established tradition at the prison. When Clawson arrived, he heard shouts of "a fresh fish," "bring him along," "we have been waiting for him," "will someone get a rope," and "lynch him! lynch him!"[33] Before Moroni Brown had arrived in July 1885, he had heard reports of how the "fresh fish" were handled—"pummeled with the gloves, thrown up in a blanket, hung up by the neck and otherwise roughly handled."[34] In October 1885 threats of "Kill him, d—n him! Hang him! Lynch him!" were directed to an incoming cohab who was also a police officer.[35] In March 1886 the initiation was to choose between singing a song, dancing a jig, standing on one's head, making a speech, or being tossed up in a blanket.[36]

Clawson's introduction to the other prisoners was about as inauspicious as his introduction to his new home. The penitentiary was located in the Sugar House area southeast of Salt Lake City and had an entrance on the west side. The sentry boxes were located at the top of the wall on the northeast and southwest corners. The interior dimensions of the yard were ninety-three yards long by fifty-five yards wide, being a little more than an acre in area.[37] Within the prison yard there were several structures. Bunkhouse no. 1 held sixty "toughs," who were the rougher or more violent convicts. Bunkhouse no. 2, which was a later extension to no. 1, held about thirty "trusties," who could be entrusted with jobs in the kitchen, laundry, or farm, all of which were located outside the prison walls. There were two or three tiers of bunks around the three inside walls of the bunkhouses. Mattresses were made of straw and two men slept in each bed.[38] The dining room was a separate structure forty-five feet by twenty feet. During the summer of 1885 bunkhouse no. 3 was built to accommodate sixty men. At the same time the dining room was extended and a two-tub bathroom attached to the east end.

Prison justice was primarily administered through the sweatbox. It was made of lumber with an iron cage inside and measured six feet by six feet by three feet. Prisoners were put in the sweatbox for major infractions of prison regulations and for comparatively trivial offenses, such as shouting.[39] Another device to restrain the prisoners was the ball and chain, which weighed eighteen to twenty-five pounds.

The punishments were generally dealt out to the other prisoners. Clawson came in contact with a wide spectrum of convicts—forgers, pickpockets, burglars, horse and cattle thieves, mail robbers, and murderers. At first Clawson was the only Mormon in prison, but he was joined during his fifth day by fifty-eight-year-old Joseph H. Evans, who was convicted of polygamy. They were the only two Mormons for six months, and then convictions for unlawful cohabitation began to escalate.

Clawson was not strictly confined within the prison walls during the whole period in which he was imprisoned. He was permitted to visit his plural wife, Lydia, and their newborn son, Rudger Remus, who was born in March 1885.[40] Lydia was not allowed a pass from the marshal because she was not recognized as Clawson's legal wife, and he was only able to see her standing on the prison wall. However, on 27 July 1885 Clawson was taken from the prison to appear in court and explain why the request of his legal wife, Florence, for a divorce should not be granted. The divorce was then finalized, which means that Clawson served longer in prison than his first marriage lasted.[41]

Then late the next month Lydia's efforts to get a pass were successful and they were allowed what was called a "private interview" in one of the two visiting rooms outside the wall of the prison. Although this episode is never mentioned in Clawson's memoirs, his letters to Lydia make clear that the resultant renewal of their conjugal relations led to Lydia's second pregnancy.[42] During the first seven months of 1886 when Clawson worked as tutor to Warden George N. Dow's two children, he went outside the prison wall during the day and taught them in their adjoining home.

The other Mormon cohabs were sometimes also allowed to leave the penitentiary for reasons other than to appear at official court proceedings.[43] Instances, at which time they were usually (but not always) escorted by a guard, include the following: George Q. Cannon to have a private meeting with Wilford Woodruff and Joseph F. Smith;[44] Nicholas H. Groesbeck, just two days after his arrival, to go to Salt Lake on business;[45] sixty-eight-year-old John P. Jones to walk around outside the prison walls to improve his health;[46] Royal B. Young to go home and see his pregnant wife, who had been "recently confined;"[47]

Andrew W. Cooley to visit his sick thirteen-year-old daughter and then the next day to visit again, but arriving just fifteen minutes after she died;[48] Henry Dinwoodey to visit his sick wife and then thirteen days later to attend her funeral;[49] Francis A. Brown to attend the funeral of a friend;[50] Joseph Hogan to attend his child's funeral;[51] John Y. Smith to attend the funeral of his one-year-old son;[52] and David John to go to Provo and attend the funeral of his one-month-old son.[53]

The meals were served with little variation. Breakfast consisted of meat, bread, potatoes, and coffee; lunch was vegetable soup and bread; and supper was bread and tea. In the winter the meat and potatoes that remained were served up the next day as hash. Concern for sanitary conditions during the preparation of food was at a low level, for one cohab witnessed the waiter "fish out an old greasy felt hat from the bottom of the tank that served for a tea pot, bah."[54] One time when the prisoners complained about the bad taste of the coffee, Warden Dow explained that "a bottle of carbolic acid had accidentally been dropped into the coffee" but the situation had been rectified.[55] However, at holidays and odd occasions there were special treats. For example, on 6 April 1887 when the prisoners entered the dining room they found that everyone had an orange on his plate, which was a gift of Elias Morris, a prominent Mormon business leader.[56] Because there was a fear by the prison officials that knives or forks might be used as weapons, only spoons were allowed, though during certain periods some of the inmates were able to use their own pocketknives.[57] In 1889 the prisoners were still not allowed to use knives or forks, but "some would make a fork out of whire & a Nife out of a spoon handel."[58]

The emphasis on the Mormon "Word of Wisdom," which prohibits the use of tea, coffee, tobacco, and alcohol, was not as strong in the 1880s as it is today. One Mormon cohab brought with him to prison his own supply of sugar, tea, and wine, and openly drank coffee with his meals.[59] Another Mormon prisoner published in a church periodical that the Mormons in prison drank "sugarless tea" and "black coffee."[60]

Bodily cleanliness was difficult to maintain. The pattern was a bath each week in warm weather and once every two weeks in cold weather.[61] Also, a sponge bath could be taken in the corner of the mess room.[62] In the summer the heat in the penitentiary often became unbearable. For six months each year—and especially during the hot months—bedbugs were a problem and nuisance that the prisoners had to contend with. They were particularly active at night. During summer the heat, the bedbugs, and the suffocatingly foul air made it hard to sleep. The ever-present bedbugs are confirmed by Clawson's July 1885 request for Lydia to "send with my clean clothes a bottle of Insect Powder, some clean sheets, and a pillow case."[63] George H. Taylor described conditions during a day in the summer: "Hunting shade all day. Pulled off my shoes, Vest, & some more of my clothes & lay in my bunk & sweat among the bugs for three hours."[64] One cohab said that the bedbugs "came down the wall from the ceiling in regular order straight for a person and almost as fast at times as one can despatch them."[65] During his last night in prison a Mormon prisoner said that they "killed by actual count 249" bedbugs.[66] Another man quipped that his bunkhouse should be renamed the "Bug House."[67]

By its very nature prison life depends on routine and is monotonous. After two months of imprisonment, one cohab expressed his feelings: "We get so tired of the sameness of things here that we often wish for wings to soar above those horid grey wawlls out into the world again."[68] Since some Mormon inmates had objectionable habits, it was not always easy for them to get along with each other, especially when two slept on each four-foot-six-inch-wide bunk. Abraham H. Cannon complained that his bunkmate, Thomas Porcher, was not a "pleasant bedfellow" since he "both smokes and drinks, as well as swears."[69] Thomas W. Kirby moaned that his bunkmate was an extremely loud snorer.[70] James H. Nelson is reported to have verbally abused Amos Maycock "in a most shameful manner."[71]

With plenty of spare time on their hands many cohabs read books. After eleven days of imprisonment Clawson had almost finished reading John Milton's *Paradise Lost* and told a newspaper reporter that "the surroundings out there make it somewhat applicable, I can assure you."[72] Some tried their hand at writing and publishing poetry.[73] Another popular activity among the Mormon prisoners was to sign their names and write their sentiments in autograph books of other prisoners or visitors. Rudger Clawson on 14 November 1885 wrote the following in the book of Mina C. Cannon, a wife of Abraham H. Cannon:

> The mother, her office, holds the Key
> Of the soul; and she it is who stamps the coin
> Of character, and makes the being who would be savage
> But for her gentle cares, a Christian man.[74]

To pass the time various physical activities were engaged in by the inmates, including calisthenics, baseball, football, boxing, quoits, lacrosse, croquet, marbles, chess, checkers, dominoes, and cards. Card playing is listed last because, even though it was the gentile convicts who gambled for money or tobacco,[75] some of the Mormon cohabs had negative sentiments about any form of card playing. For example, Angus M. Cannon had played cards but he felt very bad about this activity because, he said, "I see so much time wasted in this way, by my brethren, that should be occupied in that which will enrich their minds and develop their muscles."[76] The inmates also engaged in various crafts—making hair bridles, riding whips, gilded picture frames, ornamental wood boxes, flower carvings, ship models, canes, mats, fans, women's chains, and pincushions.

One other method of handling boredom was to play practical jokes on Oluf F. Due, a Mormon cohab who was the brunt of many prison pranks. One time the perpetrators attached a string to Due's hat and raised it to the upper bunk; at another time they threw pillows at him. In a rage Due "pronounced all sorts of curses and Judgments upon those who were tormenting him."[77] Being able to sustain a sense of humor in their dismal situation lessened the stress on the cohabs. John Nicholson related a humorous interchange that occurred when he was issued his striped prison uniform. His instinctive reaction after putting on the trousers was to thrust his hands into the pockets. One hit home and the other slid down along his leg. The turnkey, James Curtis, explained that there was only one pocket. Nicholson retorted, "That reminds me of the process that brought me here." "How is that?" "Exceedingly one-sided."[78]

Clawson's Prison Discussions with Apostle Lorenzo Snow

During the crusade against Mormon polygamists, three Mormon apostles were imprisoned: Lorenzo Snow, George Q. Cannon,[79] and Francis M. Lyman. However, the only apostle during Clawson's incarceration was Lorenzo Snow, who was in prison from 12 March 1886 to 8 February 1887. The Mormon cohabs had discussions with Snow for advice on personal problems and elucidation of church doctrine. Abraham H. Cannon, who became an apostle three years later, records a conversation between Lorenzo Snow, Rudger Clawson, and himself:

> Bro. Snow said I would live to see the time when brothers and sisters would marry each other in this church. All our horror at such a union was due entirely to prejudice, and the offspring of such unions would be as healthy and pure as any other. These were the decided views of Pres. Young, when alive, for Bro. S. talked to him freely on this matter.
> Bro. S. believes that Jesus will appear as a man among this people and dwell with them a time before He comes in His glory. The Gentiles

will hear of it and they will reject him, as the Jews did anciently, but they will have no power over him at all.

He says that if a man will place himself in a position where he is ready to sacrifice *everything* at the command of the Lord, he is then in a position to ask and receive Heavenly revelation.[80]

Helon H. Tracy records a conversation between Lorenzo Snow, Rudger Clawson, and himself:

> Speaking as to the love that ought to exist between husband and wife Bro. S. said, No man should not or ought not to take a wife unless it was one he could truly love he related an anecdote about Bro H. C. K. [Heber C. Kimball] an affair that occured at Nauvoo when plural marriage was first introduced The principle was quite a trial to Sister V. K. [Vilate Kimball] but she essayed to submit to it and went and chose two *very* old maids of quite plain and homely Appearance for her husband Bro K spoke to the Prophet Joseph about it and he said, Bro K that arrangement is of the devil you go and get you a young wife *one* you can take to your bosom and love and raise children by. A man should choose his own wife and one he can love and get children by in love. Jesus says you have not chosen me but I have chosen you [John 15:16]. Bro S. said further one reason why illegitamate children are often so bright and and intelligant is because they are begotten in love and unless they children are begotten in love they are not so liable to be so intelligent[81]

Rudger Clawson, seventeen years later when he was an apostle, remarked during a quarterly conference of the Twelve Apostles in the temple that none of the Mormon brethren in prison—not even Apostle Lorenzo Snow—"could foretell the outcome."[82] Similarly, Lorenzo Snow remarked that the church leaders "knew no more just how this crusade would terminate than himself or me. They like us were simply living by faith and trusting in God for the deliverance of his Saints."[83]

Legal Developments during Clawson's Imprisonment

On the day of his sentence and imprisonment Clawson filed a notice of his appeal to the territorial supreme court against the judgment and also applied for bail pending his appeal. Judge Zane denied his motion for bail. Clawson then appealed that refusal to the U.S. Supreme Court. On 19 January 1885 the U.S. Supreme Court decided against Clawson.[84] Clawson also appealed concerning the method of grand jury and jury selection in his case. The decision of the Supreme Court on the question of open venire in Clawson's polygamy case was given on

20 April 1885, sustaining the decision in support of its legality by the Utah courts.[85] The gentiles were reported to be jubilant.[86]

Angus M. Cannon was arrested and indicted early in 1885. At his trial on 27 April 1885 a new maneuver was used to help ensure conviction for unlawful cohabitation. Judge Zane ruled that unlawful cohabitation would be established by merely showing that a man appeared to support and live with more than one woman as a wife, without the necessity of proving marital intimacy between them. In Zane's charge to the jury, he said:

> If you believe from the evidence . . . beyond a reasonable doubt, that the defendant lived in the same house with Amanda Cannon and Clara C. Cannon [his second and third wives, respectively] . . . and ate at their respective tables one-third of his time or thereabouts, and that he held them out to the world by his language or his conduct, or by both, as his wives, you should find him guilty.
>
> It is not necessary that the evidence should show that the defendant and these women, or either of them, occupied the same bed or slept in the same room; neither is it necessary that the evidence should show that, within the time mentioned, he had sexual intercourse with either of them.[87]

This broad definition of cohabitation differed from that which Zane had used in the Clawson case the previous October. On 29 April 1885 the jury found Cannon guilty of unlawful cohabitation. He was sentenced on 9 May to six months' imprisonment and a $300 fine. Cannon appealed to the Utah Supreme Court, arguing that the trial court's definition of cohabitation was wrong, since the term necessarily implied a sexual relationship. In June 1885 the Utah Supreme Court rejected the appeal and confirmed Cannon's conviction, with Judge Jacob S. Boreman expressing the opinion that

> sexual intercourse was not a necessary element in the crime [of unlawful cohabitation]. If it were an element—a necessary element—as the defense claim, then . . . if the prosecution did not prove that [the] defendant had sexual intercourse with these women, the prosecution would have to fail. The prosecution would have to prove adultery when adultery was not charged, would have to prove fornication and lewd and lascivious cohabitation when none of these charges had been made.[88]

Angus M. Cannon voluntarily remained in prison two months longer than he actually had to so that his appeal might be considered by the U.S. Supreme Court. On 14 December 1885 the court confirmed his conviction for unlawful cohabitation. Justice Samuel Blatchford wrote the six-to-two majority opinion and affirmed (following Zane's charge to the jury) that unlawful cohabitation was demonstrated if Cannon "lived in the same house with the two women, . . . and held them out to the world" as being his wives. Concerning Cannon's promise to refrain from sexual relations with his plural wives, the U.S. Supreme Court said, "Compacts for sexual non-intercourse [are] easily made and as easily broken, when the prior marriage relations continue to exist."[89] In a minority opinion one of the two dissenting justices stated that the Edmunds Act, "when prohibiting cohabitation with more than one woman, meant unlawful habitual sexual intercourse."[90] Cannon left prison the day the decision was issued. It was this Supreme Court decision that opened up the floodgates for literally hundreds of prosecutions for unlawful cohabitation among the Mormons and encouraged anti-Mormon sentiments against the social and political system in Utah.[91]

In September 1885 Judge Zane began segregating offenses and instructed the grand jury that separate indictments could be issued for the same offense by segregating the period covered into years, months, or even weeks. In March 1886 seventy-one-year-old apostle Lorenzo Snow was convicted on three counts of unlawful cohabitation—one for eleven months of the calendar year of 1883, one for 1884, and one for 1885. He was tried in reverse chronological order so that he would not be able to claim that he had already been tried for the crime at hand and received a sentence of eighteen months and a fine of $900.[92] In February 1887 the U.S. Supreme Court rejected the segregation of offenses.[93]

The Edmunds-Tucker Act was passed on 19 February 1887 and became law on 3 March 1887, without the endorsement of President Grover Cleveland. It permitted (but did not require) a wife to testify against her husband, allowed charges of adultery to be brought by someone other than a spouse, required marriages to be certified in probate courts, dissolved the Perpetual Emigrating Fund Company, abolished the territorial militia known as the Nauvoo Legion, disfranchised women, initiated forfeiture proceedings against the Mormon church, revived the property limitation of $50,000 for a religious organization, and reaffirmed the disincorporation of the Mormon church.[94]

Clawson's Release from Prison

At the time of his release Clawson had served the longest continuous sentence of any Mormon cohab in the Utah Territorial Penitentiary.[95] After serving three years, one month, and ten days of his sentence, he was pardoned by President Grover Cleveland and walked out of prison a free man on 12 December 1887. Fourteen years later Clawson joked about having lived within the boundaries of the Sugar House Ward for three years, but was never allowed to attend church and did not have the normal privileges of membership.[96] Concerning his imprisonment and release in 1887 Clawson said that he "never once felt to murmur or complain, and as I emerged from the prison walls my faith in the principle of plural marriage was just as firm and unshaken as when I entered."[97]

As a reward for so nobly defending the principle of polygamy, Apostle Lorenzo Snow nominated Rudger Clawson to President Wilford Woodruff to receive the fulness of priesthood ordinance, or second anointing, saying that he felt "confidence in recommending him [Clawson] as worthy of this blessing from my intimate acquaintance with him in prison."[98] Clawson received this ordinance a week later. This special anointing, in Mormon belief, assures the recipient of exaltation in the highest degree of the Celestial Kingdom.[99] Later that same month President Wilford Woodruff called him as president of the Box Elder Stake at the further suggestion of Snow. Clawson was sustained in this position in February 1888, and was asked, as a newly appointed stake president, to speak at the next general conference in Salt Lake City. During this period the church was involved in a public relations campaign to get more favorable coverage in the national press and to convince the American people that a change had indeed been made with respect to Mormon polygamy. These efforts were with a view to achieve statehood for Utah. President Wilford Woodruff (who was in hiding to avoid prosecution for polygamy) forbade any discussion of plural marriage at the conference and had instructed Lorenzo Snow that "if anyone attempted to speak about polygamy to throw his hat at him."[100] However, on 6 April 1888—less than four months after being released from prison—Clawson delivered a stirring speech at the general conference, in which he said the following about his experience in the penitentiary for living the principle of polygamy:

> It has fallen to my lot to be sent to prison. In the year 1884, I was convicted of polygamy and unlawful cohabitation. I was convicted of having rendered obedience to a law of God: that was my offense. I had kept one of the commandments of God, and there are many, and they are all very important and very necessary, and for having done this I was sent to prison. . . . I was there 3 years 1 month and 10 days, and passed through many and various scenes during that time. I saw some 300 of my brethren come there during my imprisonment for the same offense, and saw 220 go from the prison.

Perhaps the Latter-day Saints would like to know how I feel in relation to this work, after an experience of 3 years & 1 month in the Penitentiary. I will simply say I feel first rate. I am not one whit discouraged. I have just as much faith in the work of God today as ever I had. I will say that my faith is even greater today than it was 4 years ago, and I trust I shall always be able to express a feeling of this kind. . . .

The Lord has revealed the principle of celestial marriage. Do we believe it is true? We most assuredly do. And will we honor this principle? By the help of the Lord we will honor it and honor him. By the help of the Lord we will not make the promise to do away with this principle any more than we will promise to do away with the principle of faith, [repentance,] baptism, or the laying on of hands for the reception of the Holy Ghost.[101]

A telegraphic report of Clawson's sermon was widely distributed, and the next day it appeared on the front page of the *New York Times*.[102] A church public relations agent issued a dispatch that categorized Clawson's sermon in support of polygamy as "reckless and unauthorized remarks."[103] President Woodruff complained that the brethren who spoke at the conference were not cautioned strongly enough to avoid speaking "on topics that at the present time, were likely to rouse prejudice."[104] Clawson, looking back three years later at the adverse publicity that was aroused, said his speech "occasioned a great deal of comment at the time, not only among the saints but to some extent among the gentiles" and put the blame squarely on the government, who were conducting a vigorous antipolygamy crusade.[105]

In October 1898 Clawson was ordained an apostle by President Lorenzo Snow and became the junior member of the Quorum of Twelve Apostles. An even more significant event occurred in Clawson's life in 1901, for he was chosen by President Lorenzo Snow and sustained at the October general conference of the church as second counselor in the First Presidency. Unexpectedly, Snow died only four days later. It was decided, however, not to dissolve the First Presidency until after the funeral on 13 October 1901. Clawson's seven days in the First Presidency earned him the distinction of having served in the highest council in the Mormon church for the shortest period of time. The closest Clawson ever again got to the First Presidency was the last twenty-two years of his life, in which as president of the Quorum of Twelve Apostles he served only a heartbeat away from becoming the next president of the church.

Clawson's Involvement in Post-Manifesto Polygamy

Discussion of Clawson's polygamy in the 1880s would be incomplete without investigating his involvement in a post-Manifesto plural marriage. Over a century has passed since two significant events for Mormonism—the 19 May 1890 U.S. Supreme Court decision that upheld the dissolution of the corporation of the Mormon church and the federal government's seizure of church property as contained in the Morrill and Edmunds-Tucker Acts[106] and the 24 September 1890 "Official Declaration," or Manifesto, by President Wilford Woodruff that (when it was ratified by the general membership of the church) officially ceased new Mormon polygamy. This latter announcement was actually the result of several years of private discussion and debate among church leaders, but personal conviction among Mormons concerning the need to continue polygamy did not stop immediately. Mormons wanted statehood to get rid of appointees from the federal government and to control their own interests. Ironically, statehood could not be achieved until they gave up the practice that "many considered their most precious tenet"—polygamy.[107]

On 4 January 1893 President Benjamin Harrison proclaimed an amnesty to polygamists, on the condition that they abstain from unlawful cohabitation. Future violations of the Edmunds Law would be prosecuted and this was done to a limited extent, for thirty-five Mormon men were convicted and sent to the Utah Territorial Penitentiary after this date.[108] Three years after this conditional amnesty, Utah became a state.

At a Thursday temple meeting of the Mormon Apostles in 1902 Rudger Clawson suggested that any women being called to church positions should be "carefully questioned" about their attitudes toward polygamy and thus avoid calling anyone to a position who was not a believer in the principle of plural marriage.[109]

Recent historical research has shown not only that Mormon leaders continued to cohabit with and father children by their plural wives after 1890,[110] but also that many general authorities entered into post-Manifesto polygamous marriages between 1890 and 1904.[111] However, concerning Rudger Clawson, one researcher stated in 1983 that "no indication has been found that he actively participated in post-Manifesto polygamy."[112] This conclusion needs to be revised. Official documentation of such banned marriages is unavailable and, in fact, records may never have been kept,[113] but cryptic diary entries, code names in correspondence, circumstantial evidence, genealogical family group sheets, official temple endowment records, and family oral tradition combine to support the position that Rudger Clawson married another plural wife, Pearl Udall, in August 1904—fourteen years after new polygamous marriages were ostensibly ceased by the Manifesto of 1890.[114]

Consider the following scenario: in August 1903, while in Arizona, Clawson typed in his diary that he had a very important discussion with David K. Udall, president of the St. Johns Stake, "upon a subject of vital interest, the nature of which I do not care to mention at this writing."[115] During the quarterly conference of the Twelve Apostles in the Salt Lake Temple on 1 October 1903 Rudger Clawson reported his recent trip to the stakes and settlements in Arizona and Mexico. Affirming that enthusiasm for the principle of plural marriage was not dying out in these areas, Clawson continued: "One young woman in the St. Johns Stake of about 18 years of age, speaking for herself and a number of companions of the same age, said that they would much prefer to take a married man in the church, who had proven his faithfulness and integrity, than to marry a single young man, who was untried." The First Presidency of the church then entered into the room and the presidency and apostles together conducted their regular weekly meeting, followed by the quarterly partaking of sacramental bread and wine. After the First Presidency had withdrawn from the room, Apostle Marriner W. Merrill bore testimony to the other apostles of the truthfulness of plural marriage and specifically exhorted the younger ones—Rudger Clawson, Abraham Owen Woodruff, and Hyrum M. Smith—to take plural wives and increase their families, so that they would be "crowned with glory and exaltation in the presence of God."[116]

Merrill's exhortation kindled Clawson's passion to practice polygamy, for a week later Clawson asked for and received permission from Lydia, his wife, to take another wife, with the only restriction being that he must inform her before actually taking such action.[117] On 6 November 1903 he sent an important letter to an unidentified person, not explaining the nature of this letter. Then on 19 December 1903 he received an important letter, which made him very happy, and sent off an important Christmas present to this unidentified "special friend."[118]

On 5 January 1904 during the quarterly conference of the Twelve Apostles in the temple, the apostles were "cautioned not to exercise the keys of sealing in plural marriage at present."[119] Anthon H. Lund's diary indicates that Rudger Clawson and Apostle Abraham Owen Woodruff opposed President Joseph F. Smith's 1904 issuance of a reaffirmation of the Manifesto. Lund records that Clawson "feared that it would do no good but make many hearts ache." The morning of the announcement the First Presidency and the Twelve Apostles had a council meeting and decided that President Smith would "make an official declaration that plural marriages should not be celebrated and any one who should undertake to do so would be liable to be cut off from the Church."[120] The second manifesto was proclaimed by President Smith in general conference on 6 April 1904.

Pearl Udall, the twenty-three-year-old daughter of David K. Udall, traveled from the south in Arizona and took out her temple endowments in Salt Lake City in May 1904.[121] At this time Clawson mentions in his diary that he is looking forward to "a very important appointment" and is concerned whether the weather will be good, and then three days later indicates that he had climbed to the top of Ensign Peak, the weather had been fine, and he "much enjoyed the view." This is the only instance in Clawson's diaries that he has both a prospective and retrospective reference to a single event—and yet he does not disclose with whom he had the "appointment." The next week he tells of a visit with someone whom he only identified as "a friend from the south."[122] In mid-May 1904 Clawson records a visit with Apostle Merrill, and after administering to him, they engaged in interesting conversation, after which Merrill blessed Clawson that "the desires of my heart would be realized."[123] The older members of the Udall family acknowledge that Rudger Clawson took Pearl Udall as his plural wife sometime in 1904.[124] It cannot at present be stated with certainty who performed the marriage, but probably Apostle Matthias F. Cowley officiated. Not all post-Manifesto plural marriages were performed in Canada and Mexico, since Cowley usually sealed in the United States.[125] On 3 August 1904 Clawson mentioned a quick trip from Salt Lake City to Grand Junction, Colorado, where he met Cowley for an undisclosed purpose.[126] Pearl was leaving Salt Lake City and returning home to Arizona during the first week of August (intending to stop in Denver for a day), and this time period correlates with Clawson's presence in Grand Junction on 3 August 1904.[127] It is most likely that the marriage was performed on this day.

Nowhere in his diaries does Clawson mention Pearl Udall by name. Though the Marriott Library at the University of Utah purchased the bulk of Rudger Clawson's papers from three of his grandchildren in 1983, there was some material that remained in the family's possession until it was donated in 1991. Among this new material were three significant items—a small 1¼-inch photograph of Pearl, a formal one taken in 1910 when she graduated from the Los Angeles College of Osteopathy (with handwritten comments by Clawson on the back), and an encoded love letter, all of which constitute concrete evidence from Clawson himself of his relationship with Pearl. This mysterious letter is a carbon copy (the original presumably having been sent) and reads as follows:

At home, Oct. 17, 1904.

Dearest Z:

Did you receive my letter of Sep. 29th, and did you answer it? If so, your letter has miscarried, for it is several days past due.

Whether it has miscarried or not, I think it would be a good idea to change the name occasionally. Don't you? So when you write me again address the letter to Alexander Stevens No. 67 East South Temple St. and I will be sure to get it. Don't forget.

I'm looking for a letter daily, but if it has miscarried, of course, I shall not hear from you until this note reaches its destination.

I trust you are well and happy, and, believe me, I pray for you always—that you may be brave and fearless, yet wise and prudent, in the dark hour of trial. A crown of resplendent glory awaits the soul that has been tried and tested and found "not wanting" [cf. Daniel 5:27]. You are now facing the supreme trial of your life. Be patient, be hopeful, be happy, and glorify the Lord in your heart, however bitter the trial may prove to be. And remember this, there is an eternity before us in which to work out our destiny. Let that thought be bright within you during all your present troubles.

I send you the choice love of one who loves thee and seal it upon thy lips with a kiss.

_ _ A _

P.S. Remember, Alexander Stevens.[128]

This letter to a woman known as "Z" is truly remarkable, and since the author only identifies himself as "A," it is necessary to scrutinize both the text and typing carefully. It is typewritten, except for the supralinear *it* (the second word of the second paragraph), the *thy* (the sixteenth word of the fifth paragraph), and the autographed A (the signature at the end of the letter), all of which are written in Clawson's distinctive script with his black pen. Internal evidence supports not only that it was written by Clawson, but also that he typed it. The address (67 East South Temple) suggested as the destination to which a reply should be sent by "Dearest Z" is the Beehive House in Salt Lake City, where Apostle Rudger Clawson worked in the office of President Joseph F. Smith. That Clawson is writing to a polygamous marital companion, and not just a close friend, is clear from his affirmation: "Remember this, there is an eternity before us in which to work out our destiny. . . . I send you the choice love of one who loves thee and seal it upon thy lips with a kiss." That this was written by Rudger Clawson is strikingly supported by the identical wording in his prison letter to Lydia, dated sometime shortly after 25 March 1885: "remember that there is an eternity before us." Examination of the

1904 *Polk's Salt Lake City Directory* shows no one by the name of Alexander Stevens, so it was safe for Clawson to use that name. Rudger Clawson did not throw away this love letter or his photograph of Pearl Udall, and this evidence clinches his connection with Pearl.[129]

Further confirmation of their relationship to each other can be made from some Pearl Udall letters that have recently been discovered. Pearl, living within the boundaries of the First Ward in Salt Lake City and attending church in the Second Ward, wrote a letter in June 1905 to her family in Arizona, and enclosed the following separate note, which was folded and addressed to her mother:

> This is a confidential sheet to tell you about a pleasant visit I had last Wednesday with A and his mother at her home. I went there in the morning about ten o'clock as had been arranged. She gave me a warm welcome and manifested unusual interest in me and our conditions. It did me good, mamma, for now I feel that I have some little claim on those to whom a girl naturally looks when she is taken so far away from her own dear ones. I was assured that if circumstances would permit I should be welcomed by the whole family.[130]

So there exists a typed letter in Rudger Clawson's possession signed by "A" and letters by Pearl Udall, referring to clandestine meetings with a person known as "A." The two sets of independent evidence mesh perfectly, with both parties using the same code name.

When Clawson was called as president of the European Mission in 1910, Lydia Clawson accompanied her husband to England, but she returned the next year, while Clawson remained in England until 1913. Coincidentally, Pearl Udall spent parts of 1912 and 1913 in England, ostensibly to do family genealogical research.[131] Pearl's brother, David K. Udall, Jr., served a mission under Clawson during the same period and acted as the intermediary to arrange secret meetings between Pearl and Mission President Clawson. The oral tradition in the Udall family is that Clawson "released" Pearl Udall Clawson from their marriage about 1913. This enabled Pearl to marry Joseph Nelson in 1919, but only after Pearl received direct assurance from the Mormon church president, Heber J. Grant, that Rudger Clawson's and Pearl's marriage for time and eternity had been canceled.[132] Though there is—and probably never will be—any indisputable proof that Rudger Clawson married Pearl Udall, the weight of the documentary and circumstantial evidence (combined with oral testimony) leads to the firm conclusion that this marriage took place in 1904. With all the secrecy involved in this relationship, it would be hard to expect any more conclusive evidence.

How can one reconcile the contradiction between a secret polygamous marriage by a Mormon apostle and the church's public affirmation in support of the 1890 Manifesto? First of all, church leaders
sometimes held private viewpoints in disagreement with the official
church position, but more important, there was a significant distinction between the policy of the church and the power of the priesthood.
Samuel W. Taylor, a grandson of President John Taylor, expressed it
this way: "When the Woodruff Manifesto of 1890 was issued, it meant
that the *Church* had suspended the practice; but the *priesthood authority* already had taken it underground."[133] Because of the duplicity
involved in the Pearl Udall marriage, Clawson again became—in a very
real sense—a prisoner for the practice of polygamy. This double life
for Clawson lasted about nine years.

Up until the end of his life on 21 June 1943 Rudger Clawson as-
serted his intense belief in the principle of plural marriage, even though
it was no longer practiced by the church. At the celebration of his
seventieth birthday he affirmed:

> Plural marriage is a principle that I do now believe and have always
> believed to be a true principle. . . . This doctrine of plural marriage is
> obnoxious to the Christian world of today for the reason, mainly, that
> they have been taught that monogamy is the only true form of marriage.
> Nevertheless, plural marriage, as practiced heretofore by the Latter-day
> Saints, is a true principle. . . . I am through with that subject, but I would
> like to say this so that you who are listening may know just exactly my
> feelings when I came out and what they are today. I suffered bonds and
> imprisonment for that principle.[134]

The Genre of Prison Literature

Separate from their historical interest, Rudger Clawson's memoirs
have value as a literary production. His memoirs can appropriately be
considered as part of the genre of prison literature. This genre is rather
rich—perhaps not suprisingly—since one in prison finds considerable
free time and usually a desire to explore inmost feelings and often a
need to justify one's presence in prison. The outlet for creative expression can be in the form of letters, diaries, or journal accounts.[135] Another avenue is to contribute to a formal prison publication, the earliest
of which was the *Forlorn Hope* of 1800.[136]

Clawson's memoirs fit more closely with the writings of those persecuted and imprisoned for their religious beliefs. Paul, the foremost
Christian apostle, was imprisoned for two years at both Rome and Cae-
sarea, and from one of these prisons he wrote the letters to Philippians,

Colossians, and Philemon, and possibly also Ephesians.[137] John Bunyan, the Congregational dissenter, spent twelve years imprisoned at the Bedford jail, and during this time he published his spiritual autobiography, *Grace Abounding to the Chief of Sinners,* and began to write his famous allegory, *The Pilgrim's Progress.*[138] In Mormon tradition, parts of one of Joseph Smith's letters from Liberty Jail have been canonized as three sections in the Doctrine and Covenants.[139]

The Clawson memoirs and letters provide many valuable insights into the Utah Territory of the 1880s—the pride that the Mormon polygamists felt in being "prisoners for conscience sake," the discussions of various Mormon doctrines, daring prison escapes, the particulars of prison life, and the sexual frustration of a husband forcibly separated from his plural wife. Clawson's memoirs provide his perspective on various issues. His racist attitudes, which were probably shared by a majority of his fellow church members, are evident. He describes with an air of superiority his repulsion at the smell of two black prisoners in a nearby bunk. Interesting comparisons to Clawson's viewpoint could be made of the writings of black prisoners concerning the prejudice and ill-treatment they face.[140]

An autobiography represents a person's self-image, which naturally changes over time.[141] All autobiographical accounts distort reality, and this is especially true if successive revisions are made years after the event. Parts of the earliest manuscript of the Clawson memoirs can be dated to 1887, while the latest manuscript was written in the late 1930s when Clawson was in his early eighties. Thus, the process of writing and revising his life story covers half a century. Clawson's polished memoirs show that he is a good storyteller and uses vivid descriptions. His narratives, character portraits, and dramatic episodes are usually compelling, but have often changed over time. Sometimes a comparatively insignificant occurrence has, over the passage of time, been rewritten into a moving religious experience. The giving of the Hosanna Shout in July 1886 was not heard at all outside the Mormon bunkhouse and even some of the Mormon prisoners begrudgingly participated. But Clawson's memoirs describe it dramatically. Likewise, the episode in July 1885 during the Sunday services of an Episcopalian minister has been transformed. Examination of successive manuscripts written by Clawson demonstrates that the account was radically rewritten to show the rightness of Clawson's position. In his narrative Clawson is the hero throughout.

NOTES

1. David S. Hoopes and Roy Hoopes, *The Making of a Mormon Apostle: The Story of Rudger Clawson* (Lanham, Md.: Madison Books, 1990).

2. John Taylor, "God's Purposes Unchangeable," *Journal of Discourses* 19 (1878): 76–83; Erastus Snow, "Difference between the Saints," *Journal of Discourses* 19 (1878): 98–104; George Q. Cannon, "The Rock of New (or Continued) Revelation," and "Actions Should Harmonize with Professions," *Journal of Discourses* 19 (1878): 104–11.

3. Linda King Newell and Valeen Tippetts Avery, *Mormon Enigma: Emma Hale Smith, Prophet's Wife, "Elect Lady," Polygamy's Foe, 1804–1879* (Garden City, N.Y.: Doubleday, 1984), 66; and Richard S. Van Wagoner, *Mormon Polygamy: A History*, 2d ed. (Salt Lake City: Signature Books, 1989), 5, 9.

4. Andrew Jenson, in "Plural Marriage," *Historical Record* 6 (May 1887): 233–34, lists twenty-seven plural wives; Danel W. Bachman, in "A Study of the Mormon Practice of Plural Marriage before the Death of Joseph Smith" (M.A. thesis, Purdue University, 1976), 333–36, lists forty-eight.

5. David J. Whittaker, "The Bone in the Throat: Orson Pratt and the Public Announcement of Plural Marriage," *Western Historical Quarterly* 18 (July 1987): 293–314. See also "Celestial Marriage," *Journal of Discourses* 1 (1854): 53–66.

6. David J. Whittaker, "Early Mormon Polygamy Defenses," *Journal of Mormon History* 11 (1984): 43–63; also see Davis Bitton, *The Ritualization of Mormon History* (Urbana: University of Illinois Press, forthcoming), the chapter "Polygamy Defended: One Side of a Nineteenth-Century Polemic."

7. Lawrence Foster, *Religion and Sexuality: The Shakers, the Mormons, and the Oneida Community* (Urbana: University of Illinois Press, 1984), 201–4.

8. "Celestial Marriage," *The Seer* 1 (Oct. 1853): 159; cf. 172.

9. "Uniformity," *Journal of Discourses* 1 (1854): 345.

10. "The Marriage Relations," *Journal of Discourses* 2 (1855): 81–82; cf. 2 (1855): 210 and 4 (1857): 259. By March 1852 Orson Hyde had already stated his view that Jesus had three wives (John W. Gunnison, Letter to Albert Carrington, 6 March 1852, Albert Carrington Collection, Marriott Library, University of Utah, Salt Lake City).

11. Rudger Clawson, sincerely believing that he was following the example of Jesus in practicing polygamy, explained in 1884 in his earliest extant diary: "I have entered into the practice of plural marriage, which consists in simply taking the same course as did old father Abraham, Isaac, and Jacob, and as I firmly believe, the Lord Jesus Christ himself, viz.: the marrying [of] more than one woman" (Rudger Clawson Collection, Ms 481, Bx 2, Fd 1, 1884 Diary, 13, which is reproduced in Appendix 2 and located at the Marriott Library, University of Utah, Salt Lake City; hereafter the Rudger Clawson Collection is cited as RC).

12. Carrel H. Sheldon, "Mormon Haters," in *Mormon Sisters: Women in Early Utah*, ed. Claudia L. Bushman (Cambridge, Mass.: Emmeline Press, 1976), 121–25.

13. *Reynolds v. United States*, 98 U.S. 166 (1879). See Randall D. Guynn and Gene C. Schaerr, "The Mormon Polygamy Cases: Politics, Religion, and Morality in the Court of Last Resort," *Sunstone* 11 (Sept. 1987): 9–12.

14. 22 Statutes 30 (1882), which is reproduced in Stewart L. Grow, "A Study of the Utah Commission: 1882–96" (Ph.D. diss., University of Utah, 1954), 288–90.

15. "A Small Scetch of Lydia Spencer Clawson," 2, RC, Bx 30, Fd 2.

16. "Memoirs of the Life of Rudger Clawson Written by Himself," 85, RC, Bx 1, Fd 3.

17. Reminiscence of Thornton D. Morris (Florence's son by her second husband, Richard P. Morris), interview with author, 2 September 1986, Salt Lake City.

18. *Salt Lake Daily Herald*, 10 May 1885, which prints the text of *Clawson v. United States*, 114 U.S. 477 (1885).

19. Thomas G. Alexander, "Charles S. Zane, Apostle of the New Era," *Utah Historical Quarterly* 34 (Fall 1966): 290–314.

20. For a transcript of John Taylor's testimony, see the *Deseret Evening News*, 18 October 1884. Two days after his appearance in court, Taylor told the Mormons in Ogden that when he was asked about sealings performed outside the temple or the Endowment House, he "could have told them I was sealed outside, and lots of others" ("Discourse Delivered by President John Taylor," *Journal of Discourses* 25 [1884]: 355).

21. For experiences of plural wives during the "Raid" against polygamy during the 1880s, see Kimberly J. James, " 'Between Two Fires': Women on the 'Underground' of Mormon Polygamy," *Journal of Mormon History* 8 (1981): 49–61.

22. Orson F. Whitney, *History of Utah*, 4 vols. (Salt Lake City: George Q. Cannon and Sons, 1892–1904), 3:313–14.

23. Papers and Files in Case No. 117 of *United States vs Rudger Clawson*, 25 October 1884, charge to the jury by Judge Charles S. Zane, RC, 1987 Addendum, Bx 24, Fd 19. Unknown to Judge Zane, Lydia was already four months' pregnant at the time of the trial. This child, named Rudger Remus Clawson, was born on 25 March 1885 and died of typhoid fever on 18 November 1904 (*Deseret Evening News*, 21 November 1904).

24. "Notes on Family Meeting at Death of Lydia Spencer Clawson, February 1941," RC, Bx 30, Fd 3.

25. Rosa Mae M. Evans, "Judicial Prosecution of Prisoners for LDS Plural Marriage: Prison Sentences, 1884–1895" (M.A. thesis, Brigham Young University, 1986), 1. Evans notes often that Judge Charles S. Zane and Judge Jacob S. Boreman were strict on the Mormon polygamists and usually imposed the maximum sentence. The religious prejudice of the judges seems indicated by how they treated Mormons and non-Mormons for the same offense. Examining five cases of men in their twenties convicted of polygamy, the two Mormons received sentences of forty-two and forty-eight months, while one non-Mormon was sentenced to only one month and the other two to six months (41). However, this did not approach the severity of the racial prejudice of Judge John W. Judd of the First District Court in Provo who, having come from Tennessee, sentenced each of three young black men (who had been convicted of rape) to twenty-four years in prison (87).

26. Sixty-four-year-old John B. Johnson was convicted of unlawful cohabitation and sentenced by Judge Zane on 24 February 1888 to a term of six months and a fine of $150 plus court costs of $43.15. Because Johnson contracted pneumonia two days later, the prison officials moved him to the guardroom, which served as a hospital. He died early in the morning of 5 March 1888 with a son at his bedside. See *Deseret Evening News*, 5 March 1888. *Salt Lake Daily Tribune*, 7 March 1888, objects to the *Deseret News*'s use of the term *martyr*.

27. Evans, "Judicial Prosecution," 36–37.

28. Henry Sudweeks (1815–1900), at the age of seventy, polygamously married Emma Sudweeks, the forty-year-old daughter of his brother. He was sentenced on 14 May 1890 and received the minimum three-year sentence allowed by the Edmunds-Tucker Act, but was released after thirteen and a half months on 27 June 1891. See Joseph Sudweeks, "Biography of Henry Sudweeks," Lee Library, Brigham Young University, Provo. In relation to uncle-niece marriages among polygamous Mormons, Jessie L. Embry, in "Ultimate Taboos: Incest and Mormon Polygamy," *Journal of Mormon History* 18 (1992): 138–39, reports that Samuel Smith, mayor of Brigham City, had five wives, two of which were nieces, and Aaron Johnson, bishop of Springville, had twelve wives, six of which were nieces.

29. *Salt Lake Daily Herald*, 24 May 1885.

30. John Adams, Diary, 31 May 1887, in private possession, and David John, Diary, 3–4 June 1887, Lee Library, Brigham Young University, Provo.

31. For example, from 1885 to 1893 five polygamous Mormons—Thomas H. Bullock, James Bywater, Nicholas H. Groesbeck, Orlando F. Herrin, and Charles L. White—each served three separate imprisonments for various convictions of unlawful cohabitation and adultery.

32. Since the Clawson memoirs are about life at the Utah Territorial Penitentiary, only those imprisoned there are considered. There were also polygamous Mormons arrested, convicted, and sentenced to imprisonment in Lincoln, Nebraska; Detroit, Michigan; Boise, Idaho; and Yuma, Arizona. See James L. Clayton, "The Supreme Court, Polygamy, and the Enforcement of Morals in Nineteenth Century America: An Analysis of Reynolds v. United States," *Dialogue: A Journal of Mormon Thought* 12 (Winter 1979): 46–61; B. Carmon Hardy, "The American Siberia: Mormon Prisoners in Detroit in the 1880s," *Michigan History* 50 (Sept. 1966): 197–210; Merle W. Wells, *Anti-Mormonism in Idaho, 1872–92* (Provo, Utah: Brigham Young University Press, 1978); and David Boone and Chad J. Flake, eds., "The Prison Diary of William Jordan Flake," *Journal of Arizona History* 24 (Summer 1983): 145–70.

33. RC, Bx 2, Fd 1, 1884 Diary, 9; evidently the mention of putting on the gloves and being thrown up in a blanket, given in the present memoirs, were in the ensuing conversation about what Clawson's initiation should be. Cf. *Salt Lake Daily Herald*, 15 November 1884.

34. Moroni Brown, speech at his prison farewell, 13 January 1886, RC, Bx 2, Fd 12.

35. O. W. W. T. [John Nicholson], "Sketches and Reminiscences of Prison Life," *Contributor* 8 (Dec. 1886): 76. After Nicholson was released in March 1886, he was so happy to be "out" of prison that he wrote this article under the pen name "O. W. W. T." Cf. the toned-down wording in his earlier work *The Martyrdom of Joseph Standing* ... Also ... *Description of the Utah Penitentiary* (Salt Lake City: Deseret News, 1886), 90–91.

36. George H. Taylor, Diary, 1 March 1886, Utah State Historical Society, Salt Lake City.

37. *Salt Lake Daily Herald*, 24 May 1885.

38. RC, Bx 2, Fd 1, 1884 Diary, 6.

39. Henry Dinwoodey, Diary, 25 March 1886, Marriott Library, University of Utah, Salt Lake City.

40. "A Small Scetch of Lydia Spencer Clawson," 2. See Hoopes and Hoopes, *Making of a Mormon Apostle*, 99, 104.

41. After the divorce, Clawson's mother and others suggested that he now remarry Lydia, since this would make it possible for her to get visiting privileges. Clawson and other cohabs were opposed to this suggestion, not simply on principle, but because Clawson "could marry a legal wife hereafter and they could not trouble him for it, ... if he did not marry Lydia again" (Angus M. Cannon, Diary, 9 August 1885, Lee Library, Brigham Young University, Provo). Clawson finally remarried Lydia on 26 October 1887. For a discussion of divorce among Mormon polygamists, see Jessie L. Embry, *Mormon Polygamous Families: Life in the Principle* (Salt Lake City: University of Utah Press, 1987), 176–82.

42. RC, Bx 16, Fd 4, Letter to Lydia Clawson, 9 September 1885, which is reproduced in this volume. The request for Lydia to get permission for another "private interview" is found in the letter of 23 September 1885, which is also reproduced in this volume. In October Lydia told him she was still "in a serious condition" (RC, Bx 16, Fd 4, Letter to Lydia Clawson, 15 October 1885). When Lydia wrote to him on Thanksgiving, 26 November 1885, she relayed that she was still pregnant, using the French word *enceinte*, misspelled as *enciente* (RC, Bx 16, Fd 4, Letter to Lydia Clawson, 30 November 1885, which is reproduced in this volume). She later miscarried. For a modern discussion of the values of conjugal visits to prisoners, see Columbus B. Hopper, *Sex in Prison: The Mississippi Experiment with Conjugal Visiting* (Baton Rouge: Louisiana State University Press, 1969).

43. The earlier laxness of prison rules is illustrated by the fact that during the one and a half years of George Reynolds' imprisonment at the Utah penitentiary, he was allowed to go home on five separate occasions, twice when children were born. See Clayton, "The Supreme Court," 53.

44. M. Hamlin Cannon, ed., "The Prison Diary of a Mormon Apostle," *Pacific Historical Review* 16 (Nov. 1947): 408–409.

45. Abraham H. Cannon, Diary, 4 August 1886, Marriott Library, University of Utah, Salt Lake City.

46. John Lee Jones, Diary, May 1887, Lee Library, Brigham Young University, Provo.

47. Joseph H. Dean, Diary, 3 November 1886, Archives, Historical Department, Church of Jesus Christ of Latter-day Saints, Salt Lake City, hereafter cited as LDS Archives.

48. Abraham H. Cannon, Diary, 30–31 March 1886. Herbert J. Foulger, in his diary, 30–31 March 1886, Marriott Library, University of Utah, Salt Lake City, says that on 31 March 1886 Cooley "received word that his Daughter [Maretta] had expired & got permission to go home" again, but Foulger misunderstood that the previous night when Cooley had returned to the prison he was given permission to visit her again the next day and had almost reached home when she passed away. His daughter, Maretta, known affectionately as Net, had died of pneumonia (Myrtle Stevens Hyde and Everett L. Cooley, *The Life of Andrew Wood Cooley: A Story of Conviction* [Provo: Andrew Wood Cooley Family Association, 1991], 166).

49. Dinwoodey, Diary, 10 and 23 March 1886.

50. Angus M. Cannon, Diary, 9 August 1885.

51. Adams, Diary, 10 April 1887.

52. George C. Lambert, Diary, 28 August 1886, LDS Archives.

53. John, Diary, 1 August 1887.

54. Adams, Diary, 25 May 1887.

55. Abraham H. Cannon, Diary, 28 May 1886, quoted in William C. Seifrit, "The Prison Experience of Abraham H. Cannon," *Utah Historical Quarterly* 53 (Summer 1985): 228.

56. Adams, Diary, 6 April 1887.

57. Angus M. Cannon, Diary, 10 May 1885.

58. Gottlieb Ence, "A Short Sketch of My Life," 194, Marriott Library, University of Utah, Salt Lake City.

59. Helon H. Tracy, Diary, 27 February and 31 October 1886, Marriott Library, University of Utah, Salt Lake City.

60. O. W. W. T., "Sketches," 78–79. Truman G. Madsen, *Defender of the Faith: The B. H. Roberts Story* (Salt Lake City: Bookcraft, 1980), 188, is not historically accurate when he states that "Mormon prisoners had cold water instead of coffee."

61. Adams, Diary, 1 March 1887.

62. Angus M. Cannon, Diary, 16 May 1885.

63. RC, Bx 16, Fd 4, Letter to Lydia Clawson, 8 July 1885.

64. Taylor, Diary, 12 July 1886.

65. Tracy, Diary, 2 August 1886.

66. James Kirkham, Diary, 19 August 1887, LDS Archives.

67. James Bywater, Diary, 259, quoted in Melvin Bashore, "Life behind Bars: Mormon Cohabs of the 1880s," *Utah Historical Quarterly* 47 (Winter 1979): 30.

68. Adams, Diary, 28 April 1887.

69. Abraham H. Cannon, Diary, 20 March 1886, quoted in Abraham H. Cannon, "Mormons in Prison," in *Voices from the Past: Diaries, Journals,*

Introduction / 29

and *Autobiographies*, comp. Campus Education Week Program, Division of Continuing Education, Brigham Young University (Provo: Brigham Young University Press, 1980), 99.

70. Dale Z. Kirby, "From the Pen of a Cohab," *Sunstone* 6 (May-June 1981): 37.

71. Abraham H. Cannon, Diary, 30 May 1886.

72. *Salt Lake Daily Herald*, 15 November 1884.

73. James M. Paxton, *The Cotter and the Prisoner or Whisperings from the "Pen"* (Salt Lake City: n.p., 1889).

74. Mina C. Cannon, Autograph Book, Lee Library, Brigham Young University, Provo. Mina was visiting her husband's uncle, Angus M. Cannon, who himself records what he wrote in such an autograph book: "Immured in prison for one's faith / I now am asked to write: / My Autograph and so relate / What I do now indite. / Of liberty I've felt so proud / What would I give for thee / Ee'en life itself I'd cry aloud, / But ne'er my families flee (Angus M. Cannon, Diary, 5 June 1885). For other examples from prison autograph books, see William Mulder, "Prisoners for Conscience' Sake," in *Lore of Faith and Folly*, ed. Thomas E. Cheney (Salt Lake City: University of Utah, 1971), 135–44.

75. Abraham H. Cannon, Diary, 30 April 1886.

76. Angus M. Cannon, Diary, 4 November 1885; cf. John, Diary, 22 May 1887.

77. Tracy, Diary, 22 and 28 June 1886.

78. O. W. W. T., "Sketches," 77.

79. For a transcription of George Q. Cannon's prison diary for September to December 1888, see M. Hamlin Cannon, ed., "The Prison Diary of a Mormon Apostle [George Q. Cannon]," *Pacific Historical Review* 16 (Nov. 1947): 393–409. In 1991 the present editor discovered the original Cannon diary in an unprocessed box at the library of Colorado College in Colorado Springs, Colorado.

80. Abraham H. Cannon, Diary, 15 July 1886, with Cannon's two dashes being changed to new paragraphs to separate the three different topics. William H. Dixon, in *New America*, 2 vols. (London: Hurst and Blackett, 1867), 1:310–11, quotes Brigham Young as seeing no objection to the marriage of a brother and sister except "prejudice" (the same term as reported by Lorenzo Snow to A. H. Cannon), and this source is nineteen years earlier than Cannon. A. Theodore Schroeder, in "Incest in Mormonism," *American Journal of Urology and Sexology* 11 (1915): 411, also refers to this view of Brigham Young.

81. Tracy, Diary, undated, 72, with Tracy's dittography, misspellings, and lack of punctuation being retained. Contrast the version of this episode related in Stanley B. Kimball, *Heber C. Kimball: Mormon Patriarch and Pioneer* (Urbana: University of Illinois Press, 1981), 95.

82. RC, Diary, 2 April 1903.

83. Tracy, Diary, 7 August 1886.

84. *Clawson v. United States*, 113 U.S. 143 (1885). Cf. Edwin Brown Firmage and Richard Collin Mangrum, *Zion in the Courts: A Legal History of*

the Church of Jesus Christ of Latter-day Saints, 1830–1900 (Urbana: University of Illinois Press, 1988), 393–94.

85. *Clawson v. United States,* 114 U.S. 477 (1885). The text is also printed in *Salt Lake Daily Herald,* 10 May 1885.

86. Abraham H. Cannon, Diary, 23 April 1886.

87. *Cannon v. United States,* 116 U.S. 66 (1885).

88. *United States v. Cannon,* 4 Utah 137 (1885).

89. *Cannon v. United States,* 116 U.S. 71–72 (1885). That the court was right in this opinion is demonstrated by the fact that after this promise Cannon had two more children (born 1890 and 1900) by his fourth wife, Martha Hughes Cannon, and that he married Maria Bennion in March 1886 (by whom he had four children from 1887 to 1897) and Johanna Christina Danielson in March 1887. See Beatrice Cannon Evans and Janath Russell Cannon, eds., *Cannon Family Historical Treasury* (Salt Lake City: George Cannon Family Association, 1967), 230–37.

90. *Cannon v. United States,* 116 U.S. 80 (1885). See *Deseret Evening News,* 15 December 1885.

91. Ken Driggs, "The Prosecutions Begin: Defining Cohabitation in 1885," *Dialogue: A Journal of Mormon Thought* 21 (Spring 1988): 121.

92. Orma Linford, "The Mormons and the Law: The Polygamy Cases," *Utah Law Review* 9 (Winter 1964): 360.

93. *In re Snow,* 120 U.S. 274 (1887).

94. 24 Statutes 635 (1887), which is reproduced in Grow, "Utah Commission," 291–300.

95. The author incorrectly stated in "Synoptic Minutes of a Quarterly Conference of the Twelve Apostles: The Clawson and Lund Diaries of July 9–11, 1901," *Journal of Mormon History* 14 (1988): 98, that Rudger Clawson served the longest continuous prison sentence of any Mormon cohab, implying that the record was not later broken. That honor belongs to George C. Wood of Bountiful, who entered the penitentiary on 29 May 1886 and was released on 5 November 1889, due to a pardon by President Benjamin Harrison. Wood served for three years, five months, and seven days—almost four months more than Rudger Clawson. Rosa Evans, through an error of arithmetic, lists Wood's time served in prison as only twenty-nine months (instead of forty-one months and seven days). Because of this error and because she lists Harvey Murdock's time as forty-two months (instead of one day less than forty-one months), Evans incorrectly has Harvey Murdock as having served longer than any other cohab (Evans, "Judicial Prosecution," 41, 94, 126, 132).

96. Rudger Clawson, speech at a High Priest social gathering in the Sugar House Ward, recorded in Brigham Young, Jr., Diary, 24 April 1902, New York Public Library, New York.

97. Nephi Anderson, "Rudger Clawson," *Juvenile Instructor* 35 (1 Dec. 1900): 775–76. Cf. Adams, Diary, 24 October 1887.

98. Lorenzo Snow, Letter to Wilford Woodruff, 13 December 1887, in Scott G. Kenney Collection, Bx 12, Fd 10, Marriott Library, University of Utah, Salt Lake City.

99. David J. Buerger, " 'The Fulness of the Priesthood': The Second Anointing in Latter-day Saint Theology and Practice," *Dialogue: A Journal of Mormon Thought* 16 (Spring 1983): 10–44.

100. Van Wagoner, *Mormon Polygamy*, 135. See Thomas G. Alexander, *Things in Heaven and Earth: The Life and Times of Wilford Woodruff, a Mormon Prophet* (Salt Lake City: Signature Books, 1991), 248.

101. This extract is derived from his journal (RC, Diary O, 21, 23). Among the Clawson papers is preserved what appear to be the original sheets used by Clawson to record this discourse in his journal (RC, Bx 22, Fd 1). The twenty-nine numbered sheets are six by eight inches, written in pencil on one side only, and folded vertically. There are penciled corrections to the text at several points and one ink correction, all of which are followed in the journal version. This manuscript is the authority for the editorial insertion of the word *repentance*. In the synopsis of Clawson's speech published in the 7 April 1888 *Deseret Evening News* and the 11 April 1888 *Deseret Weekly News* the third paragraph as quoted here was not printed at all; cf. the more accurate coverage in the 7 April 1888 *Salt Lake Daily Tribune*.

102. *New York Times*, 7 April 1888.

103. Edward Leo Lyman, *Political Deliverance: The Mormon Quest for Utah Statehood* (Urbana: University of Illinois Press, 1986), 90.

104. Wilford Woodruff to Franklin S. Richards and Charles W. Penrose, 12 April 1888, Woodruff Letterbooks, quoted in Van Wagoner, *Mormon Polygamy*, 135.

105. RC, Diary O, 17.

106. *The Late Corporation of the Church of Jesus Christ of Latter-day Saints v. United States*, 136 U.S. 1 (1890); 140 U.S. 665 (1890).

107. B. Carmon Hardy, "Self-blame and the Manifesto," *Dialogue: A Journal of Mormon Thought* 24 (Fall 1991): 46.

108. Evans, "Judicial Prosecution," 35.

109. RC, Diary, 16 January 1902.

110. For a discussion of President Lorenzo Snow, President Joseph F. Smith, and nine apostles who all together had twenty-seven wives bear seventy-six children after the Manifesto, see Kenneth L. Cannon II, "Beyond the Manifesto: Polygamous Cohabitation among LDS General Authorities after 1890," *Utah Historical Quarterly* 46 (Winter 1978): 24–36.

111. For a discussion of post-Manifesto polygamy by seven Mormon apostles and evidently even the ninety-year-old President Wilford Woodruff to the forty-nine-year-old Madame Lydia Mary von Finkelstein Mountford in 1897, see D. Michael Quinn, "LDS Church Authority and New Plural Marriages, 1890–1904," *Dialogue: A Journal of Mormon Thought* 18 (Spring 1985): 9–105, and Victor W. Jorgensen and B. Carmon Hardy, "The Taylor-Cowley Affair and the Watershed of Mormon History," *Utah Historical Quarterly* 48 (Winter 1980): 11–15.

112. Kenneth L. Cannon II, "After the Manifesto: Mormon Polygamy 1890–1906," *Sunstone* 8 (Jan.–Apr. 1983): 30, 35.

113. Jerold A. Hilton, "Polygamy in Utah and Surrounding Area since the Manifesto of 1890" (M.A. thesis, Brigham Young University, 1965), 6–7.

114. Based on D. Michael Quinn's research, Roy Hoopes, in "My Grandfather, the Mormon Apostle: Discovering a Giant in the Family," *American Heritage* 41 (Feb. 1990): 90, and David Hoopes and Roy Hoopes, in *Making of a Mormon Apostle,* 225–30, first made public Clawson's post-Manifesto marriage to Pearl Udall.

115. RC, Diary, 23 August 1903.

116. RC, Diary, 1 October 1903.

117. RC, Diary, 11 October 1903, referring to the conversation that took place on the previous day.

118. RC, Diary, 6 November and 19 December 1903. Additional references to his expecting to receive letters from, and writing "important" letters to, an unidentified person are found in the diary entries of 18 January, 23 February, 9 March, and 29 April 1904.

119. RC, Diary, 5 January 1904.

120. Lund, Diary, 4 and 6 April 1904, photocopy in the possession of Jennifer Lund, with the original at the LDS Archives.

121. Family group sheets submitted by family members indicate 9 May 1904, while the temple endowment record indicates 11 May 1904.

122. RC, Diary, 2 and 10 May 1904.

123. RC, Diary, 16 May 1904.

124. Elma Udall, Letters to Stan Larson, 14 March and 10 April 1989, in author's possession.

125. Van Wagoner, *Mormon Polygamy,* 161.

126. RC, Diary, 3 August 1904. B. Carmon Hardy mentions the Udall family tradition of their marriage being performed by Joseph Robinson, president of the California Mission, while in a ship off the California coast (and not, therefore, being in the United States), but he prefers placing the marriage on 3 August 1904 in Grand Junction. However, Hardy sees a problem: "The problem is that, had Clawson taken the earliest train from Salt Lake City on 3 August 1904 (the fastest method of travel at the time), without delay or other complication, he could not have arrived in Grand Junction before 6:35 P.M. And the next returning train did not leave until after midnight, arriving in Salt Lake City at 10:40 A.M. the next morning. Clearly, Clawson could not, as his diary describes, have returned to Salt Lake City the same evening as his departure for Grand Junction" (B. Carmon Hardy, *Solemn Covenant: The Mormon Polygamous Passage* [Urbana: University of Illinois Press, 1991], 211). The trip to Grand Junction is not as difficult as suggested by Hardy, for one must understand how Rudger Clawson kept his diary. The high point of each week was the Thursday temple meeting and often the diary entries for the previous weekdays (Monday through Wednesday) were grouped together and typed just before typing up the minutes of the Thursday council meeting. This is one of those instances. Clawson could easily have had an evening buggy ride with Lydia (telling her of his decision to marry Pearl) and then leave on

the last train to Grand Junction on the evening of 2 August 1904, coming back on the last return train the next day.

127. Pearl Udall, Letter to "Dear Mamma" [Luella Stewart Udall], 18 July 1904, David K. Udall Collection, Ms 294, Bx 2, Library, University of Arizona, Tucson.

128. "A" [Rudger Clawson], Letter to "Dearest Z" [Pearl Udall], 17 October 1904, in RC, Bx 30, Fd 1. See Hoopes and Hoopes, *Making of a Mormon Apostle*, 229–30.

129. Other considerations also strengthen Rudger Clawson's authorship of the letter. That same day he typed a letter with a similar series of spaced lines upon which he signed his name. The sheet of the 17 October 1904 letter bears the "Oriole Linen" watermark just like Clawson's diary pages at this point. The sheet was folded into three sections and on the back is written "Oct. 17, 1904" in Rudger Clawson's handwriting. The sheet is now unfolded, but the soiled edges confirm that for years it was kept folded into the size 1¼ inch by 3 inches. His grandsons suggest that it was kept in his wallet (Hoopes and Hoopes, *Making of a Mormon Apostle*, 229).

130. Pearl Udall, Letter to "Mamma" [Luella Stewart Udall], 25 June 1905. Also, in an 11 August 1905 letter Pearl says: "Aunt Ida and I, she stayed with me last night, took an early walk to the park and had a lovely visit with A from five to nearly six o'clock [A.M.]. And, I must come to the point at once and make explanations later, A and I decided perhaps it will be better for me to go home and spend the winter with you." In a letter dated "Sunday Morning" Pearl says: "Mamma the other night A and I had a fine drive in the only big rainstorm of the season. Our buggy had a top and there with an umbrella we kept dry. Drove down and up Main St and down Brigham with no fear of attracting attention that night." These letters are quoted in Maria S. Ellsworth, Letter to Stan Larson, 30 January 1991, in the author's possession, with the originals in the possession of Jeanie Udall Glazier of Rialto, California.

131. David K. Udall, *Arizona Pioneer Mormon: David King Udall, His Story and His Family* (Tucson: Arizona Silhouettes, 1959), 253.

132. Hoopes, "My Grandfather," 92.

133. Samuel W. Taylor, "Oh Say, What Is Truth? Use Only as Directed," in the John Taylor Family Collection, Bx 71, Fd 5, Marriott Library, University of Utah, Salt Lake City. Emphasis in original. Another illustration of this same distinction is Matthias F. Cowley's remarks in 1903: "While in attendance at the recent Kanab Stake conference, he [Cowley] was led by a rich outpouring of the Holy Spirit to speak upon the principle of plural marriage and to defend it. This talk seemed to be necessary because of a spirit of fault finding and complaint against the authorities that had broken out there. The present agitation [about Reed Smoot] throughout the country would doubtless result in good. The hand of the Lord is in it, so that our young people shall not lose sight of the principle. We must, of course, sustain the policies of the church, but cannot change the revelations of God. Plural marriage will stand" (RC, Diary, 1 April 1903).

DOCUMENTARY
SOURCES

The prison memoirs of Rudger Clawson have been preserved in six distinct manuscripts. In the notes MS I indicates the original holograph manuscript in Clawson's handwriting, which was written on 6½-by-10½-inch lined sheets. This manuscript was begun while Clawson was still in prison (several statements can be pinpointed to early 1887), and this earliest draft was probably finished in 1888, though certainly by 1891, since in May 1891 Clawson referred to his completed "Memoirs of Prison Life." At a point where there is either a corrected reading or an addition in this manuscript, MS I* indicates the original reading. MS I² indicates a handwritten correction to MS I. Several instances of MS I² can be dated to after Utah became a state in January 1896 and one revision of MS I² to after the death of Abraham H. Cannon in July 1896. MS I³ indicates the later handwritten additions on separate sheets inserted into MS I. There are several instances in which the paper used for MS I³ contains the watermark of the Rocky Mountain Bank Note Company, which was organized in the fall of 1907. MS I, entitled "Personal Experiences in the Utah State Penitentiary," is located in the Rudger Clawson Collection, Manuscript 481, Bx 2, Fds 2–7 and Bx 26, Fd 1, Marriott Library, University of Utah, Salt Lake City.

MS II indicates the first typescript that was made directly from MS I. MS II was typed on 8½-by-11-inch sheets of paper, but Clawson was not the typist since numerous errors demonstrate the typist's inability to read the handwritten MS I or to understand Clawson's use of certain Latin terms. MS II² indicates a handwritten correction to MS II. MS II³ indicates a later handwritten addition inserted on separate sheets into MS II. In one instance the addition of MS II³ is written on the back of a carbon copy of a letter typed in March 1921. MS II, entitled "Personal Experience in the Utah State Penitentiary," is located in the Rudger Clawson Collection, Manuscript 481, Bx 2, Fds 8–11 and Bx 26, Fds 2–3, Marriott Library, University of Utah, Salt Lake City.

MS III indicates the typescript made from MS II. This carbon-copy manuscript was typed sometime between 1926 and 1936. There are no interlinear or marginal corrections. MS III, entitled "Personal Experience in the Utah State Penitentiary," is located in the Rudger Clawson Collection, Manuscript 481, Bx 26, Fds 4–9, Marriott Library, University of Utah, Salt Lake City.

MS IV indicates another carbon copy of MS III. At a point where there is either a corrected reading or an addition, MS IV* indicates the original reading. MS IV^2 indicates a later handwritten correction to MS IV*. These revisions were added to MS IV up to the time of Clawson's death in 1943. MS IV, entitled "Memoirs of the Life of Rudger Clawson Written by Himself," is located in the Rudger Clawson Collection, Manuscript B-21, Utah State Historical Society, Salt Lake City. A microfilm (Manuscript 8912) of this autobiography is located in the Archives, Historical Department, Church of Jesus Christ of Latter-day Saints, Salt Lake City.

MS V indicates the typescript made from either MS III or MS IV*, since at their earliest stages the latter two manuscripts are identical. In several instances MS V, due to the error of homoioteleuton, omits a whole line of the manuscript being copied from. Another unique feature of MS V is an unintentional dittography of an entire page, due to unknowingly retyping the same page of the exemplar. MS V was typed in the late 1930s. MS V^2 indicates a later handwritten correction to the manuscript. MS V, entitled "Memoirs of the Life of Rudger Clawson Written by Himself," is located in the Rudger Clawson Collection, Manuscript 481, Bx 1, Fds 1–13, Marriott Library, University of Utah, Salt Lake City.

MS VI indicates a very late typescript made from MS IV^2, probably in the 1950s or 1960s. Because this typescript lacks any revision by Clawson, MS VI has not been utilized or referred to here. MS VI, entitled "Personal Experience in the Utah State Penitentiary of Rudger Clawson," Manuscript 2690, is located in the Archives, Historical Department, Church of Jesus Christ of Latter-day Saints, Salt Lake City.

To present Clawson's memoirs as he intended them, this edition is necessarily an eclectic text, based mainly on MS V (incorporating the revisions of MS V^2), with the even later revisions from MS IV^2 and various textual restorations based upon the original reading of MS I.

The notes draw attention to illustrative material in Clawson's various manuscripts, the diaries of other cohabs, and other sources. The love letters written by Rudger Clawson to his polygamist wife Lydia Spencer are selected from the letters in the Rudger Clawson Collection, Manuscript 481, Bx 16, Fds 4–6, Marriott Library, University of Utah, Salt Lake City. There are no known letters to or from his first wife, Florence Dinwoodey, or letters from Lydia Spencer. Clawson's prison letters to Lydia were preserved in her strongbox containing old photos and letters, some of which had been folded to the size of a postage stamp and smuggled out of the prison by being concealed in the seams of dirty clothes. From among those that have survived, seventeen representative letters from 1884 to 1887 have been selected. Two 1887 letters have postscripts written by Clawson in Pitman shorthand, and the five words which LaJean Purcell Carruth could not be certain about the decipherment are indicated by square brackets.

The prison journal of Rudger Clawson, which is transcribed in Appendix 2, was written in November and December 1884. Because it is a firsthand glimpse into Clawson's feelings and attitudes at the beginning of his imprisonment, it provides useful comparison with Clawson's later memoirs. This journal is located in the Rudger Clawson Collection, Manuscript 481, Bx 2, Fd 1, Marriott Library, University of Utah, Salt Lake City.

The present editor's alterations to Clawson's text of the memoirs, letters, and journal consist of inserted words and scriptural references in square brackets, adjusted paragraphing for easier reading, improved spelling, and minor changes in capitalization and punctuation. The ampersand (&) has been written as an *and*, except when it occurs in the form &c. The abbreviation *do*, used for *ditto*, has been replaced by the words intended in the context. The symbol # has been written as *no*. The wording and grammar have not been altered. Clawson's underlining of words is shown by italics. His occasional use of a sarcastic question mark (enclosed by parentheses) has been retained, since it shows the insertion into the narrative of his point of view. For example, when Clawson refers to the prison food as "luxuries (?)," he adds the question mark to indicate that he is using the term sarcastically. Words accidentally omitted by a typist and obvious typographical and transcriptional errors have been silently corrected; likewise, the few instances of unintentional dittography have been corrected. Also, where there are interlinear corrections by Clawson, only the final form is printed.

PART ONE

The Memoirs of Rudger Clawson at the Utah Territorial Penitentiary

CHAPTER 1

1884

Having been convicted of polygamy and unlawful cohabitation in the Third Judicial District Court of the State of Utah,[1] I was sentenced by Judge Charles S. Zane,[2] on November 3rd, 1884, to four years' imprisonment and to pay a fine of $800.00. There were two counts. On the first, the sentence was for three years and six months with a fine of $500.00, and on the second for six months with a fine of $300.00.

When the Judge asked me on the day appointed for sentence if I had anything to say as to why sentence should not be passed upon me, I answered: "I regret very much that the laws of my Country come in conflict with the laws of God, but whenever they do, I shall invariably choose to obey the latter. If I did not so express myself, I should feel unworthy of the cause I represent. The Constitution of the United States expressly provides that Congress shall make no law respecting the establishment of religion or prohibiting the free exercise thereof, and it cannot be denied, I think, that marriage, when attended and sanctioned by religious rites, is an element in the establishment of religion. The Anti-Polygamy law of 1862 and the Edmunds-Tucker law of 1882 were expressly designed to operate against plural marriage as believed in and practiced by the Latter-day Saints.[3] These laws are, therefore, unconstitutional, and cannot command the respect that is given to Constitutional laws. That is all I have to say, your honor."

In the subsequent remarks of Judge Zane he said that every man has a right to worship according to the dictates of his conscience and to entertain any belief that his reason and judgment might dictate. But this was followed by a flat contradiction of his own theory, when he added: "You violated the Edmunds Act, as you say, with the understanding that you had a right to do so because there was a higher law by which you govern your conduct. That being so, it makes the case somewhat aggravated. . . . I confess that I should have felt inclined to fix the punishment smaller than I shall were it not for the fact that you openly declare that you believe it is right to violate the law, in that you believe you are right in doing so."

His proposition was that belief and worship are exempt from peremptory process, but he practically contradicted himself by the judgment rendered. I received a heavier sentence on account of my belief than I would otherwise have received.

I was taken into the custody of Marshal E. A. Ireland[4] about 3:00 P.M. and entered the prison on the evening of the same day. Ah, little did I then realize how strange and distasteful would be my experience before emerging from the gloomy walls of the penitentiary, a free man!

The prison proper was enclosed by a massive wall four feet thick and twenty-two feet high, with two sentry boxes located on the diagonal corners.[5] It was divided into two compartments, one of which (room 1) was occupied by the rougher element among the convicts; the other (room 2) by such men as could be trusted to work on the penitentiary farm and the kitchen located just outside the walls in the building used by Warden G. N. Dow and family.[6] The prisoners in room 2 were called "trusties" and were much less turbulent and unruly than the others.

The warden was directed by the marshal to place me in room 1, although I had been led to believe that my lot would be cast among the "trusties." After being searched, measured, and thoroughly scrutinized, I passed through the huge gate and was led into the enclosure. As I approached the prison door, a strange and fearful noise reached my ears which fairly made me shudder. The sound issued from the room where remorseless fate had decreed that I should pass my first night in prison—a night ever to be remembered as long, tedious, and full of melancholy apprehension. Before entering I caught such expressions as "get the rope," "hang him," "the blanket—up he goes," "make him put on the gloves," "we'll fix him," etc., while the air was rent by profanity and ribald laughter. No consolation could be drawn from this dismal noise which was further aggravated by the rattling of chains worn by some of the prisoners. I paused bewildered, the lock was turned, the iron door swung on its hinges and a moment later I found myself in a room about 50 by 20 feet, and in the midst of a class of men who compose the lowest stratum of society and who haunt the dens of vice that exist in most of our large cities throughout the country.

A cloud of tobacco smoke, dense and obnoxious, filled the room. I gasped for fresh air, remaining silent, however. It would be impossible to describe the feeling of intense repugnance that seized upon me as these sixty uncouth men gathered round and stood gazing at me like wild beasts ready to pounce upon their prey and devour it. The expression of their faces was malignant and threatening. "Mormonism" is always very unpopular, and the prejudice existing against it, which is so common in the world, had found its way even into the minds of these unruly and restless spirits, and they were prepared to handle me roughly.

It was promptly decided that I must either sing a song, dance a jig, speak a piece, stand on my head, or put on the gloves. I was rudely informed that a refusal to respond would subject me to the proceeding of being thrown up in the blanket—a proceeding invariably attended by much noise, confusion, and violence. Many of the roughest characters favored the idea of sending me up in the blanket without further ceremony and at all hazards.

In a time of need friends often unexpectedly turn up. It was so in this instance, for a prisoner called "Rocky" stepped forward and said that he proposed to see fair play. He was a tall, strong man, with pleasant features and a sympathetic heart. After explaining to me the necessity of my doing something to allay the increasing clamor, he asked if I would put on the gloves. I consented, but not without some reluctance, for I could see plainly that in point of size and physical strength, I was by no means a match for many who were present.

The gloves were called for, but could not be found, although a thorough search was made for them. They had inadvertently been left outside and it was impossible to get them. Disappointment and chagrin was apparent on every face, but a sigh of relief issued from my lips at this happy turn of affairs. I was finally excused with an admonition to be prepared for a glove contest on the following evening. I learned later that in case of a glove contest, the plan was to put me up against a real "bruiser," who no doubt would have pummeled me to a finish. My friend Rocky knew nothing of this plan, however, when he suggested the gloves. The contest did not come off, for on the following night, the 4th of November, I was removed to other quarters, thereby escaping what might have turned out to be a very mournful catastrophe.

The evening of November 3rd wore away very slowly. The clanking of chains, the profanity, the vulgarity, and the brutal laughter were a constant source of offence to me. I recognized among the prisoners a man who had robbed my home a short time before of about fifty dollars worth of jewelry, and who was now serving a term of one year for the crime. He seemed quite pleased and amused to see me there. I fancied that the broad smile on his face also exhibited some signs of

malignancy. He undoubtedly blamed me for his misfortune and derived some satisfaction from our present relationship. I too was struck
with the novelty of the situation, for whoever heard of a man who
had been robbed and the robber meeting on equal terms within the
walls of a gloomy prison.

Many of my new and strange companions came up at different times
during the evening and volunteered statements of their cases, and according to their representations they were all innocent. I was as-
tounded to see so many innocent men wearing the convict's garb, and
yet the outward evidences of guilt were by no means few. Truth will
out, and as time went on, I came to the conclusion that very few who
find their way into a penitentiary are free from guile.

At 9:00 o'clock in the evening the guard appeared, as was his usual
custom, and rapped sharply upon the door—the summons to retire.
All loud talking immediately ceased, the prisoners slipped into their
bunks and five minutes later, strange to relate, an awful stillness ensued. I had been assigned a bunk on the middle tier, situated at a short
distance from a porthole or window. My bed-fellow was a harmless
sort of a man—a tramp who hailed from Ogden and whose underclo-
thing presented a decidedly unclean appearance. I refrain from going
into detail with regard to the filthy condition of his body—I leave that
to the imagination, but suffice it to say that my flesh fairly crawled at
the thought of passing the night in that bed. As I settled down to the
inevitable, it was not long ere I discovered that the room was not only
exceedingly close, but the air was filled with noxious odors issuing
from a poorly ventilated toilet in one corner of the room.

A further circumstance that annoyed me almost beyond endurance
was the constant hawking and spitting of the prisoners all through the
long hours of the night. My mind was so filled with forebodings concerning the new life now opening up before me, that I slept only
intermittently. The thought of spending four years in a place so un-
desirable was uppermost in my mind and was oppressive to a degree
almost maddening. Yet in this trying hour, I felt the sustaining influence of an invisible power—the power of the Almighty.

Morning came at last, and with it a clear sky and bright sunshine,
but oh, how dull and sluggish were my spirits! Life at that moment
certainly presented a dismal and forbidding aspect. Immediately after
arising I stepped out into the yard for exercise and fresh air. I walked
alone, for, while many had come out for the same purpose and were
moving back and forth in couples, their coarse talk and loud laughter
mingled with the noise of rattling chains attached to their ankles,

repelled rather than attracted me. I was wrapt in a loneliness not often experienced in the midst of the living.

Everything about me was strange and unfamiliar—the new faces so different from those to which I had been accustomed, the great frowning walls that appeared to fairly mock me in my new situation, the ever-present guards whose vigilant eyes seemed constantly riveted upon me, in fact everything within the range of my vision had a woeful and solemn appearance. And who can describe the feeling that comes with a realization of the loss of liberty—the realization that one's actions in life must hereafter be ordered hither and thither by the harsh command of a guard?

The meals in the prison were served in a long, low, unplastered lumber building 60 × 20 feet, with one entrance and six small windows. Breakfast was called at 7:30 A.M., dinner was served at 12:00, and supper at 6:00. The prisoners acted in turn as waiters. Those serving would proceed to the gate and there receive the victuals from the kitchen hands, which they carried into the dining room. Each man was entitled to a place at the table, which he held until released from the prison. A tin plate, cup, knife, fork, and spoon for each convict constituted the table utensils. After the food was dished out by the waiters, the men were called into line by three bells, and a moment later they filed into the dining room where they broke the line, dropped into their respective seats and, without further ceremony, began to devour their rations.

My first meal consisted of boiled beef, by no means remarkable for its tenderness, soggy potatoes, butterless bread, and coffee unaccompanied by either milk or sugar. My appetite suddenly failed and I could eat nothing. The noise and confusion that attended this meal, and in fact all other meals that followed, was simply bewildering. There was chatter, chatter, chatter, intermingled with oaths or vulgar jokes followed by shrieks of rude laughter, and sometimes it all ended in a fight. All that was left of this first repast was gathered up and sent out to the penitentiary pigs, which, in their manner of eating, were about as genteel as some of Utah's convicts.

The dining room was immediately turned into a workshop and recreation room, where the men busied themselves until noon. Dinner was served at noon and as at breakfast the edibles were hastily portioned out, three bells sounded, and the men rushed into line pell-mell. Tramp, tramp, tramp, and once more we found ourselves face to face with a duplicate of the morning meal, with the single exception that the potatoes, not having been soaked in water all night, were less soggy. Long experience had suggested to Utah's ravenous criminals many ingenious methods of sweetening and improving the otherwise unpalatable food set before them. I will mention one method. A large, circular, old-style heating stove, with bulge, stood in the center of the room. This stove seemed to exert a fascinating influence over the minds, or rather the stomachs, of many of my companions; for, no sooner had they entered the room than, armed each with two or three slices of bread which had been soaked in water, they made a rush for the stove and plastered the slices on the heated iron. When ready for mastication, the slices presented an unsightly appearance, but were nevertheless esteemed a great delicacy. I had previously observed that tobacco spittle occasionally found its way on to this same stove, so it would naturally be supposed that I had my prejudices against the new method of toasting bread. Dinner being over, the remnants were soon swept out of sight, and the men busied themselves as before until supper.

The evening meal was scarcely worthy of notice. Two slices of butterless bread and a cup of mild tea to each man constituted the bill of fare, and about fifteen minutes were sufficient to dispose of these luxuries (?). After supper most of the men found their way into the yard for exercise. When I say that the convicts were served three times a week with vegetable soup, and in the winter season with hash every other evening, you will get some idea of our prison diet the year round. The soup, as a rule, was so inconceivably weak and tasteless as to be only a few degrees removed from water, and the hash was often so rank that "it smelled to heaven."

As has been indicated, the dining room was turned into a workshop and study room after each meal, where all the men in rooms 1 and 2 passed the day engaged in the manufacture of various articles, such as hair bridles, riding whips, gilded picture frames and horse shoes, fancy work boxes ornamented with wood carvings of flowers, figures of birds, animals, etc., ship models and other things.[7] It must be admitted that these articles exhibited a beauty of design and a completeness in finish deserving of the highest praise. The industry displayed by many whose moral natures were very much depraved was something of a surprise to me.

I observed with pleasure that some few were intellectually inclined and applied themselves diligently to the acquisition of knowledge. One man, Joseph Biddlecome, who had been convicted of murder in the first degree and sentenced to life imprisonment, was quite illiterate when he came into the prison, a lad of seventeen, but by application and perseverance he had acquired a pretty thorough knowledge of shorthand, and a clear understanding of the French language. He seemed to derive great pleasure and profit from reading History, Biography, and Fiction by our standard authors.

Joe Miller, a Frenchman convicted of burglary and sentenced to two years, was also studying shorthand with good success. He acted as tutor of the warden's children (a boy about twelve years old and a girl about five), besides teaching French to some of the men in the yard. The fact that he had lost his right arm and was compelled to do his shorthand and other work with the left, detracted nothing from his ability.

Oliver Accord, who was convicted of robbing the U.S. mails and sentenced to five years, had made excellent progress in the study of the French language, and later on, under my tuition, took a thorough course in Bookkeeping. Composition and Rhetoric, Mathematics, and Penmanship were also receiving his attention.

Fred Moss, convicted of grand larceny (horse stealing) and sentenced to seven years, had succeeded in mastering the Spanish language and spoke it with fluency. He was gifted with an unusually good memory and attained this result after only a few months' study.

The prison was not without its artist, who was no other than Frank Treseder, a young man well known in Salt Lake City, and serving out a four years term for burglary committed in Ogden, Utah. An examination of some of his work proved beyond question that he had talent for painting and would under proper training distinguish himself; still his lack of application was ever a serious barrier in his way to success. His efforts with the brush were directed largely to landscape painting. I was pleased with his two pictures of the penitentiary, interior and exterior, and purchased them.

While thus engaged in contemplating some of the pleasant features of our prison life, I did not fail to notice several gaming tables located in different parts of the room, which appeared to be well patronized. Small stacks of silver coin ($2.00 to $20.00) and tobacco in the plug were in sight and passed rapidly from hand to hand. The baleful influence that emanated from these tables and spread itself among the prisoners was pernicious and blighting. The hard-earned means of those who were inclined to be industrious thus soon melted away and left the losers completely demoralized. I also discovered, much to my disgust but not surprise, that a few of the more degraded and hopeless cases—morally—seemed to derive their chief delight from telling stories of the filthiest and most obscene character.

When the bell announced the time for turning in, the second evening, much to my gratification, I was directed to fall into the line that led to room 2. The difference between the two rooms was due, not so much to the accommodations, as to the society; and yet, it must be owned, that profanity, vulgarity, smoking, chewing, and spitting also prevailed here to an alarming extent. In my new surroundings I breathed a little more freely and began to make observations. This room was about twenty-five feet long by twenty feet wide, and contained approximately thirty men. Like room 1, it was surrounded with three tiers of bunks attached to the three sides of the room. An unpleasant feature in this room was a toilet, the odor from which, combining with tobacco fumes, well-nigh overpowered me at times, but I managed to get through the evening in pretty good condition, and thereafter met with fair success in fighting off these health-destroying agencies.

There was also turmoil and uproar incident to life in room 2 and the confusion was greatly augmented by the antics of Jack Emerson, who gave expression to his feelings from hour to hour in the strumming of a banjo. If at any time during the evening he showed signs of weariness, "Shorty" McDonald, then serving a three years sentence for having stolen a "silver service" from the Episcopalian church in Ogden—shocking crime—came to his aid with a pair of bones, and the effect of this combination of sounds was most distracting. Jack, besides being an expert on the banjo, was also an accomplished clog-dancer, and a good singer, and his voice, blending with the music of his instrument, occasionally touched a tender and responsive cord in me.

Six years had passed away since Emerson, who was a genial and obliging fellow, came into the prison, and though convicted of complicity in the murder of young John Turner and sentenced to life, he was generally believed to be innocent. If outward evidences could be accepted as reliable, I should certainly take this view of the case. Whenever speaking of the matter, he invariably and stoutly affirmed his innocence. Through the strenuous efforts of my father, Hiram B. Clawson, and John Nicholson, each of whom served a six months' term for unlawful cohabitation in [1885-]1886, young Emerson was finally pardoned out.[8] At the moment of release he wept like a child, asserting before high heaven that he had had no hand whatever in the fearful tragedy with which his name had been connected.

Two nights and a day had come and gone since I entered the prison gate, an exile from the world—a very short time to be sure, but to me O how long! Every hour, as it dragged its slow length along seemed like an age; and when I looked forward to the day of release, the awful barrier—four long years—which separated me from that happy moment, almost overwhelmed me with its magnitude. The justice of my cause and an implicit confidence in the Almighty, however, gave me courage and enabled me to reconcile myself to the terrible situation. During the day the prisoners were allowed the freedom of the yard for exercise, a provision which contributed much toward preserving the health of the men. The boxing gloves were not infrequently called for, and the sparring, not to mention "slugging," that quickly followed always commanded the most wrapt attention. The "slugging" feature of these contests, I fancied, gave them a popularity much beyond their merit. This led me to the conclusion that the minds of my fellow prisoners had been molded by the *Police Gazette*. The fascinating waltz, the entrancing schottische, and the delightful quadrille also received a generous share of the boys' attention, as the hours wore away. All these doings were so new to me that I looked on in astonishment and surprise.

I was not long in discovering, among other things, that it was almost a universal custom in this prison for the inmates to engage in the despicable practice of slander. Tearing each other's reputations into shreds was easily accomplished in most cases, owing to the publicity of facts in connection therewith. "There is honor among thieves" is a trite saying, but when applied to the inmates of the Utah penitentiary, it lost much of its force. In addition to many other bad practices, prisoners often sought to build themselves up and gain influence with the warden by carrying tales to the gate derogatory of the character of their associates. In such instances honor cut but a sorry figure. So, it might have been truly said this was a veritable "school for scandal."

One necessarily comes in contact with a great variety of characters in prison, such as pickpockets, burglars, horse and cattle thieves, mail robbers, and murderers. Jack [William] Bryant of no. 2, a professional and accomplished burglar, attracted my notice. Unlike many of his companions, he appeared to borrow no trouble whatever from his imprisonment, but on the contrary was particularly jolly and sociable at all times. When dilating upon past exploits, his face fairly beamed with delight. One day shortly after my entrance into the prison, he communicated to me, in a confidential tone, the secret of making a successful burglary. This he did in view of the fact, he said, that some day I might be in a position to use the information advantageously.

The substance of his instruction I give below. General admonition: *Always work in the dark.* Arm yourself with a "bull's-eye" or dark lantern and skeleton keys. After selecting the field of operation, glide softly up the front steps, remove your shoes and pause at the front door. All being quiet, insert skeleton key and gently swing the door open. Darkness ahead. Light from the "bull's-eye" flashes through the hallway, and all is dark again; but in the meantime you have noted the position of the door leading into the dining room, and you quickly pass through it. The darkness is once more dispersed for an instant by the "bull's-eye," showing the door communicating with bedroom. Cautiously and noiselessly you move along in that direction and, standing at the door, pause, listening attentively, then pass in. [It is] still darkness, but a low breathing in one corner of the room apprises you of the presence of others. By means of your faithful friend, the "bull's eye," the room is suddenly illuminated, bringing into bold relief a man and wife quietly reposing on a richly furnished bed, with man's pantaloons on a chair at one side. Intense darkness succeeds the flash, but, with throbbing heart, you reach forth, clutch the pantaloons, step to the window and roll out. Never lose your presence of mind and, above all, make no attempt to retrace your steps; but vanish like the shadow of a dream, through the nearest exit. When at a safe distance from the house, you removed pocket book from the pantaloons, and go on your way rejoicing.

Jack took occasion to inform me that he was then serving out a term of five years for having practically carried out the above directions in a residence at Ogden City, U[tah] T[erritory]. He secured $750.00, but was *afterwards* arrested on suspicion, tried, and convicted. As he hurried away from the house after the burglary, he extracted from the pantaloons a wallet containing this large sum of money in currency. Passing a lumber yard, he paused long enough to throw the trousers, incriminating evidence, over the high board fence enclosing it. He then breathed more freely. After appropriating $20.00 for immediate needs, he buried in the earth the balance of the money, with the firm determination of returning later to carry off the prize. In a self-satisfied mood he proceeded to the Union [Pacific] Depot, Ogden, which he reached at an early hour. Here he found very few people astir and this he interpreted as a good omen for a safe "getaway." Stepping up to the ticket office, he asked for a ticket to Evanston, handing the agent the $20.00 bill. The ticket and change were promptly handed to him. Thus armed, he boarded a U[nion] P[acific] train and was soon out of the Territory and, as he supposed, absolutely out of danger. He naturally showered congratulations upon himself for the signal success of his undertaking.

Although the deed was committed in the dark, he failed to note the all-seeing eye of justice that intently gazed upon him, followed him through the house and down the street to the place where the money was buried, followed him to the railroad station and saw him enter the train and was now following him with a relentless, piercing gaze to his doom.

Shortly after his train pulled out, the police officers who had already been notified of the robbery, hardly knowing which way to look for the culprit, entered the Union Station. They critically scanned the faces of all whom they saw there, but utterly failed to detect any suspicious-looking characters. Stepping up to the ticket agent, they casually enquired if he had noticed any doubtful characters in the building that morning. "Why, yes," he said, "a party called this morning and asked for a ticket to Evanston. The request was not unusual, but the fact that he offered a $20.00 bill attracted my attention, because he looked like a man who would not ordinarily be in possession of bills of that denomination." The police felt confident they were on the right track, and, after getting a description of the man, wired his arrest to the sheriff at Evanston; and as Jack Bryant left the train, he walked into the arms of an officer.

It was but a brief interval from the time he was arrested until he was committed to the Utah Penitentiary where, for two years he was given the opportunity of pondering upon the solemn fact that it is well nigh impossible to escape the consequences of one's evil deeds. And yet Jack clapped his hands with glee, exulting over the lucky circumstance that he had outwitted the officers of the law, judge, and jury by burying out of sight and beyond their recovery the precious wallet of money. This he intended to secure at his liberation from prison, and would go on his way rejoicing. It cannot be said that Jack was a scripturarian, but he seemed to feel that two years imprisonment would pay the "uttermost farthing" [Matthew 5:26] of his offending. He would then go forth feeling that he had paid the penalty and could now enjoy to the full the fruits of his skill. To him it was the money that counted. It was plainly apparent that Jack Bryant had an easy conscience and an accommodating mind.

The notorious fraud, [Andrew S.] Hill, who had robbed his own wife of $10,000.00 and was being held to answer the charge, was pointed out to me during the second evening. He was a short, heavy-set man, with round face and dull blue eyes. A short chin beard gave him very much the appearance of a Southerner. That any man could be guilty of a deed so base and degrading seemed almost incredible, and, as I eyed him curiously, an involuntary shudder crept over me. The coolness and indifference with which he appeared to accept the situation denoted, if anything, a "conscience seared as with a hot iron" [1 Timothy 4:2]. Instead of being placed under strict surveillance, as the case justly demanded, he enjoyed privileges little less than actual freedom guarantees. It was no uncommon thing I found, for Hill to attend a dance in the Sugar House Ward meeting house, returning in time for the morning meal, or to spend a whole day in the mountains hunting and fishing. When thus seeking pleasure he invariably went and came unaccompanied by a guard—a significant fact when considered in connection with the circumstances of his final discharge. Who shall say that money, when freely expended, will not accomplish wonders?

Being more or less exhausted by the excitement growing out of my peculiar situation, I experienced considerable relief each evening when the guard made his appearance at the door and roughly said: "Nine o'clock, roll in." The noise instantly ceased, and each man slipped into his bunk and out of sight with extraordinary celerity, reminding one very much of the scene often witnessed in the vicinity of standing pools, when a hundred frogs, disturbed by human approach, suddenly rise in the air, then shoot down into the water, and instantly vanish from view.

When comfortably settled and about to seek forgetfulness in sleep, one night, I became conscious of the presence of a peculiarly obnoxious odor in the air. It was so distinctly different from the smells one ordinarily comes in contact with that my curiosity was aroused, and I sought an explanation by submitting the matter to my past experience. It was of little avail, however, for I did not remember, in all the varied scenes of my life, to have encountered a smell just like this. I was about to discontinue the investigation when my eyes rested on two of Africa's sons with skins as black as coal, who occupied the bunk next to mine, and the mystery was solved.

As the long hours of each night slowly sped away, I did not fail to note that the guard made a circuit of the building every fifteen minutes, to satisfy himself that its wretched inmates were not burrowing their way into the outer world. As he would pass around each time, the guards on the walls were required to make a signal to him to denote that they were wide awake and alert. A failure by these guards to make the required signal was cause for dismissal. These precautions on the part of "Uncle Sam" had a tendency, of course, to make the prisoners feel very secure, and to dispel all fears of midnight intruders.

On the afternoon of the my fifth day, Joseph H. Evans, much to my surprise, and in one sense delight, walked leisurely into the yard, having been convicted of polygamy and sentenced to three and a half years imprisonment and to pay a fine of five hundred dollars.[9] I shook him warmly by the hand and eagerly inquired for news from the outside. It is impossible to tell how much I appreciated that first meeting with this friend behind the dreary walls of Utah's penitentiary. The prospect of having an associate, whose hopes and aspirations were similar to my own, filled me with joy.

To show what amusing reports reached our friends outside the Pen, it was reported of Joseph in Salt Lake that on one occasion, when a number of roughs fiercely attacked me with evil intent, he promptly stretched six of them along the ground, and with intrepid calmness invited the others, who were slinking away, to step forward. This they modestly declined. Now, this heroic exploit, though it reads very beautifully, never in fact occurred. Propriety would seem to suggest, under such circumstances, that I should take my own part inasmuch as Joseph was about sixty years of age and I twenty-eight.[10] During the long winter months that followed, I spent many a pleasant moment in Joseph's society.

A week had now passed since my leaving home, and I began to feel the importance of taking a thorough bath; but alas! I found the accommodations for bathing to be very meagre. In fact there were none, so I was reduced to the sad necessity of bathing in a small tub which I placed under my bunk in the bunkhouse—a practice I indulged in weekly for many months. While engaged in the performance of this duty, a cold piercing draft would *often* steal in through the door and cause me to shake with great violence.

My example was by no means generally followed. Many did not bathe at all, while others preferred to wash themselves in the yard, with no protection but the blue canopy of heaven. One man, however, had the impression that his health required his taking a plunge bath in cold water every morning, both summer and winter. His devotion and unswerving faithfulness to that impression, unreasonable as it appeared, won my admiration. More than once, aye many times, I have seen him break the ice in the tub to get at the water; and to watch the movements of his naked body as it writhed under this self-imposed torture was not a little amusing. Splash—splash—sputter—sputter—heavy breathing—now sitting—now standing—arms in motion—rub—rub—rub—and the nude figure would melt out of sight, immediately reappearing in a suit of clothes. Where reason prevailed, the men would bathe in the middle of the day when the sun shone out brightly and warmly. If some of the visitors who came on the wall did not witness some of these scenes, it must have been due to short-sightedness.

NOTES

1. This first sentence of Clawson's memoirs contains an anachronism, since Utah did not become a state until January 1896. *Of the state of Utah* is an interlinear addition in MS I², which is followed in MSS II, III, IV*, and V (Rudger Clawson Collection, Ms 481, Bx 2, Fd 2, MS I, a-1, which is located

at the Marriott Library, University of Utah, Salt Lake City; hereafter the Rudger Clawson Collection is cited as RC). An effort has been made by an unidentified individual to rectify this problem in MS IV², where an interlinear *Territory* is surrounded by square brackets. For other anachronistic references to the state of Utah after the production of MS I*, see pp. 56 and 69.

2. Charles S. Zane (1831–1915) attended McKendry College in Lebanon, Illinois, and studied law in Springfield, Illinois, being admitted to the bar in 1857 and soon thereafter forming a law partnership. In 1873 Zane was elected judge of the Fifth Circuit Court of Illinois. In July 1884 President Chester A. Arthur appointed Zane as chief justice of the Supreme Court of the Territory of Utah. He arrived in Utah at the end of August 1884, and Governor Eli H. Murray assigned Zane to the Third District Court in September 1884. He continued in this office until 1893, when he resumed the practice of law. When Utah became a state, he was elected to the Supreme Bench of Utah, holding this position from 1896 to 1899. See Thomas G. Alexander, "Charles S. Zane, Apostle of the New Era," *Utah Historical Quarterly* 34 (Fall 1966): 290–314.

3. The Morrill Antibigamy Act of 1862 made polygamy a crime for anyone living in a U.S. territory. The Edmunds Act was passed in 1882. Clawson's reference to the Edmunds-Tucker Act is an anachronism, since this act dates to 1887. This paragraph, the one preceding, and the one following were not in MS I*, being inserted in the no-longer-extant MS I³ and first appearing in MS II. Notice that the next paragraph does contain a correct reference to the Edmunds Act. For two other anachronistic references to the Edmunds-Tucker Act after the production of MS I*, see p. 41.

4. Elwin A. Ireland (1843–98), born in Maine, served with the North during the Civil War. He then worked in New York as a clerk in a customs house for Chester A. Arthur. When the latter became president, he appointed Ireland as U.S. marshal in April 1882. Ireland continued in this position until his resignation in October 1886, when he became involved in the livestock business. In February 1898 Ireland went to Alaska to search for gold, but he died there in May 1898 of dropsy of the heart. See *Deseret Evening News,* 27 May 1898, and Stephen Cresswell, "The U.S. Department of Justice in Utah Territory, 1870–90," *Utah Historical Quarterly* 53 (Summer 1985): 209–10.

5. Clawson approximates the height here. The four-foot-wide wall was twenty feet high on the outside and twenty-four feet high on the inside. This difference created a catwalk on which one could walk around the prison wall (William Fotheringham, Letter to Daniel Tyler, 11 June 1885, newspaper clipping, William Fotheringham Collection, Marriott Library, University of Utah, Salt Lake City). According to Richard D. Van Orden, in "A History of the Utah State Prison, 1950–1980" (M.A. thesis, University of Utah, 1981), 6, the wall was originally only twelve feet high.

6. George N. Dow (1839–1904) worked for the Louisville and Nashville Railroad, rising from braketender to baggage master to freight master to passenger conductor. During the Civil War he continued to run trains. In 1882 Dow moved to Utah to accept the position as warden of the territorial penitentiary and remained in this position until his resignation in October 1886.

At this time he began raising sheep and became interested in various mining operations. When Utah became a state, he again served as warden from January 1896 until his death in February of 1904. See *Biographical Record of Salt Lake City and Vicinity, Containing Biographies of Well Known Citizens of the Past and Present* (Chicago: National Historical Record, 1902), 101–3, and the *Deseret Evening News,* 27 February 1904.

7. Some of the "other things" are canes, mats, fans, women's chains, and pincushions. See Abraham H. Cannon, Diary, after 5 September 1886, "Cash a/c with "Pen,"" 224, photocopy located at the Marriott Library, University of Utah, Salt Lake City, with the original at the Lee Library, Brigham Young University, Provo, Utah; George H. Taylor, Diary, 20 April 1886, located at the Utah State Historical Society, Salt Lake City; John Adams, Diary, 18 May 1887, in private possession; Abraham A. Kimball, Diary, 1 December 1888, copy located at the Utah State Historical Society, with the original at the Archives, Historical Department, Church of Jesus Christ of Latter-day Saints, Salt Lake City.

8. John Emerson, alias McCormick, was convicted of murder and sentenced on 11 December 1881 to life imprisonment at hard labor. Due to the governor's pardon, Emerson was released on 22 April 1886 and he then again affirmed his innocence: "I have now spent 6 years within those walls for a crime of which God and angels know that I am innocent" (Abraham H. Cannon, Diary, 22 April 1886).

9. Joseph H. Evans (1826–1909), who worked in the church blacksmith shop in City Creek Canyon, married Ruth Evan on 27 December 1848, by whom he had twelve children from 1849 to 1870. On 6 May 1880 Joseph F. Smith married Evans and twenty-five-year-old Harriett Parry, who bore his child in November 1881. The estranged wife, Harriet, testified at the trial that Evans wanted the marriage kept secret, "because he didn't want the other wife to know" that they were married. The jury convicted Evans of polygamy, after deliberating for fifteen minutes. At the day of sentencing, Judge Zane said that Evans knew of his wife's opposition to this second marriage and sentenced him to three and a half years imprisonment and a fine of $250, not $500 as stated by Clawson. Perhaps Clawson was led to this error, because his own conviction for polygamy had a fine of $500. Evans entered prison on 8 November 1884 and was released on 15 March 1887. See *Salt Lake Daily Herald,* 7 November 1884.

10. The designation of Evans's age as "about sixty years" is appropriate since Clawson's prison autograph book and the Utah State Prison Admission Records give his age as fifty-eight. Actually, at this time Clawson was only twenty-seven, as he would not turn twenty-eight until 12 March 1885. The question of his age came up during his sentencing on 3 November 1884. When Judge Zane described him as being about thirty, Clawson interjected that he was only twenty-seven. See RC, Bx 2, Fd 13, and transcript in *Salt Lake Tribune,* 4 November 1884.

CHAPTER 2

1885

Day followed day in slow succession, until the winter wore away, and the spring of 1885 came in with all its beauty and freshness. What a wonderful experience and what varied scenes I had passed through since November 3rd, 1884!

Many curious phases of human nature had come under my notice. I was now familiar with the circumstances connected with the charge, trial, and conviction of nearly every man in the yard, and often conversed with them, thus getting a good insight into character. I had previously looked upon the pickpocket, burglar, horse-thief, forger, etc., as a kind of monster, whereas, by this time I had found that these men who were convicted of such crimes, degraded though they were, were in possession of many good qualities, such as generosity and sympathy. They also admired goodness, purity, and virtue in others, though apparently deficient in these qualities themselves.

To show their generosity toward each other, it is very necessary to note that a prisoner, whose time had expired, seldom went out into the world entirely destitute, but was generously supplied by his convict brothers with hat, coat, vest, pantaloons, shoes, and sometimes with money. Letters from home often brought tears into the eyes of exiled sons, while audible regrets for wrong-doing not infrequently reached the ear.

Divine service was held every Sabbath afternoon at the State Penitentiary by ministers of the different sects in Salt Lake. On these occasions, perfect order prevailed, and the listeners appeared eager to catch every word that was spoken; but, strange to say, as soon as the preacher had departed, the noise and confusion were as great as ever; dancing, singing, profanity and vulgarity being freely indulged in. I could not help thinking that, if proper influences had been thrown around these rough, rude men in their childhood and youth, many of them might have become intelligent and virtuous citizens, a power in society for good, and a credit to the country. This suggests another thought, that in judging such characters we should place ourselves for the moment in their position, look at matters from their standpoint, and enter into their views, and feelings—and not fail to consider the circumstances by which they were surrounded in early life. What an important part, therefore, should *charity* play in our dealings with the human family! Will these men go down to hell and suffer? Yes, if they do not repent, but, on the other hand, they will be eventually redeemed, if we may rely upon the revelations of God, and receive a glory far beyond our finite conception.

The prejudice that existed in the minds of my fellow prisoners against the "Mormon" people seemed to grow stronger and stronger as time went on. Patrick Callaghan of Irish extraction, serving a term of fourteen years for murder, but afterwards pardoned, wielded an influence in the yard out of all proportion to his merits. A facility in writing *mediocre* poetry constituted his sole accomplishment—an accomplishment, however, which won the profound admiration of his fellow convicts and made him the hero of the hour. Pat's opinion on any subject was generally accepted as orthodox, and he brought all his influence to bear unfavorably on the "Mormon" question in general and upon me in particular. He seldom lost an opportunity, when I was present, to speak disrespectfully of the religious faith of the Latter-day Saints, and appeared to take infinite delight in vulgar and filthy slurs on some of our leading men. Nor did the worthies of the Old Testament escape his vituperative tongue. His remarks were never addressed to me personally, but to someone nearby, and were always spoken in a loud clear tone that every man in the room might hear. As a result, quite a bitter feeling was aroused against me. My only weapon of defense was "silent contempt" and it did me excellent service. It might perhaps be interesting to state that Pat was not entirely devoid of seeming religious culture. An evidence of this was shown in the fact that during religious services he was the only man who assumed a kneeling posture when prayer was offered up. This, with his suavity of demeanor and genteel politeness in the presence of the minister and his assistants, at the close of the services, though deeply affecting, illy corresponded with his unseemly conduct at other times, and made him to be a striking example of superb hypocrisy.

Joseph and I were not the only ones destined to suffer imprisonment for conscience sake. May 2nd, 1885, our number was increased by the addition of Parley P. Pratt, Jr., who was convicted of unlawful cohabitation, and sentenced by Judge C. S. Zane to six months imprisonment and to pay a fine of three hundred dollars. He met with a hearty welcome from Joseph and myself.

About this time cause for serious complaint grew out of the fact that sour *hash* was often served up for breakfast. The smell that came from it sometimes caused us to beat a hasty retreat from the dining room. Therefore, whenever this dish was served, I regarded it with suspicion, and invariably subjected it to a close inspection before partaking thereof, thus saving myself much unnecessary discomfort.

During this first spring of my incarceration (1885) several diverting incidents occurred, one or two of which I will mention. Michael [William] Sullivan, a son of Erin, having been convicted of murder, was sentenced to fifteen years imprisonment. He entered the penitentiary in 1884. Until now he had been looked upon as a quiet and inoffensive man, and so I found him to be; but a change was taking place in his mental status. From some cause or other, reason was apparently departing from him, and I fancied it was the result of constant brooding over his crime, combined with constitutional weakness of mind. He first attracted attention by taking great draughts of scalding hot water, which scorched and blistered his mouth and throat as it passed into his stomach, causing violent purgings. It was a most painful sight also to see him dig into his ears and nostrils with a rough sharp stick with the apparent intention of removing some fancied obstruction.

His personal pride had become very great as evidenced by the fact that he often appeared in the yard with coat turned inside out, pantaloons rolled up above the knee showing lower half of drawers, and socks drawn over his shoes. Thus arrayed, he would walk the yard, gesticulating wildly with his arms and addressing imaginary beings. His tongue displayed an activity truly astounding in giving expression to the multitudinous fancies of his diseased mind.

One bitter cold night after all had retired to rest, Mike quietly arose and with amazing coolness, plunged into a tub of freezing water that had been previously used by one of the prisoners for bathing purposes. With his underclothes thoroughly drenched, he crawled into bed apparently unconscious of any discomfort, and there remained quietly until morning. These singular freaks of Mike's madness, while they afforded considerable amusement for the boys, did not in the beginning suggest any danger or cause for alarm. One day, however, an awful change suddenly came over the "spirit of his dream." He grasped a fork, in a moment of fierce anger, and thrust it violently into the back of Willard Ivy, wounding him severely. Mike expiated this offense in the sweatbox and though somewhat subdued by the severe treatment, he was only temporarily conquered.

The real climax came later. Scene: dining room; hour, 12:00 o'clock m., three bells—tramp—tramp—tramp—and the prisoners, according to their usual custom, proceeded to devour the noon-day meal. Suddenly Mike's familiar form darkened the door-way—he paused for a moment, then made a dash for the iron fire shovel, clutched it firmly in his right hand, darted along the aisle, passing a number of startled convicts, and struck Joe Kylie a terrific blow on his side, breaking several ribs. Kylie fell from his seat senseless. At this moment, when all was confusion, Dick Kelly, a light, strong, active man, bounded to his feet, and, in the most artistic manner, planted a stinging blow against Mike's nose, which sent him headlong to the floor. He gathered himself up, the blood streaming from his mouth and nostrils, and hastily retired, a sadder, and though irresponsible, a wiser man. From that time until he was removed to the mental hospital at Provo, Mike was closely watched day and night by prisoners detailed for the purpose.

In the early part of this year, John Aird, commonly called "John the jailor" from having been employed at the City jail, was remanded to the custody of the U.S. marshal, on a charge of unlawful cohabitation, but as he promised to obey the law, he escaped punishment.[1] During his brief stay with us he met with not a little ill usage. Those inmates of the penitentiary who had served terms in the city jail, did not appear to have admired his method of handling men, hence his unpopularity in this place. Constant dread of an open rupture with the rougher element of the prison haunted him. His fears were well founded; for one morning shortly after John's advent into our midst, a thrilling scene occurred in the dining room. Breakfast was well under way when the door unexpectedly swung open and a man stood there armed with a club to prevent egress. In the twinkling of an eye, John's arms were pinioned to his side by two strong burley fellows who had approached from behind. "A rope! a rope! a rope!" was the cry heard in all parts of the house. Violent hands were then laid upon his massive shoulders and he was hustled to the center of the room. The noise and confusion all this time was very great. Tom Murray, a wild Irishman, arose and calling the house to order, said: "Gentlemen, we have before us a man who deserves nothing but scorn and contempt at our hands. His course, as jailor at the city prison, with which many of you are familiar, proves him to have been a brute. That he had a hand in the killing of the negro who shot Andrew Burt, captain of Salt Lake City police, there can be no doubt.[2] This is further evidence of his depravity. We now propose to make an example of him." Turning to the supposed culprit, he said: "John, prepare yourself for the awful fate that awaits you. You will be allowed three minutes for the indulgence of silent prayer."

For a moment John stood there pale and motionless. The abject terror that had taken possession of him found expression in the following language: "Gentlemen, you are mistaken. As jailor of the city prison I always treated you with kindness and consideration. I had no hand whatever in killing the negro." His neck was bared, the noose adjusted, the rope thrown over a cross-beam just overhead, and O sickening sight! John's body was dangling in the air. The matter was really becoming serious, when some of the men, fearing to carry the "joke" as they afterwards termed it any further, cut the rope. The victim gasped for breath, staggered toward the table, drank off a cup of coffee with great difficulty and hastily withdrew from the building. It was six or seven days ere John could swallow his food without suffering severe acute pains in his throat. The affair was promptly reported to Marshal Ireland, who, instead of ordering a thorough investigation, simply instructed the warden to guard against its reoccurrence in the future.

On the 9th of May, 1885, Angus M. Cannon, A. Milton Musser, and James Watson, were convicted of unlawful cohabitation and sentenced to six months imprisonment each, and to pay a fine of three hundred dollars. They entered the prison the same afternoon, and were duly installed as members of our society. Having heard of the many inconveniences connected with prison life, Brothers Cannon and Musser had wisely provided themselves with hammocks attached to movable frames, which, when properly arranged for the accommodation of our new guests, left but little unoccupied space in the bunk room. Hammocks in a dungeon! The idea created a great amount of merriment, as well as dissatisfaction, among the prisoners who winked and smiled and growled until sleep came along and stole away their senses. The scene affected even me and I must admit that the air of refreshing comfort which surrounded those hammocks caused an envious feeling to steal over me, which was not easily subdued.

Owing to the crowded condition of the prison, the newly arrived brethren, together with Joseph H. Evans and Parley P. Pratt, Jr., were permitted, after this first night, to occupy the dining room as a bunk house. Their beds, which were kept in the yard during the day and which were exposed to the heavy dust storms that often blew up, were carried into the dining room every evening and removed every morning. The procession of ten men with five beds (two men at each) that passed across the yard every day at dusk and into the dining room, presented quite a fantastic appearance. I was very sorry I was not among these favored few, and was still doomed to occupy bunk room no. 2, as heretofore.

For several reasons the warden, G. N. Dow, and I could not get along very pleasantly together as jailor and prisoner, as the following instances will show. A certain convict, [T. M.] Johnson by name, like a hideous monster in a dream, only with all the reality imaginable, crossed my path time and time again. He was a man of medium stature with large head, long face, massive jaw, high forehead, big nose, and blue eyes. His features were far from being interesting and attractive. He was an accomplished rogue, combining cunning and shrewdness with a good education. At the time mentioned he had served part of a twelve months' jail sentence for forgery, while his accomplice in the crime, though less guilty than himself, received two years. It was thought that he (Johnson) would have fared much worse had not the Rev. Mr. [C. M.] Armstrong, an Episcopalian minister, whose sympathy he had won, interceded for him at court. An evidence of his lack of appreciation and gratitude was shown when he afterward robbed the Rev. Mr. Armstrong of sixty dollars while partaking of his hospitality.

That this man, who was then acting as tutor to the warden's children, had nothing against me personally, I am perfectly aware, but that he was actuated in his malice toward me by a deep-seated prejudice against the "Mormon" people, was evident. His mind seemed to be surcharged with venom. A constant stream of falsehoods and misre-presentations concerning my movements in the yard was poured into the warden's ears by him. He watched me as a beast watches his prey, and magnified the most frivolous acts into an evidence of cunningly devised schemes, to prejudice the warden against me. The fact that I was non-committal with regard to these charges, instead of trying to vindicate myself as would ordinarily be the case, only militated against me, thus showing what prejudice will do. As a result it was the consensus of opinion among prison officials that I was secretive, full of subtlety, and, therefore, most dangerous. A victim of Johnson's spleen and misrepresentation, I was compelled to do battle in a very unequal contest. It is no agreeable matter for a prisoner to come into unpleasant contact with the warden, inasmuch as the latter, by virtue of his position, has a prodigious advantage over the former. Therefore, time and time again I was called into the warden's private office, closely questioned about fancied violations of the rules on my part, and sharply rebuked.

An instance or two will suffice. Prisoners had been forbidden to carry money in the yard. Having been called to the gate one morning, the following dialogue took place. The warden, his eyes flashing fire, said to me:

W[arden]. Have you any money about you?

C[lawson]. Yes, sir.

W. Do you not know that it is against the rule to carry money in the yard?

C. Yes, sir.

W. Why, then, do you violate the rule?

C. Because many of the prisoners are doing the same thing. Money is freely circulating in the prison.

W. That is not so. I do not think there is a single dollar inside except what you may have.

C. Mr. Warden, I just came from the dining room; there were several games of *Poker* in progress and not less than fifteen to twenty dollars in silver in sight. Please step in or send a guard and satisfy yourself.

W. I cannot believe it. I am fully posted as to what is going on in the prison. You are mistaken.

C. I do not ask you to believe it. Send a guard in to investigate.

W. You must understand that I shall require you to observe this and all other rules of the prison. That is all.

C. Good day.

As the warden took no steps to ascertain the truth of my statement, I very naturally concluded that this rule was intended to apply to me only.

On another occasion I was visited by my family. There were other prisoners and visitors in the room. A table separated the prisoners from their friends. The blending of numerous voices caused not a little noise and confusion. The prisoners were required by rule to speak sufficiently loud for the guard who sat at one end of the table to overhear all that was said. I was seated near the end opposite the guard, and spoke in an ordinary conversational tone, but this did not seem to satisfy him. "Clawson," said he, "speak louder." "Yes, sir." That evening I was reported to the warden as having violated the rules by whispering to visitors. "Your visitors and mail will be stopped for the present," said Mr. Dow, after administering a severe reprimand. Realizing that I had not indulged in the luxury of whispering, I stoutly protested against such treatment, but it was of no avail—the fiat had gone forth.

Shortly after entering the prison it became evident to me that by a judicious management in the purchase and sale of hair bridles, which were manufactured by the convicts, I might secure some means to aid in the support of my family. This being in my opinion a laudable desire, I employed Mr. Alex Howard, one of the prisoners, as an agent to buy up bridles at the very lowest figure. A market was soon found for the bridles outside, but true to his usual treatment of me, the warden threw many blocks in my way and I met with innumerable difficulties.

About this time I became profoundly conscious of the fact that as a rule a man is extremely sensitive on points touching his financial interests. The warden was furnishing tobacco to the prisoners at 75¢ per plug, which proved to be quite a profitable traffic.[3] My agent informed me that the men were taking tobacco at this price for bridles. I acted upon the hint, perhaps a little imprudently, and deciding to extend my business sent for ten plugs of "Horse Shoe" at forty cents per plug, which, according to instructions, was addressed to Howard. The tobacco came along in due season and after being examined by the warden, was passed into the yard.

A day or two later the warden called Howard to the gate and desired to know who sent him the tobacco. He replied that it came from a friend but believing the warden to be actuated by prejudice, declined to give the friend's name. I was next called and upon entering the office found the warden in a furious passion, as the following conversation will prove.

W. Howard has received a large package of tobacco from the city. As he has no friends there, I cannot understand it. I presume, however, that it was for you and that it is now in your possession.

C. No, sir.

W. Is it in your trunk?

C. No, sir.

W. Are you not handling it—that is, paying it out to the prisoners for bridles?

C. No, sir.

W. Where is it then?

C. I suppose Howard has it; it was sent to him.

W. Is he not bargaining for bridles with it?

C. I think he is.

W. Now answer me this: Did you or did you not send to the city for that tobacco?

C. Yes, I sent for it.

W. In what way did you send, by mail or otherwise?

C. By verbal message.

W. Why, then, was the package addressed to him and not to you?

C. As I never use tobacco I supposed you would not let it in if it were directed to me. Mr. Dow, is it not customary, when tobacco is sent to any of the prisoners by friends, to admit it?

W. Yes.

C. I cannot understand then why there should be any question in relation to this lot. It certainly was not smuggled into the yard, but came through the mail, and after being thoroughly examined by yourself, was passed. Is it not a little inconsistent to call for explanations regarding a matter that has already received your sanction? Why was not the tobacco detained at the gate, if there was anything wrong about it?

W. It looks to me very much as if there is some crookedness connected with this whole affair.

C. I am free to say, Mr. Warden, that you are mistaken.

Here the interview terminated. I was now fully aware that without any intention on my part I had antagonized the warden again and that it would be useless to continue my operations in the bridle and tobacco traffic. I might observe in passing that a number of prisoners were engaged in this business and, being encouraged by the prison authorities, met with good success.

On the 18th of May we had a new arrival in the person of William Fotheringham of Beaver, who was convicted of unlawful cohabitation, and sentenced to three months and three hundred dollars fine.[4] Brother William was a genial, pleasant man, strong in the faith and full of hope. His lot was cast in room no. 2, and I was thus furnished for a short time with an evening companion, the other brethren still being occupants of the dining room.

Independence Day, 1885, a time of general rejoicing throughout the United States, dawned upon our fair Territory and lo, what did we see? Seven of her respected citizens, peaceable, inoffensive men, undergoing imprisonment for conscience sake. Being practical men, they carried out in their daily lives the commands of Almighty God, and so, our great Government, which claimed to extend to her people the utmost freedom in religious matters, stepped forth and blinded by prejudice and popular clamor cast them into prison.

It was a bright beautiful day. In the forenoon Brother Fotheringham delivered a short oration in the dining hall, confining his remarks to the life and character of George Washington. As the last words fell from his lips, stirring strains of music reached our ears. We rushed out into the yard pell-mell, to learn from whence they proceeded, and there we beheld the Sixth Ward Silver Band on the wall. The musicians remained about two hours and played many beautiful pieces. In response Jack Emerson sang a solo or two, "Shorty" McDonald gave "Home Rule for Ireland" with banjo accompaniment and chorus by the crowd, and President A. M. Cannon heartily thanked the serenaders in behalf of the prisoners for their timely visit.

While the music was being played, ice cream, the gift of Bishop John Sharp to the brethren, was passed around. Many other dainties such as fruits, cakes, pies, jellies, etc., had also been sent to the brethren by their families and friends, all of which were greatly appreciated and thoroughly enjoyed.

The great event of the day, however, occurred in the afternoon. Preparations had previously been made for a "go as you please" foot race, and quite a number of the men had been in training for it for two or three weeks. Much wild talk was indulged in as to the probable winner. Many small bets were offered and taken among the sporting element of the prison. At 2:00 o'clock the race was called, the judges were selected, and about ten contestants appeared on the scene, partly stripped. The schedule was as follows: time for running, one hour, with seven laps to the mile; first prize five dollars, second prize three dollars. The word was promptly given and away went the racers, helterskelter. The excitement was intense.

At the end of half an hour about one half of the original number had fallen out of the ranks from exhaustion. Every man in the yard, of course, had his favorite, and as the runners passed the judges stand, spoke words of encouragement or dashed cold water upon them to counteract the fierce heat of the summer sun. Some few of the spectators being entirely carried away with enthusiasm and with a desire to see those of their choice come out ahead, would fall in with the runners as they passed and accompany them part way around the yard with palm leaf fans in hand. These fans were kept in constant motion to supply the weary men with a breath of fresh air. Brother Angus M. Cannon was among this number. At the end of three quarters of an hour, all but two had withdrawn from the contest. The winner of the first prize was Martin Moss, who had made about sixty-three laps or nine miles; of the second prize, Hank Wheeler, eight and one-half miles. In lieu of something stronger, a barrel of lemonade was consumed while the race was in progress.

About 5:00 o'clock in the afternoon the prisoners all joined together and gave an impromptu open air concert on the shady side of the dining room. The program consisted of songs and dances, with violin and banjo solos, as the striking features of the pleasant affair. The exercises also included several stirring hymns rendered by the brethren. Thus ended the amusements of the day.

During the first six months of my prison life I witnessed a great many personal combats among the prisoners. There were on an average from one to two fights a week, and I doubt not would have been [a] still greater number had not the fear of the sweatbox exercised a restraining influence over the violent and aggressive spirits of the prison. The prisoners had been repeatedly notified by the guards that in case of trouble arising in the dining room, they were to disperse instantly. Failing to do this they would be exposed to serious danger from bullets which the guards threatened to shoot through the roof. But the fascination that a rough and tumble fist fight exercised over the minds of Utah's criminals generally overcame the fear of being shot, and so this injunction was not very well observed, nor did the guards at any time shoot through the roof.

However, investigations were always instituted by the warden, and the party who was in the wrong, or appeared to be, usually passed the night, and very often several days, in the "box." The inmates of the prison had a perfect horror of this place of torment. An iron cage in shape very much like an ordinary dog kennel, six feet high by three feet wide, and enclosed by a lumber framework of two-inch plank, constituted the "box." In summer it was called the sweatbox, and in winter, the ice-chest, both terms being singularly appropriate. The man who was so unfortunate as to spend a season in the box, slept on a hard bare floor with no bedding and lived on bread and water. When the door was closed there was continuous darkness, both day and night, and little less than suffocation threatened the inmate. In the winter the cold stole in through the crevices and shook the sufferer's frame until he was numb. Aggravated offenses were committed now and then, and invariably secured to the offender a long term in the "box"— from two to six weeks. The demands of justice being satisfied, the penitent would come forth weak and pale and haggard. "Horrible! O horrible! Most horrible!"

Jack Bryant, of whom we have already spoken, passed many a weary hour in the "box." Owing to his peculiar adaptability to laundry and kitchen work, he was honored with a place among the "trusties." The soiled linen belonging to the warden's family received his special attention. This he washed and ironed in first-class style. In his general deportment Jack appeared to be influenced by neither fear nor favor. If the spirit so prompted, he would simply state that he proposed to work no longer and, suiting the action to the word, would settle down into absolute inactivity. Such conduct could not, of course, be tolerated in a penitentiary, and he would be promptly "fired" into the "box," there to remain until willing to go to work again. He sometimes held out a week or two, but confinement in "durance vile" usually conquered his obstinacy in a much shorter period, and induced him to seek consolation at the washtub.

Being afflicted with a violent temper, Jack was imprudent enough on one occasion to call a guard a s–n of a b——h and a few moments later found himself languishing in solitary confinement. After several days in solitude, upon the solicitation of Mrs. [Alice] Dow who insisted upon his release that he might again preside at the washtub, Jack was ushered into the presence of the warden. "Your offense," said the warden, "is very serious, but if you will apologize to the guard, and ask for forgiveness, I will release you from the sweatbox and reinstate you as a 'trusty.' " " "I'm sorry," said Jack, "but I really cannot do it." "Why can't you do it?" said the warden. "Because," replied Jack, "as a matter of fact he is a s–n of a b——h and I can't help it."[5] The prisoner was instantly rushed back into the place of torment. A day or two more elapsed when Mrs. Dow, still feeling the great need of Jack's help in the laundry, urged his release at once. He was again brought "onto the carpet," and given another opportunity to ask the guard's forgiveness, but he again refused and for the same reason.

After eleven days confinement Jack was the third time directed to ask the guard's forgiveness, and for the third time refused. The warden then said: "Well, if you will not apologize willingly, we will compel you to do so," whereupon Jack was securely tied to a tree with face outward and arms pinioned to his side. The garden hose was adjusted by two prisoners, one operating the pump and the other holding the nozzle. A steady, continuous stream of cold water shot into Jack's face, entering his nostrils and filling his mouth. He struggled and choked and spluttered, but fearing strangulation, finally gasped out: "I'll ask the guard's forgiveness," which he did. He was immediately released from further punishment and to the joy of .Mrs. Dow, was reinstated as a "trusty" and put to the washtub. That evening before retiring, Jack related his experience to an interested company of fellow prisoners, concluding his remarks by the following observation: "The warden compelled me to ask the guard's forgiveness, and I did so, but he is a s-n of a b—-h just the same." Defeated, but not conquered, might in very truth be said of Jack Bryant who was more than ordinarily stubborn and unyielding in his nature.

John Smith, one of the prisoners who had been arrested on a charge of train robbery, and was awaiting trial, gave the prison officials considerable trouble at different times. He was short in stature, but of powerful build, and, therefore, not easily handled. On one occasion, having been guilty of a misdemeanor, he was ordered by the guard to the sweatbox, but positively refused to go. Three other guards were called in and, after a severe struggle in which one of them barely escaped being stabbed in the neck by John with a case knife, the latter was duly disposed of and left to languish in the "box" for many days. At another time in mid-winter while undergoing punishment, he became quite restless and, with a view of giving vent to his feelings, hammered away against the iron cage with great vigor. The noise thus created, not only disturbed, but irritated one of the night guards, who was trying to get some sleep close by. He arose and in a firm voice requested John to desist, but the noise, instead of dying away, increased in intensity. The guard's patience was soon exhausted and, securing some ice water, he dashed several bucket-fulls over the culprit, who fairly gasped for breath, withdrew into a corner and preserved a judicious silence until morning. With wet clothes clinging to his body, and the floor glassy with ice, his sufferings from the cold must have been intense.

The exploit by which John Smith, this desperado, was drawn into the toils of the law was both foolhardy and daring. Single-handed and alone he held up a passenger train on the old Utah and Northern Railway. With superb self-composure he relieved the travelers of their valuables as they stood trembling in his presence. Upon being captured he feigned insanity with such perfect success as to deceive the examining physician and he was, therefore, committed to a private mental hospital.

His experience at this institution, as related by himself to me, was unique. Every night, regularly, when the inmates had retired to rest, he left his bed and silently passed into the pantry. With careful deliberation he helped himself to the good things usually found in such places; namely, milk and cream, cakes, pastry, and canned fruit. After appeasing his hunger he withdrew, but instead of retiring to his own room, he sought the apartment of one of the female patients. There he would pass the remainder of the night. At an early hour he would quickly slip into his own quarters preparatory to the morning visit of the attendant. Thus he eluded detection for a series of weeks. The strange disappearance of edibles from the pantry finally aroused the liveliest curiosity among the officials of the institution but remained a "hidden mystery." The climax came, however, upon one occasion when John, having overslept, was found in the room of the female inmate alluded to. He was at once adjudged to be sane and rushed off to the Utah Penitentiary.

He related this story to me with much gusto, laughing inordinately at the deception wrought upon the hospital officials. It may be of interest to the reader to know that after rather a lengthy period of incarceration at the "Pen," John Smith feigned insanity a second time and he did it so perfectly and cleverly that the examining physician pronounced him mentally unsound and recommended his transfer to the State [Territorial] Mental Hospital at Provo, where he was finally taken. The prison officials, as well as the prisoners, without exception believed him insane. He was a consummate actor and those who witnessed his "antics" were constrained to say: "Well, if he was not crazy before, he certainly is now." I was of the same opinion.

Shortly after he was sent to Provo a letter written by him to A. Milton Musser of Salt Lake City, and which he tried to smuggle out, was intercepted by the guard. In words of undoubted sanity, he confided to Brother Musser the trick he had played on the physician and prison officials and earnestly invoked the latter's assistance in having him released from the hospital. There was no reason to believe that Brother Musser sympathized with Smith or would have rendered him any aid whatever. However, John Smith was unceremoniously returned to the state prison where he served out his sentence.

That he was a truly desperate character was further shown in the following sensational incident. He remarked in my presence a number of times that upon his release he fully intended to get the "scalp" of O. W. Powers,[6] the trial judge before whom he was convicted and sentenced. At the time the threat was regarded as an idle joke. However, one day long after he had left the prison and apparently disappeared from among men, Judge Powers received by mail a neat looking package. That he did not open it without hesitation was a matter of wonder. In some unaccountable way the idea that danger was connected with the package popped into his mind. Accordingly, he turned it over to the police who, after plunging it into a bucket of water, carefully opened it, when an infernal machine was disclosed to view. It was no doubt the messenger of death sent by John Smith to Judge Powers, who narrowly escaped with his life, for it cannot be doubted that if the Judge had opened the package he would have been killed instantly. Subsequent to this stirring incident, it was reported that John Smith, the bandit, had committed suicide.

With all the hardships of prison life, there was still some compensation. During the first six months of my incarceration, we were allowed visitors and were permitted to receive provisions from family and friends, and to make purchases for ourselves. The rule governing the visits of relatives and friends was rigid in character and strictly enforced. A fixed day of each week was designated as visiting day and only such persons as held a written order from the U.S. marshal were permitted by the warden to see the prisoner or prisoners named in such order. Visiting day was always looked forward to by the cohabs with intense interest, as it gave them half an hour's interview with loved ones and thus for a few moments, took their minds away from the dreariness of prison life. It was truly an interesting sight to see twelve or fifteen visitors seated on one side of a long table, their prison relatives and friends on the other side—all earnestly engaged in animated and oftentimes serious conversation. A guard armed cap-à-pie invariably sat at the head of the table, being delegated to see to it that the prisoners not only did not make their escape, but did not pass written communications to the visitors.

Owing to the inferior quality of the food furnished by the prison, the privilege of receiving supplies was highly esteemed. It was also a source of considerable revenue to the warden, who supplied the men with tobacco, sugar, butter, cheese, canned goods, etc. As time went on, however, prejudice began to assert its sway over the minds of the prison authorities. All at once (July 1885) it was announced, as a rule of the prison, that visiting days would be reduced to *one* each month and confined to members of the prisoner's family.[7] It was also announced that no provisions whatever, except the prison fare, which, as we have already seen, was exceedingly simple, would be allowed to come into the yard. Thus, in order to annoy and discourage the brethren, early precedents were trampled upon and Warden Dow was even willing to forego the financial gains he had enjoyed in order to humiliate the brethren.

It was a heavy blow made with telling effect; but the brethren, though deeply moved, preserved an outward composure, and occasionally sang in concert "Hard Times Come Again No More," which of course was far from being a truthful expression of their inward feelings. The rule was rigidly enforced for several months, when a slight reaction took place and milk was allowed. Milk! Glorious milk! If I were a poet, I should certainly have written an ode to milk. After our enforced abstinence, it operated upon the system like the elixir of life, renewing our strength and making us young again.

The sultry months of summer were now upon us. The scorching rays of the sun struck the massive walls that surrounded us on all sides, and were reflected into the yard, thus withering every object that came in their path. Myriads of bedbugs made their appearance in the bunk rooms, and tormented the prisoners almost beyond endurance. I was told, and my own experience confirmed the statement, that a man could write his name with the blood of bugs by pressing his finger against them as they crawled along the wall and over the framework of the bunks. Newly whitewashed walls soon told an awful tale of blood and carnage, and, until the novelty wore off, it was quite amusing to watch the convicts war against their powerful enemies at all hours of the night. Vermin, it must be admitted, also abounded in some of the bunks, and multiplied and flourished on the persons of many of the prisoners. An evidence of this was sometimes shown, when an undershirt that had been worn for several weeks was thrown upon an ant bed in the yard. The busy little insects would immediately begin an exploration in quest of prey, seize upon the numerous vermin, and drag them away to their storehouse for winter consumption. By exercising the utmost care, I was comparatively free for a long time from this foe to cleanliness.

After about two years, however, I was attacked with severe itching which was very annoying and which I attributed to some ordinary skin trouble. I went on scratching for several days when one afternoon as I was in the act of bathing, upon looking rather closely at the parts of my body that were afflicted, I discovered to my great surprise and horror, the presence of body lice. With all diligence I put myself to the task of ridding my body of this insidious foe, and thereafter exercised a watchfulness that went far to secure my peace of mind.

The prison was rapidly filling up and there was a prospect that there would be many new arrivals in the fall from among the polygamists who were being convicted. As a result, the marshal decided to erect a new bunkhouse and to make other changes. The bunkhouse was patterned after the other two rooms, and furnished accommodations, though meager, for sixty men. The dining room was enlarged by extension and a bath room with two tubs was added to the east end. Some of the prisoners, when any good fortune overtook them, were in the habit of saying: "'Tis far better than a pardon." If the new bathing facilities were not "far better than a pardon," they were certainly next thing to it. Those who had no taste for the pleasures of the bath were compelled by rule to take a weekly ablution, while all others, of course, cheerfully took advantage of the opportunity. The brethren and a few "trusties" who had occupied the dining room up to this time, as a sleeping apartment, were located in the new bunkhouse, and appeared to enjoy the change, as their new quarters, though far from being elaborate, were fresh and clean.

On the 11th of July Brothers Francis A. and Moroni Brown of Ogden City were convicted of unlawful cohabitation, and on the 13th, Brother Job Pingree, also of Ogden. They were each sentenced by Judge

Powers to six months imprisonment and to pay a fine of three hundred dollars, and entered the prison the same evening.[8]

The prison was often visited by the marshal, who came either for the purpose of inspecting our condition and surroundings, or to show friends through the institution. At such times the prisoners were driven into one corner of the yard like so many cattle, and there compelled to remain until he had withdrawn. It was evident from this that he reposed but little confidence in his wards, and foresaw the possibility of being attacked by them and roughly handled, although, so far as I could judge, the danger was purely imaginary. The brethren were often called out from among their fellow convicts to be interviewed by strangers. On one occasion, while a party of distinguished visitors accompanied by the marshal were passing through the yard, "Nosey" [John] Banks, the burglar, being dissatisfied with the prison diet, called out lustily: "Soup! Soup! Soup!" and disappeared from sight in the crowd. This little indiscretion was fatal to him, and as a result he spent a night and a day in the sweatbox.

I never so fully realized my helpless and in one sense humiliating situation, as when general searches were ordered. These searches were made once in every two or three months, the object being to guard against the circulation among the convicts of such articles as saws, files, knives, etc., which it was supposed might be smuggled into the prison and which would aid the owners in making an escape. Without any previous notice, an order would be issued for the men to take their trunks and boxes with keys in the locks, to the gate, and then retire into one corner of the yard. Being thus taken by surprise, the prisoners were left without an opportunity to hide away or get rid of any condemned articles that might be in their possession. The trunks were passed out through the gate and carefully inspected by the warden before being returned to the owners. In the meantime two guards were stationed in the dining room for the purpose of examining the prisoners themselves, who, after being called out from the crowd by twos, were compelled to *strip off* their clothing, which was taken by the guards and subjected to a thorough scrutiny. At the close of these examinations, the men were directed to go into another corner of the yard, when the dining room, bathroom, and bunkhouses were thoroughly searched. Notwithstanding the thoroughness of these searches, which were never completed in less than six or eight hours, the prison authorities seldom reaped a rich harvest. I rather incline to the view, from what I saw, that this result was due to the shrewdness of the prisoners rather than to the fact that there were no contraband articles in their possession.

The following incident might be interesting in this connection. One afternoon word was conveyed to the guard that the room no. 1 men had a file in their possession. After being locked up for the night without supper, they were invited by the guard to deliver up the file, "otherwise," said he, "I'll starve you until you do." The night wore away, morning came, and hunger too, but no breakfast. By noon the men had grown desperate and, headed by the notorious Fred Welcome, they ripped off a plank from one of the bunks and commenced to pry open the heavy iron door, that held them secure.[9] The guard, who stood nearby with a pistol in his hand threatened to shoot. "Shoot and be damned," responded the men, who worked on with increasing vigor. Rushing out into the yard the guard, pale with terror, notified the sentinel on the wall of the state of affairs. A truce was soon arranged for and the men were released and supplied with food. No file was discovered.

One of the most serious evils we had to contend with during the heated term was the prison diet. Stale meat and maggoty soup were often set before us. Those whose stomachs revolted against such sickening and disgusting fare were obliged to confine themselves almost exclusively to bread and tea or coffee or milk. The new rules against prisoners receiving provisions from the city and from friends greatly aggravated the situation. Brother Parley P. Pratt took occasion to remark, one day, that he did not believe we could be lawfully subjected to such inhuman treatment, and that he intended to report the matter to Marshal Ireland. I quite agreed with him but predicted that any appeal to the marshal would be fruitless, basing my opinion on past experience. A few days later the desired interview with Marshal Ireland was accorded to Brother Pratt. I happened by chance to be standing nearby and consequently overheard the following dialogue:

Pratt: Mr. Ireland, I desire to call your attention to the meat and soup furnished us by the prison; they are not fit for a dog to eat.

Ireland: Why, Mr. Pratt, such language from you astonishes me.

Pratt: It is, nevertheless, true. This very morning the meat was dished up in a rotten condition, maggots appearing on some portions of it. I saw them myself.

Ireland: Mr. Pratt, I really cannot believe what you say. Yours is the first complaint of the kind that has ever been made by any of the convicts. Mr. Dow, how is this?

Dow: Really, I cannot say. I was not aware there was anything wrong with the meat. Mr. Pratt certainly must be mistaken.

Pratt: I am not mistaken, sir. There are many others in the yard who will confirm my statement. I would suggest that "Government Kid,"[10] James Cowley, Jack [Frank] Clinton, Dick Price, or any of the other prisoners be called. There's Clawson. Ask him.

Ireland: Mr. Clawson, did you see any maggots in the meat this morning?

Clawson: No, sir.

Ireland: Did any one remark in your hearing there were maggots in it?

Clawson: Yes, sir, quite a number of the prisoners.

Ireland: Did the meat smell strong?

Clawson: Yes, sir, it was not fit to eat. Some of the prisoners took portions of it to the gate for the warden's inspection but were sent back by the guard, who threatened them with the sweatbox for their pains.

Ireland: Well, Mr. Pratt, it is just possible that some tainted meat was sent into the prison by mistake. I thank you for calling my attention to the matter, and beg to assure you that it will not occur again. I shall take it as a favor if you will report to the warden when anything goes wrong.

Pratt: Thank you, Mr. Ireland, that is all we ask.

Ireland: Good day, Mr. Pratt.

Pratt: Good day, sir.

There was an improvement in the food for a time succeeding the foregoing interview, but the evil was not entirely remedied for occasionally still spoiled food was served at the prison.[11]

This kind consideration that Bro. Pratt had received at the hands of Marshal Ireland in connection with the promise mentioned, inspired him with a feeling of genuine satisfaction. His face beaming with delight, he afterwards favored the prisoners with a synopsis of the interview, and gave it as his opinion that no more bad meat would be sent in. This announcement by no means created the enthusiasm which the prospect of a change would ordinarily excite, for Marshal Ireland was noted for his suavity of manner. I smiled and murmured low, "we shall see." For a week or so there was a decided improvement in the diet, and many of the convicts, though often disappointed before, began to look for better things; but alas! their hopes were raised only to be dashed to the ground. Tainted meat, soggy potatoes, and thin, tasteless soup found their way into the bill of fare, not once or twice only, but many times.

The convicts again became furious and spoke of the marshal and warden in terms far from complimentary. The brethren also felt keenly the indignity thus placed upon them. Bro. A. M. Musser being naturally of a combative disposition was particularly active during this trying period in advocating and demanding our rights. His popularity among the prisoners became very great, but, like popularity in the world, it was evanescent in its character. This will be apparent as we proceed. The bad feelings of the convicts toward the prison authorities were finally embodied in a strong remonstrance, which was written by Bro. Musser and signed by about seventy of the convicts. It was addressed to Marshal Ireland and Warden Dow, and read as follows:

Utah Penitentiary
August 22, 1885

To Marshal Ireland
and Warden Dow:
Gentlemen:

On entering the mess room this morning, when breakfast was announced, one of the waiters was heard to say: "The meat has a vile smell, the bread is sour, and the 'spuds' are not cooked"; and we will add that 90% of the whole vomity mess was rejected and emptied back into the swill tubs in which it was brought. If this condition of things occurred but once in a while, we would not complain; but the warden, at least, must know that about 50% of the meat and 25% of the potatoes and bread have been rejected by your boarders for a number of months past. You must know that the meat has been many times full of maggots and so putrid that, on entering the mess room door, the stench was almost stifling; and that the soup (no doubt made from the rejected meat, but so highly seasoned with onions etc. as to conceal its true character) has many times been served to us full of maggots.

You must know that the old, rusty, and broken tin plates and cups (many of the cups being old fruit and oyster cans) and spoons are not fit for a dog to use, and that the tubs (old whiskey and vinegar barrels sawn in two) in which the "feed" is sent to us from the kitchen, are fit only for swill tubs and cannot be cleansed. You know all this which has been repeatedly brought to your notice, yet you pay no more attention to our respectful protestations against the inhuman treatment than as if we were so many hogs.

We need say nothing about the unwholesome well water which without any doubt receives the percolations of the public privy vault deposits, and which the warden, in ridiculing opposition to the opinions of all the men in the corral, says is pure, good water.[12] When asked to let us bring our drinking water for use during the day from the outer well, as the "trusties" always did in the evening when they came in, he refused us.

Without knives or forks (which were taken from the prisoners for fear they might dig down the prison walls with them, notwithstanding there are two armed guards on the walls and two inside the corral, night and day) we are obliged to eat the food with our fingers; nor are we permitted to purchase any supplies—not even when we are sick. This was allowed for a time before a certain class of prisoners came here, for whose benefit (?) no doubt the change in this regard was made.

With now and then an exception, we have not had a square, wholesome meal of victuals since we entered this Andersonville. We know not, gentlemen, what you get from the general Government, or the Territory, for boarding us, nor do we care; but we do know that much better fare than we receive can be furnished for fifteen cents per day, per capita; and there are responsible men among the undersigned who are willing to obligate themselves to do it, providing they are furnished with the same inexpensive facilities you have.

With the hope that our prayer for relief will not be disregarded, we respectfully subscribe ourselves [y]our temporary wards.

The climax was reached. The marshal and warden in their turn became furious. They construed this action to be an insult, and instituted an immediate investigation. Many a countenance was pale with anxiety as one after another slowly but sadly wended his way into the warden's office to be interviewed. Out of the whole number of signers not more than eight or ten had the moral courage to stand by their expressed sentiments. When interrogated, they boldly stated that they had been persuaded to sign by A. M. Musser, not knowing the exact purport of the remonstrance. This will be considered a little surprising when it is known that the document was read aloud in the presence of the prisoners, and only those who fully endorsed it were permitted to sign. Those who remained firm, after being severely reprimanded, were informed that their mail and visitors would be stopped for the present.

Bro. Musser, as the chief offender, was finally called out to give an account of his part in the transaction, which he did in a masterly manner, and a terrific, wordy combat ensued. The outcome was by no means discreditable to Bro. M., although his mail and visitors were also stopped. I have reason to believe that the warden hoped all the signers would repudiate the remonstrance and thus give him an opportunity to accuse Bro. M. of shameful misrepresentation; but, happily, there were a few who were not susceptible to intimidation.

It was confidently expected by all that Bro. Musser would be remanded to the sweatbox, in which event a number of the men expressed a strong determination to interfere and prevent so great an outrage. How far they would have carried this resolution into effect, had such an order been given, can only be conjectured, as a breech-loading rifle leveled at one's head has a wonderfully persuasive influence. This conflict was followed by a temporary improvement in our food—I say temporary because there was more or less cause for complaint during the whole summer.

From this time until after the expiration of his term, Bro. M. was closely watched by the prison authorities, who appeared to be haunted by the fear that he would bring about a revolution in the yard, which might lead to bloodshed. I strongly suspect that the warden heaved a deep sigh of relief as our veteran brother bade him an affectionate (?) farewell. Just prior to his release, a general search was ordered and conducted on the plan heretofore mentioned. Nothing of importance developed, however.

Bro. Musser's parting shot at the moment of departure was a point-blank refusal to allow the warden to examine his trunk, which was securely locked. He claimed that, having served out his sentence, he was no longer a convict, and that consequently the warden had no right to demand the keys of his trunk. "You will do so at your perils," said he to Mr. Dow, who threatened to break it open. After being retained several days, the trunk was turned over to its owner unopened.

I now come to a very singular feature of my experience in the penitentiary. From the course pursued toward the Polygamist convicts by the Crusaders, including Marshal Ireland and his deputies, one would naturally suppose that any sort of religion was obnoxious to them. Yet they seemed determined to force religious observance upon these convicts. As to whether a man should or should not attend divine service, or, being present, should or should not sit or stand, or take part in the service by repeating the prayers and saying "amen" thereto, was simply a matter of choice when I entered the prison. To remain seated during the service, had never been regarded as a mark of disrespect to the preacher. But after the arrival of Cannon, Musser, Watson, Fotheringham, Brown, and other brethren, there seemed a splendid opportunity for the prison authorities to exhibit their narrowness of soul, and they failed not to avail themselves of it.

The first indication of trouble came in the conduct of T. M. Johnson, choir leader, with whom the reader is already familiar, who impudently boasted that "if these damned 'Mormons' didn't arise to their feet at certain times during religious service, he would have them jerked up by the collar." This was astounding language to come from a convict, yet his influence over the warden amply justified it. We were, therefore, not very much surprised when the guard directed our attention to an edict posted on the dining room door, which set forth that every prisoner in the yard would be required to attend divine service and observe the formalities incident thereto. This announcement was received very ungraciously and seemed to arouse a spirit of antagonism, even among the hardened criminals who had been regular attendants at these meetings. They did not fancy the idea of being forced into church and gave expression of their feelings in language that would fairly make a minister of the Gospel shudder. That it is almost impossible to reform the wicked, or to drive them into the Kingdom of Heaven by force, was strikingly exemplified in the rebellious attitude of these men.

The cohabs (there were seven of us) held a council meeting to determine what our attitude should be regarding this obnoxious rule. We, as well as the toughs, were offended. I took the ground strongly that the warden was without authority to enforce a rule of that character, as it clearly invaded the conscience. I was perfectly willing, I said, to attend divine service no matter what denomination conducted, but I rebelled in my feelings at the thought of being compelled at the signal of the minister to take a responsive part in the service. I had made up my mind, I said, to ignore the rule and take whatever punishment might be inflicted. The brethren took a view similar to mine and we thereupon entered into a solemn compact to stand together and resist the rule. I remarked that if we were true to our mutual agreement, notwithstanding we might be charged with insubordination, and brought before the warden, he would experience some difficulty in meting out punishment to seven of us—the problem would be a little "white elephant on his hands"—but if he caught any one of us singly in a rebellious attitude he would deal harshly with him.

The Sabbath day came; meeting was called at 3:00 P.M. The convicts reluctantly fell into line and slowly entered the dining room. The evidence of suppressed rage was visible on every countenance. [James] Doyle, the guard, was in charge, Johnson, the burglar, presided at the organ, and Rev. Mr. Putnam, an Episcopalian, conducted the service.[13] The seven cohabs of the "secret conclave" sat in different parts of the hall. In referring to them later I will not give their correct names for obvious reasons.

The minister, with a sort of leer in his eyes, opened by announcing a hymn and saying that he "would be very glad if all present would *stand upon their feet and take part in the service.*" This invitation, though couched in polite terms, was extremely galling to his unwilling auditors, the most of whom after a severe inward struggle managed to get into a standing position.[14] *The seven cohabs remained seated.* Doyle, the guard, his eye flashing, turned his attention to the cohabs and said in an authoritative tone: "Jones, stand upon your feet." This was a critical moment, a testing time. The other six cohabs turned their eyes with fevered anxiety upon Jones, wondering, hoping he would stand by the compact. There was a moment of tense silence. Jones seemed to be in an uncertain state of mind, but upon a second command from the guard his body swayed to and fro and he slowly rose to his feet. The spell was broken, the battle seemed to be lost, for immediately Doyle turned to the other five, saying, "Price, Williams, White, Hatch, Cannon (Angus M.—true name), stand up." Slowly, reluctantly the four stood up, but Brother Cannon remained seated. At this juncture Doyle came striding down the aisle and, standing over the offender, said insultingly, "Cannon, stand up." Meekly Brother Cannon continued to sit and looking up said in the gentlest tone: "Mr. Doyle, I cannot stand." "What is the matter with you?" asked the guard. "I'm afflicted with the piles," said the prisoner. "Then," shouted Doyle, pointing to the door, "get out of here." Forgetting his malady, if it really existed, Brother Cannon reached for his hat, moved with incredible alacrity, and passed out of the room. Of the seven cohabs and in fact of the entire congregation I was the only one now who sat while all others rose and stood or knelt in response to the request of the preacher. Finally, the guard with a most malignant expression on his face noticed me sitting far back in the room, noticed that I persistently kept my seat. He was evidently very angry and glared at me like a wild beast, but did not, however, again indulge in a further demonstration of authority in my case.

The prisoners were frequently asked "to stand upon their feet and join in the responses," etc.; consequently, there was a continual rising, sitting, and kneeling down. The meeting being over, many a malediction was launched at Mr. Putnam as he passed through the entrance gate and disappeared from view.

I was reported to the warden, by Doyle, as having been guilty of insubordination, and soon found myself standing in his awful presence. Brother Joseph H. Evans was called out at the same time, and as we wended our way toward the gate everybody supposed that the intention was to put irons on me, as Joseph did all that kind of work, being a blacksmith. This, he afterwards informed me, he would have declined to do at all hazards. The warden was in a furious passion.

Dow: Evans, I have called you out to be a witness to this interview, as I cannot trust Clawson. He is not truthful, and when called out at any time to give an account of himself, misrepresents to the prisoners what passes between us. Clawson, how is it that you did not arise to your feet this afternoon when spoken to by the guard?

Clawson: The guard did not speak to me.

Dow: You knew it was against the rules to remain seated?

Clawson: Yes, sir.

Dow: Why then did you violate them?

Clawson: Simply, Mr. Dow, because I did not fancy the idea of being forced into church against my will and then be compelled to take part in the service. You'll understand, Mr. Dow, that I'm not an Episcopalian but a Mormon, and do not accept the doctrines or approve the rites of the Episcopal Church.

Dow: You were not compelled to take part in the service, but you are expected to show due respect to the minister.

Clawson: It looked very much like compulsion, for we were requested to stand up and assist in the singing, praying, etc., which I could not conscientiously do.

Dow: It is certainly ridiculous to take that view of the matter. I wish it to be distinctly understood that you are expected to observe every rule of the prison, including the rule respecting attendance at and participation in divine service held in the prison here.

Clawson: Mr. Dow, you cannot enforce such a rule and will have to withdraw it. Every prisoner under your charge must be left free to worship God according to the dictates of his conscience.

Dow: You have given me more trouble than any other prisoner in the yard; scarcely a week passes but what you are reported as having been guilty of some misdemeanor. This thing must cease. That will be all.

At this point the interview ended and we were unceremoniously marched back into the yard. About an hour later I was placed in solitary confinement—not in the sweatbox, but in a small lumber building containing an inner iron cage that was originally designed for the accommodation of Mike Sullivan, the lunatic.[15] In shape and construction it was similar to the sweatbox, but sufficiently large to admit of my cot, which I was permitted to take in with me. As I passed the brethren on my way to this infernal abode, they cast upon me an anxious and sympathetic look. First the outer, then the inner door closed. I passed in and a moment later found myself surrounded by midnight darkness. I was not long in exploring my new quarters by the sense of touch. The iron cage that held me fast was about six feet long by five feet wide and five feet ten inches high. It will be seen from this that there was little space to stir about in, when allowance was made for my cot, as its dimensions were six feet by three feet by two feet.

The fierce rays of an August sun beating down upon the roof created a heat well nigh intolerable, while an almost entire absence of ventilation increased the misery of this inhuman torture tenfold. I felt the necessity of taking immediate steps to guard against being melted into oil, and so I stripped off my clothing. Throwing myself upon the cot and collecting my scattered thoughts, I began to ruminate on the probability of being attacked by vermin. The darkness prevented a satisfactory examination of the place, yet I imagined I could feel their mysterious presence, and was correspondingly uncomfortable. However, being some two feet above the floor, I escaped this aggressive foe.

The simplicity of my diet was simply startling to me; bread and water three times a day composed the bill of fare, which, though not very nutritious, supplied just sufficient vitality to keep soul and body together. Some of the brethren asked permission to furnish me with milk, but it was peremptorily denied.

Three days and nights passed away ere I emerged from this place of awful gloom, the intensity of which one cannot comprehend until he has endured it. As the time dragged its slow length along, every hour seemed like an age, and when released I could scarcely realize that I had been in solitary confinement only three days. But for the timely appeal presented by the brethren and addressed to the warden, and for the influence exerted by my father, I would doubtless have remained much longer in "durance vile." While this paper which set forth the injustice and cruelty of such treatment in strong terms received the warden's careful consideration, he was evidently very much annoyed for he afterwards referred to it several times. He intimated that he was not only annoyed but said he was very much surprised at such audacity on the part of convicts, and he seemed to question in his mind their right to criticize his official conduct.

The reference to an influence used by my father, who was quite diplomatic, to secure my release from "solitary confinement" may be explained as follows: hearing that I was undergoing punishment for an infraction of the rules of the prison, father called upon the warden. "Mr. Dow," said he in substance, "I understand that my boy has broken one of the rules of the prison and for this he is undergoing punishment. Is that true?" "Yes, sir," answered the warden. "May I be permitted to see him?" "Yes, Mr. Clawson," said Mr. Dow. I was then ushered into the presence of father and the warden.

With a sly wink of the eye, which was intended for me and which did not escape my notice, father assumed a severe attitude and in a stern voice that was frigid in its coldness, said: "My son, I understand you have violated a rule of the prison and for this are undergoing punishment?" "Yes, father," said I in a meek, humble tone of voice. "I am very sorry to hear it." "Yes, father," I reiterated. "You must know that I cannot approve of such action on your part." "Yes, father." "And now, my son, I advise you to conform to the regulations of the prison, and give heed to the rules laid down by the warden." "Yes, father," was my answer. The interview ended; I went back to solitary confinement.

Father's parting word to Warden Dow was: "I do not think after what I said to the boy that he will give you any further trouble. I trust you may see your way clear to release him." Father acted his role well and left an excellent impression on the mind of Mr. Dow, who was delighted with what he thought was a father's reasonable attitude towards an erring son. The foregoing interview, together with the remonstrance alluded to, brought to me the needed relief. The rule pertaining to religious worship at the prison was almost immediately abrogated, because of the determined stand taken by the cohabs.[16]

When I again rejoined my brethren, the cohabs, I said to them: five of you failed to keep the compact we entered into, Brother Cannon met the issue in a most diplomatic manner and is exempt from reproach. The brunt of the warden's displeasure, therefore, fell upon me, and I was made to suffer. Had we stood together I think the result would have been different. The brethren were embarrassed and had nothing to say. I think they really repented of their weakness.

September of this year was an eventful month. Notwithstanding the stringency of the prison rules, the brethren maintained a quiet and cheerful demeanor. No murmur escaped them. Their equanimity under conditions so unfavorable to one's peace of mind was truly admirable. The prison authorities could not well endure the spirit of resignation manifested. It seemed to be galling to them. Something must be done to humiliate these indifferent men. A crushing blow was thereupon aimed at them in the introduction of striped clothing.[17] The brethren, however, received the blow with their usual equanimity and smiled complacently as they passed into the warden's office, one by one, to be fitted with the new suits.

But who can describe the demonstration made by the other class of prisoners? Their fury knew no bounds. Pacing the dining room in extreme agitation many of them cursed and swore in a frightful manner. Thunderbolts of wrath were hurled at Marshal Ireland's devoted head for thus seeking to make a display of their degradation. The shot fired at us glanced off, but struck and wounded them deeply.

While the new suits were a decided, though hideous, success in the matter of stripes, they were sadly deficient in pockets, there being but one in the pantaloons in lieu of three, none in the vest and two only in the coat; but this defect was soon remedied by the prisoners themselves, many of whom were expert with the needle. As a sequel to this introduction of additional pockets the men were all ordered into a line the next day and instructed by Doyle, the guard, in mellow tones to sew up the newly improvised pockets, which was done with the utmost dispatch. After all, the new suits did not appear to satisfy the marshal. They did not seem to be conspicuous enough, and were accordingly replaced by heavier suits with larger stripes.

To add to the humiliation of the "Mormon" prisoners, the United States marshal not only introduced striped clothes to be worn by the inmates of the penitentiary, but required that all, without exception, should submit to a clean shave and a close hair cut. In some cases the more aged and feeble under this new rule were exposed to serious discomfort, resulting oftentimes in dangerous colds.

One man of rare diplomatic ability, namely H. B. Clawson, approached the prison doctor with a five dollar gold piece hidden away under his thumb and said: "Doctor, I'm afraid that if my moustache is shaved off it will be detrimental to my health." "What is your trouble, Mr. Clawson?" inquired the doctor. "Why," replied the man as he took the doctor's hand into which the gold piece slipped and disappeared, "there is a weakness in my throat." With a knowing smile the doctor said: "Mr. Clawson, I'm sure your health would be much impaired if your moustache were removed. I shall, therefore, give strict instructions that you be not shaved." He was the one and only prisoner who moved among his fellows with a fine moustache that was the envy of all.

During September and October there were many new arrivals. I give a list below: H. B. Clawson, Edward Brain, Charles Seal, A. W. Cooley, Isaac Groo, Alfred Best, Charles L. White, John Connelly, William Rossiter, Emil O. Olsen, John Nicholson, Andrew Smith, Aurelius Miner, W. D. Newsom, all of Salt Lake City, John Lang of Beaver, and D. E. Davis of Tooele.[18] John Lang was sentenced to 3 months, $200.00 and costs, for unlawful cohabitation, W. D. Newsom to 3½ years, $800.00 and costs for polygamy, and the remaining members of the group were sentenced to 6 months, $300.00 and costs, respectively, for unlawful cohabitation. These brethren were duly installed as members of the penitentiary brigade, that is, they were shaved, clipped, and put in stripes.

Father was consigned by request to cell no. 2 that he might bunk with me, while most of the others were appointed to no. 3. My pleasure at meeting father, though very great, was not without a tinge of sadness. The prospect of having his society, counsel, and instruction for six consecutive months seemed to remove a mountain of trouble from my shoulders, and yet I would gladly have added six months to my own sentence to save him from imprisonment. The equanimity with which he accepted the situation—taking everything that came under his notice as a matter of fact and being surprised at nothing—stamped him a philosopher, a man of wide experience, indeed as a man of the world.

A few days after his arrival the warden decided to move father into no. 3, but he preferred, he said, to remain in no. 2 on my account. "In that case," replied Dow, "your son may go with you." We were accordingly removed into the new quarters. The change was very agreeable to my feelings, but it came as I had resolved it should do, if at all, unsolicited on my part.

Brother Parley P. Pratt had been sentenced to 6 months and to pay a fine of $300.00, but as the judge failed to state that he should stand committed until the fine was paid, he could only be held 6 months, less the copper.[19] While serving this sentence, Brother Parley kept a journal in which he noted the bad as well as the good features (if there were any) of the prison government, and, as the day of his release approached, he saw or thought he saw the necessity of getting the journal out without the warden's knowledge. He accordingly took the first opportunity to pass it secretly to his wife, but was detected in the act by the guard. A deprivation of 10 days copper was the punishment meted out to Brother Parley for this offence. This was a most unexpected sequel to his bold resolution, and though plunged for a short time into despair, he bore with fortitude the disappointment of not being released on time. People who feel inclined to condemn him should pause and consider the fact that [although] journals were not classed among contraband articles and while he knew the danger of passing out written information secretly, he felt justified in doing this and was willing to take the risk and suffer the penalty. Had not father and Brother Cannon exercised a strong influence in his behalf, it is probably that Brother Pratt would have fared much worse.

An amusing incident occurred relating to one of the brethren who, though possessed of an excellent appetite, was naturally thin, presenting a cadaverous appearance. It seemed utterly impossible for him to put on flesh. One day he accosted the prison physician and said to him: "Doctor, I'm seriously in need of a tonic—something that will build me up and impart greater strength than I now enjoy." Answering the doctor said: "Well, what kind of a tonic do you think would help you?" The brother replied: "A little good brandy." "Very well, I will prescribe a little brandy for your health," said the accommodating doctor. A few days later the brother was called to the gate and received a small flask of brandy, which he carried unwrapped in his hand. Walking into the dining room he put the liquor into his cupboard and securely locked the cupboard door. He then returned to the "yard," with a broad smile on his face, feeling he now had the means of toning up his system. However, his movements with the exposed brandy had been carefully noted by some of the "toughs" from the time he left the gate until he reached his cupboard and retired. Immediately thereafter the cupboard was ripped open and the liquor disappeared. When the brother later discovered his loss, which under the restrictions of that period seemed almost unbearable, he wept. The warden instituted a vigorous investigation, but no trace of the missing tonic could be found other than the compelling evidence furnished by the uncertain walk of two "toughs," who were later sent to the sweatbox for theft.

Brother A. Milton Musser and James Watson, having paid their fines, were released [on] October 12, 1885. Brother Angus M. Cannon was held about two months longer to await the decision of the U.S. Supreme Court in his appeal case.

Father's advent into the prison had an important bearing on the warden's attitude towards the brethren. It will be seen from what is already recorded that Mr. Dow's prejudices had been thoroughly aroused against us. He had seldom neglected an opportunity to make us feel the helplessness and misery of our situation. It was soon apparent, however, that father had a wonderful influence over him—an influence which he exerted exclusively for the benefit of the brethren.

A gradual relaxation of Dow's severity towards us and numerous improvements in our surroundings took place. At father's suggestion, a new and much needed toilet was erected, skylights were put into the dining room, an inside door was added to room no. 3 to shut out the cold, a large calendar clock was permitted to furnish us with the time, and many other changes of an important, though minor, nature were made. The beards of aged brethren were not, as heretofore, taken off. The rule prohibiting admittance of supplies from outside sources into the prison was not so rigidly enforced as it had been, and the further good feelings of the prison authorities were shown in permitting the brethren to give an entertainment in the dining room on Thanksgiving Day. This holiday entertainment, which was a marked success, was superintended by father, who combined some of the best musical talent of Salt Lake City with that of the prison.

Many and various had been the schemes instituted by the prisoners from time to time at the penitentiary to effect an escape, but, it is curious to note, that few if any were ever brought to a successful issue. This result may be attributed, I think, not so much to the efficiency of the prison discipline as to a lack of unity among the convicts. Where several were leagued together for the purpose of making a sudden and hasty flight, there was generally one who would secretly betray their design to the warden. Being in communication with such contemptible characters, the warden could very consistently say as he often did, that he knew everything that was going on in the yard.

However, he was sometimes outwitted as will be seen by the following incident, which occurred just prior to my conviction: Joe Davis, Bob Tait, Dave Fennel, and Edward Watterson, four desperadoes, put their heads together and evolved a bold and daring adventure. Choosing a favorable opportunity, they entered and took possession of the dining room. One stood at the door armed with a club, while the other three tore down some cross-beams from the unplastered ceiling and proceeded to fashion them into a ladder. Prisoners in the yard who happened to wander into the dining room while this work was going on were not intercepted, but none were permitted to leave the building. This precaution was taken to guard against betrayal, and the wisdom of it needs no defense. The ladder being completed, the "big four" hastily left the building, glided swiftly across the yard, placed it against the wall, ascended one after another and, ere the guard could interpose a barrier, they had dropped to the ground and were directing their nimble footsteps toward the mountains. At the very moment of success, however, misfortune overtook them. They rushed into the arms of a guard who chanced to be out in the field in the line of their flight, and were captured. As an expiation of this offence, they were each compelled to wear twenty-five-pound balls and chains on their ankles for ten months.

Bob Tait, it seems, who was the last to ascend the ladder, stood erect on the wall for a moment and then jumped to the ground below, twenty-two feet, spraining his ankle. Thus crippled, he would have made poor headway in the race for liberty, had other things been favorable. The guard who discovered this formidable movement became wild with excitement and rushed towards the fleeing convicts waving his hand in the air, imploring them in doleful accents to return. Ordinarily in such a case the air would have reverberated with the report of pistol shots, but this would have denoted a presence of mind that this particular guard did not possess.

Of these four, Joe Davis was by far the most desperate character. Previous to his present term he had served a sentence of two years for having waylaid and robbed a Chinaman of the paltry sum of 75¢. His troubles did not end there. He went forth from prison only to be returned soon after for another two years. This was brought about in the following manner. While serving out the first sentence he was taken into the field one day with another convict to work. The guard who directed their movements stood over them with a double-barreled shotgun. At a preconcerted signal, both men dropped their tools, rushed upon him, and without much regard for his official dignity, wrenched the gun from his hand. With this deadly weapon in their possession, they made good their escape, much to the delight of their fellow companions in misery. Marshal Ireland offered a reward of $200.00 each for their recapture. Davis made his way to San Francisco, where he remained for several months. In a moment of exultation, he related the above adventure to a "pal," who with a covetous eye on the $200.00 betrayed him into the hands of Ireland. Having served out the balance of his term, he was brought to trial on a charge of grand larceny, preferred by the marshal. The taking of the gun from the guard to effect an escape was construed into theft of United States property and, as stated above, he was sentenced to another two years. Davis was later shot and killed by an officer of the law, while seeking to evade an arrest for horse stealing.

Joseph Biddlecome, of whom I have spoken favorably in another place, though quite young when he entered the prison, was justly considered a hard case. He gave the warden any amount of trouble. A determination to break jail seemed to be constantly uppermost in his mind, and he seldom neglected an opportunity of putting his resolves into execution. But it was of no avail—failure invariably followed each attempt. His rebellious attitude, of course, invited harsh treatment, and he was kept in chains or the sweatbox not a little of the time. He generally managed, however, by cutting the rivets of his shackles with a small saw, made from a knife blade, to have them so that they could be taken off at pleasure. The work was so neatly done as to deceive even the guard by whom the chains were examined every night and morning. While scuffling one day with another prisoner, the chains suddenly flew off and thus exposed the trick. An additional punishment of eleven days in solitary confinement was imposed for this offence.

His native shrewdness, however, is more fully exemplified by an incident which he related to me. At the time of its occurrence, religious services were not held, as now, in the dining room, but in the yard, the minister standing on the wall. The services were somewhat noted for the lengthy prayers offered up to the Throne of Grace, at which times the guard, who stood near the preacher with his head bent forward and eyes closed, appeared to be perfectly oblivious to all that was going on in the yard below. Here it seemed was a rare opportunity to utilize this devotional exercise as a means of escape, and Biddlecome seized it. He smuggled three large iron hooks into the yard, which he afterwards tied together, the prongs pointing out from a common center. This peculiar combination was attached to the end of a rope made from a blanket, and the preparations were completed. I will simply state in this connection that there is a parapet running around the entire enclosure, outside the wall, about three feet from the top, which is used by the guards as a patrol. Sunday came and with it the pious minister, who after a few preliminaries launched forth into the customary long-winded prayer, while the guard in accordance with his previous habits, was soon lost in apparent abstraction. Biddlecome quietly withdrew from the crowd and, making his way to the other end of the yard, displayed the utmost activity in his efforts to scale the walls. He hurled the triple-headed hook into the air. It cleared the wall but fell short. He threw it again, and again it fell short, but the third time, it dropped below the parapet and, in being drawn up, grappled it firmly. With renewed hope, Biddlecome grasped the rope tightly and began to ascend, but the loss of time was fatal to him. The prayer was already ended, the guard looked up and, taking in the situation at a glance, leveled his gun on Biddlecome, who was half way up the wall, with a stern command to "halt." The unhappy convict dropped to the ground exhausted, and was soon after loaded with chains.

Several other attempts at breaking jail came under my own observation, two of which will justify a passing notice. A number of room no. 1 men, among whom was the convicted murderer, Fred Welcome, one evening concocted a plot to overcome the night guards and then to attempt an escape. It was well known by the prisoners that the inside guards were allowed to carry firearms only when the prisoners were under lock and key at night; and as firearms were needed to carry out the plan—the scene was carefully laid for night. As the evening slowly wore away, a piercing yell rent the air, and then the cry of "Murder! Help! Help! They are killing me," suddenly came from one corner of the room. Six or seven of the most turbulent spirits had jumped upon an inoffensive convict, Knowland by name, and were beating and kicking him unmercifully. The guard appeared at the door but, though the poor miserable wretch appealed to him in piteous tones for assistance, he neither spoke nor moved. It was fondly anticipated by the plotters that at this stage of the proceedings, the guard would open the door and enter the cell for the purpose of removing some of them to the sweatbox, but his sublime composure, under circumstances so distressing, completely disarmed them, and soon all was quiet again.

Had not the whole scheme been previously betrayed to the warden, it is morally certain that the guard would have ventured into the cell, in which event he would have been seized, bound, and gagged. Armed with his pistols, these desperadoes would then have rushed out into the yard and opened fire on the wall guards. Just how the affair would have ended can only be conjectured. It is probable, however, that some of the prisoners would have been killed and others might have escaped. Knowland, the man who submitted to the beating, was remanded to the sweatbox the next morning, and came out at the end of two weeks heavily chained. He also forfeited his copper. Welcome was placed in solitary confinement, where he lived apart from the other prisoners for many months, and all the others who were suspected of complicity in the affair were closely watched.

The other attempt alluded to occurred during the winter of 1884, and was no less an undertaking than to burn down the prison, regardless of consequences. In the manufacture of hair bridles, which was largely carried on in the penitentiary, ball cotton was required. A large number of these balls were saturated with kerosene and were passed, a few at a time as opportunity afforded, into the loft of room no. 1, through a small aperture in the ceiling of the lavatory. The preparations being completed, a lighted paper was one night thrown in among the cotton balls and all were instantly ablaze. Ere the fire had made much headway, however, the guard on the wall, who happened to be a little more vigilant than usual, observed a light through some crevices in the building, and gave the alarm. The excitement in both cell rooms, when it became generally known that the building was on fire, was intense. The prospect of being roasted alive carried terror to the soul of every man present, and steps were at once inaugurated to force open the massive iron doors. This action was only prevented by the promptness of the guards, who made an entrance into the loft from the outside and extinguished the blaze. Following this incident, an investigation was instituted, and though every possible means was employed to discover the guilty parties, they eluded detection. An accusation was brought against John Green and Al Moore, who were strongly suspected of being associated with the instigators of the plot, but they stoutly affirmed their innocence. However, because they declined to disclose what they knew of the affair, the sweatbox opened its ravenous maw and swallowed them up. They came forth at the end of six weeks fearfully emaciated, but still unconquered.

In November and December 1885, our number was increased by the following brethren, who were convicted of unlawful cohabitation and sentenced to six months, $300.00 and costs, respectively: Thomas Porcher, Robert H. Swain, Frederick H. Hanson, John W. Keddington, James E. Twitchell, Culbert King, and Henry Gale.

Christmas day, 1885, was memorable, not only for the excellent dinner furnished by the prison officials consisting of roast turkey, mashed potatoes, sugared tea and coffee, and "sauer kraut," but also for a generous donation to the brethren of canned goods, sugar, nuts, raisins, candies, etc., made by the merchants of Salt Lake City. This collection of good things was made and delivered at the penitentiary by Brother James Watson, an ex-convict for conscience sake. Father was appointed by general acclaim to the pleasing task of dividing out these supplies, and a busier man for an hour or so could not have been found in the wide world. It will be seen from this account that our Christmas was not altogether joyless.

In December 1885, T. M. Johnson, tutor to the warden's children, was discharged from the prison, having served out his sentence.[20] It, therefore, became necessary for the warden to select a successor.

NOTES

1. John Aird (1850–1917), who was assistant jailer at the Salt Lake City Hall, was arrested on 25 November 1884 and appeared before Commissioner William McKay on the charge of unlawful cohabitation. Failing to secure his bail, he was kept that night in the city jail where he worked and the next night at the Utah Territorial Penitentiary. His trial was on 30 April 1885, but since he pleaded guilty to the charge and stated that he intended to obey the law and live with only one wife, he was fined only $300 with costs of $21. However, since he could not pay this amount, he was kept in prison for thirty days and released on 29 May. The evening of 30 April (according to the *Salt Lake Tribune*) is when he received a mock hanging as his initiation ceremony. The *Tribune* quipped that being allowed to pay off his fine by thirty days imprisonment "is good luck, for it is equivalent to $10 per day, professional wages, and nothing to do" (*Salt Lake Daily Tribune*, 26 November 1884, and 1, 2, and 30 May 1885).

2. Andrew H. Burt (1828–83) became captain of the Salt Lake City police in 1859 and city marshal in 1876, which position he held until his death on 25 August 1883. In response to a call for help from a local business leader,

Burt was murdered with a needle gun by a man named Harvey. The murderer was captured, but while being taken to jail he was lynched by an angry mob, hanged from the roof-beams of a shed near the city hall, and then dragged about the streets of Salt Lake City. See *Deseret Evening News,* 25 and 28 August 1883, and 8 September 1900.

3. The seventy-five-cent price of the tobacco as sold by the warden to the prisoners has been added to the text due to its presence in MS I. MSS II, III, IV, and V have no price indicated at this point but simply a blank space for the amount to be inserted. The reason for this is that when MS II was being typed (while looking at the handwritten MS I), the typist thought that Rudger Clawson's distinctive 7 was a *1* (that is, the price appeared to be only fifteen cents). The context indicates that Clawson was buying the tobacco at forty cents per plug, so it did not make sense to the typist. However, the correct amount was never filled in.

4. William Fotheringham (1826–1913) was found guilty of unlawful co-habitation on 16 May 1885. Judge Jacob S. Boreman sentenced him on 20 May to a three-month imprisonment and a $300 fine, and he was taken to the prison, arriving during the evening of 23 May, not 18 May (*Salt Lake Daily Herald,* 24 May 1885). Fotheringham served out his prison term (less fifteen days off for good behavior), but he did not have to pay the fine because when he was sentenced the judge did not specify that he must stay in prison until he had paid the fine. It was determined that he was too poor to pay it, so he was released. The date of 9 August 1885 for his release is supported by Angus M. Cannon, Diary, 9 August 1885, Lee Library, Brigham Young University, Provo, Utah; the *Deseret Evening News,* 10 August 1885; and William Fotheringham, "Part of My History Book A," 47, William Fotheringham Collection, Marriott Library, University of Utah, Salt Lake City, who correctly remembered that this occurred on a Sunday. Rosa Mae M. Evans, "Judicial Prosecution of Prisoners for LDS Plural Marriage: Prison Sentences, 1884–1895," (M.A. thesis, Brigham Young University, 1986), 121, which is based on the official prison records, has 11 August 1885 instead of 9 August 1885.

5. The earliest form of Jack Bryant's verbal abuse to the guard is stronger and probably more historically accurate, for the reading of MS I* is "to call a guard a 'G-d d—n s-n of a b—-h' " (the Rudger Clawson Collection, Ms 481, Bx 2, Fd 4, MS I, 64, Marriott Library, University of Utah, Salt Lake City, hereafter the Rudger Clawson Collection is cited as RC).

6. Orlando W. Powers (1850–1914) graduated from the Law Department of the University of Michigan in 1871. Six years later he was elected city attorney of Kalamazoo, Michigan. He was re-elected to this office and stayed in this position until President Grover Cleveland appointed Powers as associate justice of the Supreme Court of Utah Territory in May 1885. In August 1886 he resigned, returned to Michigan, and edited the Grand Rapids *Daily Democrat.* He returned to Utah in 1887 to practice law and was also active in politics. See *History of the Bench and Bar of Utah* (Salt Lake City: Interstate Press Association Publishers, 1913), 184–85.

7. The official visiting day became the first Thursday of each month. The half-hour visit was scheduled between nine to eleven o'clock in the morning and two to four o'clock in the afternoon (Angus M. Cannon, Diary, 10 May 1885). At the end of the visiting period a prisoner would sometimes have a chance to kiss and hug his baby (George H. Taylor, Diary, 6 May 1886, Utah State Historical Society, Salt Lake City). After the visit those who had come to the penitentiary would often go up onto the prison wall and stand for fifteen to twenty minutes, where they could be seen by the inmates. The prisoners would pass binoculars around to look at them. One old bishop joked with the young George C. Wood, after the latter's plural wife was seen on the wall, that "she was well worth coming to the pen for" (George C. Wood, Diary, 7 April 1887, Archives, Historical Department, Church of Jesus Christ of Latter-day Saints, Salt Lake City, hereafter cited as LDS Archives).

8. In the case of Job Pingree (1837–1928) of Ogden the sentence by Judge Orlando W. Powers was not the usual six months, but only five months. Pingree was released twenty-five days early for good behavior and returned to Ogden on 17 November 1885. Arlene H. Eakle, ed., *The Pingree Legacy* (Salt Lake City: Job Pingree Family Organization, 1983), 127, 129–30, correctly gives his conviction on 6 July 1885, his sentence on 13 July 1885, and his release on 17 November 1885, but the chronology on page 16 of section 2 has all three dates incorrect. See the *Deseret Evening News*, 14 July 1885.

9. Though Clawson does not so inform the reader, the Fred Welcome mentioned here and later in an account of an escape attempt is the same person as the Fred Hopt who signed the 26 November 1886 appreciation concerning the Thanksgiving program and who was executed by a firing squad on 11 August 1887. The twenty-two-year-old Fred Welcome, a harness maker, was tried and convicted four times for the 3 July 1880 murder of John F. Turner at Park City. In November of 1884 Clawson felt that "the world at large will not seriously regret the departure from this earth of such men as Fred Welcome" (RC, Bx 2, Fd 1, 1884 Diary, 30, which is reproduced in Appendix 2). However, after his execution in August of 1887, Clawson poignantly reflects: "I do not remember to have passed a more unpleasant day during my long imprisonment." See Kay Gillespie, *The Unforgiven: Utah's Executed Men* (Salt Lake City: Signature Books, 1991); Jean Ann Walters, *A Study of Executions in Utah* (n.p., 1973); and *Deseret Evening News*, 11 August 1887.

10. Robert W. Lourey, alias "Government Kid," a twenty-nine-year-old soldier from Kentucky, was indicted for "enticing females to a house of ill-fame." See *Deseret Evening News*, 26 November 1884, 3, and *Salt Lake Daily Tribune*, 28 February 1885, 4.

11. In the original account of Clawson's memoirs there is a graphic account of A. Milton Musser's remonstrance to Marshal Ireland and Warden Dow about the prison food (RC, Bx 2, Fd 4, MS I, 79–88). These pages of MS I were pinned together for some unstated reason and were separated from the rest of the manuscript. These missing pages not only have the original account but also show evidence of penciled revisions by Clawson. This section is now restored to its original place in Clawson's memoirs, following the various

corrections of MS I². This is the only instance in which non-crossed-out wording in MS I was left out of the later manuscripts. For a reference to the Musser letter, see RC, Bx 16, Fd 4, Letter to Lydia, 9 September 1885, which is reproduced in this volume. See Angus M. Cannon, Diary, 17 and 31 August 1885 and 1 September 1885.

12. James E. Mandell, who was inmate number 5984 in the prison, relates a story that was current in the 1930s about the sanitary condition of the water in the early period: "The water conditions were in close harmony to the rest of the prison conditions. It was carried up in buckets from Parley's creek, which flows just below the short hill outside the south wall. There is a story which bears out the statement and goes something like this: A newcomer, sitting at the mess table with his ration of water before him, reached out across the next man's plate for the pepper and salt. Not being permitted to converse with one another in the dining room, he whispered to his dinner mate: 'This soup needs a little seasoning.' Another prisoner elbowed him and muttered out of the corner of his mouth: 'The soup ain't up yet; ain't as dark as that. That's yer water' " (James E. Mandell, *History of the Utah State Prison, 1850 to 1935* [Salt Lake City, 1935], 2). He was still in prison in 1938 and asked newspaper reporter, William H. McDougall, Jr., for help in getting employment on the outside.

13. Nathaniel F. Putnam (1839–91) served as rector of St. Mark's Cathedral from 1882 until his death in April 1891. See John Dixon Stewart, *A History of Saint Mark's Cathedral Parish, 1867–1967* [Salt Lake City, 1967], 22, and *Salt Lake Tribune,* 27 April 1891.

14. At this point there is a significantly different version of this episode in MS I. There is nothing in the original version about a "council meeting," a "solemn compact," or a "mutual agreement" between the Mormon prisoners. There is no mention of using code names and the four names given are all identifiable—the gentiles Alex Howard, James Cowley, and Dick Price and the Mormon Angus M. Cannon. The following is from MS I*: "Some few, however, did not respond, or, if they did, it was but for a moment, as they immediately sat down again. This action of course demanded a prompt rebuke. Jas. Doyle, the guard, who sat near the preacher, arose and came striding down the room, pale with anger. 'Howard, Cowley, Price, Cannon,' said he in an authoritative tone, 'stand up there.' Bro. Cannon explained that he was not feeling well and preferred to sit. 'Take you chair and leave the room,' which he did with astonishing alacrity. When the guard had returned to his seat and the singing was well under way, he perceived that I was in a sitting posture. He said nothing, but glared at me like a wild beast" (RC, Bx 2, Fd 5, MS I, 57). Essentially the same narration is found in MS II, but some time after it was typed a replacement version was inserted as MS II³, and a marginal notation in MS II² to "Insert true story." Clawson consistently refers to there being seven cohabs; there were just seven from 18 May through 10 July 1885. By 11 July 1885 there were nine Mormon prisoners; and by 13 July, ten. Clawson, using the wording "the fierce rays of an August sun," dates the time of his three-day solitary confinement to August 1885. However, evidence com-

bines to specify the date of Sunday, 12 July 1885. In Clawson's own letters
to Lydia, on 24 July 1885 he refers to the episode in the sweatbox (RC, Bx
16, Fd 4, which is reproduced in this volume). This places the episode sometime
before 24 July and after 8 July (his previous letter to Lydia). The Sunday is
narrowed down to 12 July 1885 by the diary entry of one of the participants,
who gives an account much closer to Clawson's MS I than the radically rewritten story in MSS II³, III, IV, and V: "Meeting commenced at 3 P.M. When
Rev. Putnam, episcopal, held service and requested all to rise. I not being well,
guard Doyle requested me to stand or go out. After standing twice, not being
able to do more, I went out. Bro. R. Clawson got up when requested at opening
but not afterwards. In evening he was called out and asked his reason for not
standing up when he said: he could not do so without violating [h]is consionce,
so he told me. This evening he was ordered into swett box, on bread and water
twice a day" (Angus M. Cannon, Diary, 11 [12] July 1885). Clawson was not
singled out for punishment because he was a Mormon prisoner, for Cannon
also records that two weeks previous to this a non-Mormon who did not
remain to the end of the Sunday service was punished by being put in the
sweatbox the next day (Angus M. Cannon, Diary, 29 June 1885).

15. The twenty-eight-year-old William Sullivan, usually known as Michael
Sullivan, was convicted of murder and sentenced on 25 May 1884 to an imprisonment of fifteen years. John Nicholson gives the following description
of the structure that housed Sullivan: "Near the north-west corner [of the
prison yard] stands an insignificant and squatty structure, as will be judged by
its interior dimensions, its width being about ten and its length twelve feet.
The height is proportionate. Inside is a strong iron cage, which monopolizes
most of the space, as it is about seven feet long and six wide, the height being
probably six feet six inches. This sad-looking edifice is used for a variety of
purposes. . . . Another capacity in which it has figured has been that of an
insane asylum on a small scale, that being the place where the notorious Mike
Sullivan has spent a good many lonely hours, in order that he might be prevented from doing bodily harm to his fellow convicts, being a lunatic of the
desperate and dangerous type" (John Nicholson, *The Martyrdom of Joseph
Standing; or, The Murder of a "Mormon" Missionary* [Salt Lake City: Deseret
News, 1886], 82–83). On 8 May 1886 Sullivan was transferred from the penitentiary to the insane asylum at Provo (Abraham H. Cannon, Diary, 8 May
1886, Marriott Library, University of Utah, Salt Lake City).

16. While his father's influence with the warden in securing his release
from solitary confinement was originally only mentioned in passing, the last
three paragraphs explaining how this came about are an addition in MS I³.
However, "because of the determined stand taken by the 'Cohabs,' " was not
added to the text of the memoirs until MS II². It is clear from the original
version that the stand taken by the cohabs was mixed and indecisive, but
Clawson's memory over the years has considerably idealized what happened
that Sunday afternoon.

17. On the afternoon of 20 September 1885 the prisoners were alphabet-
ically called out, two at a time, to receive their new prison clothes, which

featured horizontal gray and black stripes about 1½ inches wide (Angus M. Cannon, Diary, 20 September 1885). Clawson viewed the new striped uniforms as an effort by the marshal to humiliate the Mormon prisoners (RC, Bx 16, Fd 4, Letter to Lydia Clawson, 23 September 1885, which is reproduced in this volume). Clawson, along with other prisoners who had sentences of more than thirty days, was also shaved and he sent to Lydia what was left of his moustache (RC, Bx 16, Fd 4, Letter to Lydia Clawson, 26 September 1885). Some prisoners comically expressed the view that their striped prison clothes made them look like zebras (Joseph H. Dean, Diary, 27 September 1886, LDS Archives; John Adams, Diary, 24 February 1887, in private possession).

18. George Romney (1831–1920), who was born at Dalton, Lancashire, England, has been accidentally omitted from the list of those entering prison during this period. Both he and William Rossiter were convicted of unlawful cohabitation and sentenced on 10 October 1885 by Judge Charles S. Zane to a six-month imprisonment and a $300 fine plus costs of $28 and $92.75, respectively. They were both released on 13 March 1886.

19. "The copper" refers to the Copper Act of 1880, which provided for the commutation of prison sentences for good behavior. For a six-month sentence, prisoners were able with good conduct and following all the rules to serve just five months. On 11 March 1886 a more liberal copper act was passed by the legislature. For a transcript of the act, see "Convict Bill: A Bill to Lessen the Terms of Sentence of Convicts for Good Conduct," *Deseret Evening News,* 12 March 1886.

20. The thirty-four-year-old T. M. Johnson, alias C. W. Carson, was convicted of forgery on 14 October 1884 and released on 21 August 1885, not in December 1885. The original wording of this short paragraph in MS I* provides clarification: "T. M. Johnson, tutor to the warden's children, had served out his sentence and withdrawn from our midst. Joe Miller, his successor, had been released for the same reason" (RC, Bx 2, Fd 5, MS I, 115). This not only confirms the statement made earlier that Joe Miller had also acted as a tutor to the warden's children, but also it avoids the historical incongruity of specifying Johnson's release as December of 1885. Actually, Johnson was back in prison in December 1885.

CHAPTER 3

1886

The new year broke in upon us and brought with it some few changes. Friendly relations continued to exist between Warden Dow and father, which resulted in my sudden elevation to the vacant tutorship. Doubtless feeling somewhat embarrassed over his past ill usage of me, the warden did not approach me personally, but expressed to father a wish that I should take the children. I felt disposed to decline the honor, but being guided entirely by father's advice, I was installed preceptor on January 2, 1886, to George R. S. Dow, aged eleven years, and Florence A. Dow, aged five years.[1]

Before entering upon the duties of my new calling, I was ushered into Mr. Dow's private office and informed by him in most gracious terms that my relatives and friends would now be permitted to visit me at any time without a pass, that they would not be limited to time, as formerly, and that no guard would be in attendance at such interviews. He also stated that if I chose to do so, I might take my meals outside with the "trusties," or if not, would have the privilege of passing in and out to the school room at any hour of the day.

I was visibly affected by the warden's altered manner toward me. Is it possible, thought I, that this is the man who but a short time before was so full of blind prejudice and unreasoning vindictiveness? I remembered his remark to Joseph Evans, that I was untruthful and not to be trusted, and I could not but feel a secret gratification at what now commended itself to my judgment as a complete vindication. I was indeed pleased to accept all of the courtesies extended to me by the warden except permission to take my meals outside. I explained to him that I preferred to take my meals in the yard with father and my friends.

The Dow children were bright, intelligent, and interesting, and made rapid progress in their studies. The boy's time was fully occupied with athletics, reading (5th Reader), writing, arithmetic, geography, grammar, spelling, history (U.S.), French, bookkeeping, and elocution. The little girl took lessons in reading (2nd Reader), writing, spelling, and elocution. While the more solid branches enumerated were by no means neglected, I made elocution a speciality, and with untiring diligence and perseverance drilled the boy in this fascinating art. His success for one so young was phenomenal.

Having been a student of Professor Hamil, I adopted his method of teaching elocution, and we proceeded as follows: standing face to face, I spoke the words and the boy repeated them, following my gesticulations. Thus he learned his pieces by repetition, and when one verse was thoroughly committed to memory, we went on to the next, and when one entire piece was mastered, we passed on to another. By this means he acquired a large number of selections.

Every morning the windows of the classroom were thrown wide open and from 9:00 to 9:30 Georgie's voice rang out in clear strong tones, filling the room with a volume of sounds, the reverberation of which passed through the windows into the open air. The attention of the guards and others was often arrested and upon one occasion a guard was heard to say to his fellow guard: "What in hell is going on in that room up there?" The answer came: "Elocution." My purpose was already partly attained, as I aimed with this particular study to attract attention to the boy that I might thereby obtain greater influence with the father and mother. I hoped by this means to alleviate in part, the hardships incident to the prison life of the "Mormon" inmates.

When, in my opinion, he had attained sufficient proficiency to appear before others, I said to him: "Georgie, would you like to recite before your parents?" "Yes, indeed," he answered. "Go in then, and recite 'The Charge of the Light Brigade.' " This he did and the parents were delighted.

From then on, I was regarded with increasing favor. One day, seeing an opportunity to still further strengthen myself with the warden and his wife, I said to Mrs. Dow—"Why, do you know, Mrs. Dow, I was startled the other day when little Florence asked me if I would like to hear her recite 'The Charge of the Light Brigade.' In wonder I said, 'Certainly, Florence, by all means.' She then recited it without hesitation and without a blunder, giving it the appropriate inflection and gesticulations." I explained to Mrs. Dow that I was astonished beyond measure for I had given Florence no lessons in elocution. She had learned this piece merely by hearing Georgie constantly recite it, and according to her years, she did it quite as well as he. I told her it was my intention from now on, when Georgie had learned to recite a piece perfectly, to give it to Florence. Mrs. Dow was delighted, and the impression made upon her was manifested in this way: every now and then, upon coming into the classroom, I would find a piece of cake, or pie, or a dish of pudding on my desk. It was a silent peace offering that strongly appealed to me, not so much by gratifying the gustatory organs, as that it indicated my improved standing with her and her husband. Another significant fact: oftentimes when prominent visitors called to see the warden, he would have the children recite for them, and the favorable impression made naturally reflected credit and prestige upon his teacher.

One day I imparted a little lesson in politeness to the boy. In speaking of his former tutor, my predecessor, he referred to him as Johnson. I asked: "Whom did you say?" He answered, "Johnson." I again and again asked as to whom he meant. He answered each time with some impatience, "Johnson, my former teacher." "Oh," I said, "you mean *Mr.* Johnson." "No," he repeated, "I mean Johnson." "No, you don't," said I, a second time, "you mean *Mr.* Johnson." "Well," he answered, "father calls him Johnson and so will I." "Next thing you will be calling me 'Clawson.'" "Yes," said he. "No, you shall not," said I, "If your former teacher, a prisoner in stripes, was considered worthy to become your tutor, he certainly was entitled to be called *Mr.* Johnson and more especially as he was a grown man and you but a child. And for the same reason you must call me *Mr.* Clawson. When you get to be as old as your father, you may be justified, if at all, in saying 'Johnson,' instead of 'Mr. Johnson.'"

For a short time after, assuming my new role, Georgie applied himself with due diligence to his lessons. And then he grew somewhat careless and indifferent, and appeared to think it was optional on his part as to whether or not he prepared his lessons. He also presumed on the fact that I was a prisoner and often failed to heed my admonitions. One day I said to him: "Georgie, I perceive that you are becoming careless and neglectful of your studies, and I have therefore decided to institute punishment proportionate to your offence." "What will be the punishment?" he inquired. I answered: "Whenever you fail to prepare the lessons assigned you, I propose to keep you in after school and require you to add up a column of figures on the blackboard and prove the sum total." Georgie smiled and said: "Do you call that punishment? Why, that will be great fun." "Yes," said I, "but wait a moment. You haven't understood. That is but the beginning of the punishment. On the second day of your failure in preparation there will be two columns to add and prove, and on the third day, three, etc., until, if need be, the entire blackboard will be covered with a vast sum."

The punishment then outlined was so novel in character that the boy appeared eager for it and so became a little more negligent in his duty than usual. The first day's punishment, and the second and third, seemed to afford him great delight. As the sum on the blackboard grew in size, however, the boy's enthusiasm waned and when the hour of punishment came he would weep desperately and beg to be excused. I was inexorable. The punishment was duly inflicted when the occasion justified it—inflicted now for the good of the boy. It served two purposes, namely: it became a real punishment and at the same time caused him to become expert in adding figures.

For example, one day the warden came into the room and Georgie said to him: "Father, do you see that large sum on the blackboard?" "Yes," was the answer. "Do you think you could add it up and prove the sum total as quickly as I can?" "Yes," said the father. "Very well," answered the boy. "Let's try it." Starting together both father and son matched their ability on the large sum before them. Before the father had added up the columns and had come two-thirds back in proving the figures, Georgie completed the work and gave the answer. Warden Dow was delighted, and commended the progress attained by Georgie.

My star was now greatly in the ascendant. I had gained an influence over the warden, through his children, that might be thought to be a little inconsistent with my position as a convict. The past was forgotten, favors were no sooner asked than granted. I found myself in a position to benefit the brethren in many ways, and the remembrance of having done so always gives me genuine satisfaction.

Not to weary the reader with further lengthy details, I will merely state that for a period of seven consecutive months I met with fairly good success in my efforts to advance the warden's children intellectually. It was at this juncture that I approached Mr. Dow and said: "Georgie and Florence have been closely confined with their studies for about seven months and I would therefore suggest a vacation for them. In view of the progress they have made, it seems to me that it would be eminently appropriate to have them give a brief closing program of exercises of an hour's duration." The warden readily assented. "Mr. Dow," said I, "the giving of this program, if I shall be in charge, is contingent upon one condition, namely, that my brethren in the prison be invited to witness it." "How many of your brethren do you want invited?" asked the warden. "All of them, some twelve or thirteen in number," said I. "Preposterous," said he. "The idea of permitting twelve prisoners to come from within the walls and into the warden's residence to witness an entertainment. Your request, sir, is unusual and unreasonable and cannot be granted." "Mr. Dow," said I, "forget it, let there be no closing exercises. It's immaterial to me. These are your children and your affairs. I supposed, of course, you would be delighted with my suggestion, but it must be evident to you that a program rendered without an audience would be a dull affair. However, I'm perfectly satisfied to let the matter drop." The warden then said: "Well, I will speak to the U.S. marshal about it, but I have no idea he would consent to such a request." Some two days later, Mr. Dow met me and said: "Go ahead with your program."

At 9:30 A.M. July 16, 1886, the turnkey inserted his key and the penitentiary gate swung open. The "Mormon" prisoners, headed by the late President Lorenzo Snow, then the President of the Twelve,[2] passed single file and wended their way upstairs and into the largest and best living room of the warden where they were provided with comfortable seats. The company consisted of Mr. and Mrs. Warden Dow, the brethren mentioned, the children Georgie and Florence, and myself. An armed guard stood at each of the two doors.

The following program was then given under my direction:

Closing Exercises of the Penitentiary Institute
Gymnastics... By the School
Recitation, "Bernardo del Carpio"..................... Geo. R. S. Dow
Select Reading, "The Children and
    the Moon"... Florence A. Dow
Exercises on Blackboard.................................... Geo. R. S. Dow
Exercises in Spelling.. Florence A. Dow
Select Reading, "A Morning Conversation" ...... Geo. R. S. Dow
Recitation, "The Charge of the
    Light Brigade" .... Florence A. Dow
Select Reading, "On the Waste of Life"............. Geo. R. S. Dow
Select Reading, "Suppose" .... Florence A. Dow
Recitation, "The Bells".....................................George R. S. Dow

Generous applause was accorded the children at the conclusion of each number, and the brethren gave verbal expression to the pleasure the entertainment had afforded them. It is perhaps needless to say that Mr. and Mrs. Dow were exceedingly delighted with the performance and looked upon me afterward with ever increasing favor.

In December 1885, just prior to my acceptance of the tutorship, T. M. Johnson again made his appearance in our midst. The charge preferred against him was burglary committed in Ogden City. Conviction followed trial and he was sentenced to a term of three and one-half years imprisonment. The prospect of having again this shrewd, treacherous, and unprincipled man to deal with, who had ever been my evil genius from the first, was by no means inviting. He proved to be a veritable thorn in the side of the brethren also, and succeeded in annoying them in a thousand different ways, in spite of the fact that this time he did not enjoy the confidence of the warden. He was extremely anxious to secure his former situation as tutor, and made several applications for it, but was met with a prompt refusal and stinging rebuke. Mr. Dow thought it would be very imprudent to place the children under the influence of one whom he had come to consider unworthy of confidence. Being deemed unfit to associate with the better class of criminals, Johnson was consigned to room no. 1.

Contrasting our relative positions at this time with those of a year prior thereto, I was struck with the radical change that had taken place. *He* then was Professor Johnson, and *I*, a common convict. The wheel of fortune made one revolution, and *I* was now Professor Clawson and he, a common convict. Once before he had been instructed by the warden to record that "Clawson was placed in the 'box' for insubordination," whereas now it so happened that I was called upon to make a minute of the fact that "Johnson was placed in solitary confinement for insulting one of the guards."

Smothering his chagrin and disappointment at not being restored to the full confidence of Mr. Dow, he turned his attention to the organizing of a general school among the prisoners which was well patronized.[3] Though prompted altogether by malice and hatred in his intercourse with the brethren as a convict (for he soon worked his way into room no. 3), I will do him the justice to say that he was an efficient teacher and met with fair success in his efforts to advance the students intellectually. He numbered among his pupils many of the brethren who acted, it seems, upon a maxim that has been attributed to Joseph Smith, the Prophet, viz., "If I can use the devil for good, I will do it." A more striking example of getting good out of evil, I do not remember to have witnessed.

During the months of January, February, and March 1886, the following brethren who were convicted (some pleaded guilty) of unlawful cohabitation and sentenced to 6 months imprisonment and $300.00 and costs, except in the cases noted, came to share with us the hardships of enforced confinement: James H. Nelson, W. W. Willey, John Penman, polygamy, 2 years, $25.00 and costs,[4] Thomas Burningham, John Bowen, Robert Morris, 6 months, $150.00 and costs, W. G. Saunders, 12 months, $25.00 and costs, D. M. Stuart, S. H. B. Smith, Henry Dinwoodey, Joseph McMurrin, Amos Maycock, 11 months, $100 and costs, H. S. Gowans, W. H. Lee, C. H. Greenwell, Helon H. Tracy, 12 months, $300.00 and costs, H. J. Foulger, J. P. Ball, John Y. Smith, Thomas C. Jones, James O. Poulsen, George H. Taylor, Samuel F. Ball, James Moyle, O. F. Due, Hyrum Goff, William J. Jenkins, Frederick A. Cooper, John W. Snell, A. H. Cannon, Lorenzo Snow, 18 months, $900.00 and costs, Robert McKendrick, and L. D. Watson.

It is pleasing to note that, while the brethren in general entertained a horror of prison life, yet they maintained from the first a spirit of quiet and cheerful resignation. When fully persuaded of the truth of a principle, what will not honest hearted and conscientious people endure for its sake! Bonds and imprisonment? Yes, death itself! Why, as well might one expect to be able to dam up the Mississippi River as to conquer the human heart by violence. History has proved this truth and history repeated itself in the crusade against the "Mormons." It must be apparent to the thoughtful that a religion which will enable men to relinquish cheerfully all the comforts of home will also make them unconquerable. These "Mormon" convicts accepted a loathsome prison in lieu of pleasant homes when a simple promise to obey the law would have secured their liberty. The presence of so many of our brethren in the penitentiary brought about a very remarkable change which was especially noticeable to me. It will be seen from what has already been written that during the fall of 1884 and the spring and summer of 1885, there was one constant scene of turmoil and confusion among the convicts. Attempts at breaking jail were of frequent occurrence; fighting was freely indulged in and thieving became a common practice. It would be impossible to give an adequate idea of the language that hourly fell upon the ears. This condition of affairs before the brethren came, made it extremely unpleasant for the warden, whose time was fully occupied in keeping the turbulent spirits under his charge in subjection. As one sweatbox was not sufficient to meet the requirements of stern justice, another was erected. Seventeen men out of about seventy were wearing the shackles at one time. The guards who were called to go on duty in the yard could never feel entirely safe.

Now, the mere presence of the brethren in the prison, with their high ideals and splendid example did more toward accomplishing the reformation and securing the obedience of these men to prison discipline than the punishments inflicted by the warden would have done in twenty years. The brethren exerted a most powerful restraining influence. Stubborn, rebellious men who were acquainted with every form of vice and lawlessness and who laughed at the sweatbox and paid little or no attention to the chains seemed utterly unable to resist the spirit of peace, tranquility, and resignation that accompanied the "Mormon" convicts. The brethren's example was contagious. Profanity did not cease altogether, but it was by no means indulged in to the extent that it had been; the sweatboxes fell into disuse, except at rare intervals, and the chains gradually disappeared from the yard. Jail breaking was a thing of the past. The heavy responsibility, the anxiety, and the fears that constantly harassed the warden's mind, both day and night, were measurably removed.

The guards felt as much at ease among the prisoners as they possibly could have done at home. The marshal abandoned the practice of driving the men into one corner of the yard like so many cattle when visiting the prison. In fact, the change was so marked as to excite the astonishment of every official connected with the penitentiary, although they were slow to give the despised "Mormons" credit for it.

I call to mind an amusing incident that occurred during the imprisonment of my father, who was always fond of a good joke. In his early life, reaching as far back as Nauvoo, he had attained to some repute as a comedian. He appeared in performances which were witnessed by the Prophet Joseph Smith and he was often seen during pioneer times in plays presented at the Old Social Hall and the Salt Lake Theatre, when the late President Brigham Young and other church authorities were interested auditors. Father was also something of a reader. He rather excelled in giving the well-known but always difficult piece entitled the "Maniac." The setting of this thrilling recitation was a prison cell with a liberal supply of chains for use in rattling at certain periods of the recital. The incident to which I am alluding was a grim practical joke planned by father and worked out with my assistance. After being locked up one evening as usual, I proposed to the "honorable" company present, consisting of the late President Lorenzo Snow, Abraham H. Cannon, and about twenty-two other brethren, together with a number of other prisoners, that father be called upon to give a recitation, the selection to be of his own choosing. The proposition met with instant and hearty approval. Father consented and said he would recite the "Maniac," as the surroundings seemed most suitable for that particular piece.

He then turned down the light to a point that gave the room a somber and gloomy appearance and stationing himself in a dark recess near the iron grating of the entrance door, he projected himself into the character of the "Maniac." Whatever of dramatic skill and power he possessed was exhibited in the rendition. The "Maniac" shrieked out his awful complaints, and the chains by which he was bound rattled against the grated iron door. So realistic was the scene that a shudder perceptibly swept over the auditors, who sat apparently transfixed with some evil foreboding. At the psychological moment, when father had reached the climax of this remarkable declamation, and the audience was sitting breathlessly in semi-darkness, under great nervous tension, I gave an awful yell. The effect was that of a bursting bombshell. Several nearly collapsed from the shock and one man fell over backwards.

Father, ever desirous of furnishing amusement for the brethren and obtaining permission from the marshal, went to work with his usual energy and prepared a most interesting program for Washington's birthday, February 22nd, 1886. He secured, in addition to the prison talent, speakers and singers from Salt Lake City, and the occasion was so thoroughly enjoyed that the ordinary prison gloom was dispelled for many days thereafter.

A man is judged not necessarily by his personal appearance but rather by his character. Oftentimes a gentle and refined spirit is hidden beneath a rough exterior. This was strikingly true of Brother Amos Maycock, who came into the Pen during the spring of 1886. With large irregular features, and an awkward unwieldy body, he was truly one of the homeliest men I ever saw. When he entered the prison all eyes were turned upon him. The "toughs" smiled broadly; some of them even laughed outright at his ungainly figure and homely features. For a number of days they seemed to take great delight in making uncomplimentary remarks within his hearing, relative to his personal appearance. The insulting attitude of the prisoners would have ruffled the temper of an angel, but this brother maintained perfect self-control. He positively ignored them—passed them by as if they were non-existent. Their coarse gibes and hilarious sallies fell to the ground unnoticed by him. He lived in an atmosphere far above them. Thus did he proclaim himself to be a man. By his quiet demeanor, genial manner, and good common sense, he finally won the respect and esteem of every prisoner and all the officials of the penitentiary.

The prison rapidly filled up as time went on. I know of no place that furnished better opportunities for the study of human nature than the penitentiary. Every imperfection of one's character, as well as one's every virtue, stands out in bold relief. A person who is of an irritable disposition has innumerable chances to indulge his weakness, while the quiet, patient man succeeds in preserving his equanimity only by a silent but constant struggle with self. The brethren, be it said to their credit, maintained a spirit of charity and forbearance, though packed in the cell rooms like sardines, so closely crowded together that they were continually jostling one another.

Brother John Nicholson was one of the many men incarcerated in the Utah Penitentiary during the fall of 1885 and the spring of 1886, of whose acquaintance and friendship I feel proud. We were together much of the time. While I was speaking on one occasion of my experience in the Southern States, he became deeply interested in the cruel murder of Elder Joseph Standing. I furnished him with the details of that fearful tragedy, which he wrote up at odd moments, and afterwards published under the title of *The Martyrdom of Joseph Standing*, with an addendum giving a description of the Utah Penitentiary and some data connected therewith.[5]

Upon one occasion in the daytime, when the brethren had exclusive possession of the bunk room, President Lorenzo Snow made a startling and interesting announcement.[6] He spoke to this effect: "I propose, if it shall meet with the unanimous approval of all the brethren present, that we give the sacred shout. I realize that this is an extraordinary thing to do in a prison house. It has never been before, but inasmuch as we are incarcerated here for conscience sake, I'm sure we would be fully justified." In response to President Snow's invitation, every one present arose in turn, and expressed himself as being heartily in favor of the proposition.[7] President Snow then rehearsed the brethren in this important undertaking. At a given signal led by the president, the brethren gave a mighty shout, waving their handkerchiefs above their heads, in which the following words, "Hosanna, Hosanna, Glory be to God and the Lamb forever and ever, Amen and Amen," three times repeated, rang out, filling the room with a great volume of sound, which I am sure escaped through the windows and entrance into the open air.[8] The shout was given with earnestness and force almost sufficient to raise the roof, and yet, strange to say, not a prisoner outside of that little company in the bunk room appeared at the door, nor did any one of the guards rush up to learn the case of so great a disturbance. What to us was a tremendous but glorious shout, to others was apparently not heard. Of all my experiences in the penitentiary this to me has always been a mystery.

March 2nd, 1886, like September 29th, 1885, was to me a day of lights and shadows, of pleasure and sorrow. Father had reached the termination of his imprisonment and upon payment of the fine was released. It was with no small degree of satisfaction that I saw him released from prison bondage, and yet when I remembered the many pleasant moments we had passed together—moments never to be recalled—my soul was filled with gloom and despondency. The loss I had sustained in his departure was even greater than I had pictured it to myself.

About this time Marshal Ireland, with the intention of adding, if possible, to the brethren's humiliation, decided to establish a "Rogues' Gallery." Accordingly, a photographer by the name of "General" C. H. M. y Agramonte, the wife beater, was employed to come to the prison and take a photograph of each convict.[9] When the object of his mission was made known and while he was setting up his camera in the vestibule just outside the gate, a scene of fearful consternation took place among the "toughs." A perfect storm of curses rent the air. Some of the more accomplished and dangerous crooks—those who would have the most to fear from leaving their pictures with the officers of the land—fairly grew livid with rage. "General" Agramonte came on to the wall for a few moments: Cowley, one of the toughs, was the first to espy him, and called out in angry tones, "Who whipped his wife?" "Agramonte" was the murmured response of his companions. Cowley promptly "walked" into the sweatbox for this offence, and came not thence during the space of twenty-four hours.[10]

Various were the means adopted by the non-"Mormon" convicts to disfigure their faces. Mustaches that had escaped the barber's knife were taken off from one side of the lip only; heads and eyebrows were shaved; shoe blacking and soot were freely used, and, as a consequence, large black rings appeared around the eyes of some, while other faces showed perpendicular, horizontal, and diagonal lines, both light and heavy. It must not be supposed that the brethren felt no annoyance in complying with the new order, but as heretofore, their real feelings were hidden beneath a placid countenance.

Great was the astonishment of the "General," Warden Dow, and Curtis, the turnkey, when these men, who had disfigured their faces, were called one by one and presented their hideous faces at the gate. Dow tried to look severe but failed; he smiled and that, of course, is rare in a warden. Curtis who was noted for his austerity of demeanor laughed vehemently. The "General" looked thoughtful and sad. A wash dish and water being provided them, some were directed to remove the soot and black stains from their faces and others to shave. This they did with a reluctance that signified how galling the situation was to them. Full of anger and chagrin, and still bent on outwitting the warden, they twisted their features into every conceivable shape while seated before the camera. When about half the prisoners had passed through the ordeal singly, two and two were called. In consequence of this change many of the brethren were taken with murderers, horse and cattle thieves, burglars, and highway robbers, one with a negro, and one with an Indian. Two days were required for the accomplishment of this important undertaking, whereupon the "General" gathered up his traps and fled.

It is rather interesting to note that this was the first time up to date that the inmates of the Utah Penitentiary had ever been subjected to a process which I considered an indignity, and it was plainly evident that the photographing was done not to establish better police efficiency, but to embarrass the brethren and gratify the personal malice of the prison officials.

In April, May, and June 1886, our numbers were further augmented by the entrance of the following brethren who were sentenced to 6 months, $300.00 and costs for unlawful cohabitation, except in the cases noted: Stanley Taylor, Andrew Jensen, George B. Bailey, Nephi Bates, 4 months, $100.00 and costs,[11] John Bergen, unlawful cohabitation, 2 years, $1200.00 and costs,[12] George C. Lambert, H. W. Naisbitt, Levi Minnerly, 5 months, no fine, R. C. Smith, 6 months, no fine, Ambrose Greenwell, 12 months, $300.00 and costs,[13] M. L. Shepherd, W. G. Bickley, Peter Wimmer, W. J. Cox, George C. Wood, polygamy and unlawful cohabitation, 5 years and 3 months, $800.00 and costs, Royal B. Young, unlawful cohabitation, 18 months, $900.00 and costs, Charles Denney, Ludwig Berg, Jens Hansen, William Stimpson, 5 months, $300.00 and costs, and W. H. Pidcock, unlawful cohabitation, 13 months and costs.[14]

With the object of promoting the health of the brethren, whose habits were necessarily sedentary, I organized a class in athletics during the summer, which met every morning at an early hour.[15] We went through a great variety of movements both with the arms and body, and thereby succeeded in bringing every muscle into play. Breathing exercises were especially emphasized. These exercises very materially aided digestion, which was ever on a strain from eating the inferior prison food, and therefore were productive of much good. By the activity of U.S. Prosecuting Attorney, [William H.] Dickson, in apprehending and convicting cohabs, the class was replenished with new members twice every year.

In addition to this recreation I felt the need of some mental activity. Prison life at best is monotonous and if one's mind is not fully occupied, [it] becomes almost unendurable. Having early discovered this fact, I therefore applied myself to reading and study with reasonable diligence.

A one-armed burglar [Joe Miller] taught me French in exchange for lessons in bookkeeping. He also read to me regularly that I might enhance my knowledge of shorthand and acquire speed. I took from his dictation the entire story of the Scottish chiefs, and also much other matter. Conditions in the penitentiary did not furnish much opportunity for speaking French. I therefore did not attain any proficiency as a linguist; however, I derived much pleasure from reading the entire Book of Mormon in this language. A young burglar in the pen [Frank Treseder], who had risen to some eminence as a landscape painter, gladly turned over to me a number of scenes from his brush, including a picture of the interior and exterior of the penitentiary, in lieu of lessons in bookkeeping. Thus, by an exchange of courtesies we were all profited.

At the solicitation of some of the brethren, I later organized classes in bookkeeping, recruiting the classes with new arrivals from time to time.[16] The course consisted of sixty lessons at 25¢ each or $15.00, and notwithstanding the smallness of the fee, I earned $500.00 through this activity during my incarceration, which was of material assistance not only to myself but also to my family. My pupils were also greatly benefitted. The course included general merchandising, commission, jobbing and importing, farm accounts with six column journal, and administrator's books. Among those who took the course were such well-known men as Henry Dinwoodey, George C. Lambert, Royal B. Young, William Rossiter, [and] Bishop William Bromley of American Fork. The late President Snow was a frequent visitor to my classroom and seemed to be interested in the work I was doing. He liked my method of teaching, he said.

Bishop Bromley approached me one day and said: "Brother Clawson, do you think I could master the science of bookkeeping?" I answered: "Why do you ask the question?" He further said: "Well, I'm about sixty years of age and am pretty well set in my ways. I wonder, therefore, if I would be able to master this science. I'm very much in need of the knowledge." "Bishop Bromley," said I, "it depends upon yourself. If you'll clench your fist and set your teeth and say 'I will master bookkeeping' then I'll say 'the victory is half won and you'll surely succeed,' but if on the other hand you weakly say, 'I cannot, no, I cannot master bookkeeping,' then I'll say 'no you cannot, you've failed already.' " Thereupon Bishop Bromley clenched his fist and set his teeth and said: "I will master bookkeeping." "The victory is half won"; said I: "Surely you will succeed." And he did succeed, for he was one of my ablest students. He was manager of a store, and upon returning home discharged his bookkeeper and opened a new set of books on the double entry system.

An affirmative attitude determined his success. Upon learning of this and other cases, one of the Salt Lake daily papers, which at that time was inimicable to the "Mormons," was led to say that the "Mormon" prisoners at the Utah Penitentiary—criminals in the eyes of the law—went into prison to suffer for their (alleged) crimes, and came out with professions.

In speaking of Bishop William M. Bromley, who entered the prison during the fall of 1886, I am tempted to relate here the following story which he told to President Snow and me a few years later. It illustrates how terribly prison life may affect one. He said that after leaving the pen, he determined he would never again submit to an arrest by a United States marshal. Rather than be taken he would shoot to kill and from the day of his release he carried a revolver. One night after retiring he fell into a deep sleep, he said, and dreamed as follows: he seemed to be sitting quietly in a large room before an open fire. A knock was heard at the door and upon invitation of the bishop a strange man entered. Approaching he said: "Is this Bishop Bromley?" "Yes," was the answer. The man, putting his hand in his pocket, said: "Here is a paper I wish to read to you." Raising his voice the bishop answered in an authoritative and emphatic tone: "Don't you read that paper to me. I will not listen to it." The stranger said in an equally decisive tone: "I am an officer of the United States Government and was directed to serve this paper upon you. It is my duty and I shall certainly do it." He thereupon proceeded to read, when the bishop whipped out his revolver and shot him dead. This sudden act of violence on his part seemed to react upon the overwrought nerves of the bishop, who rushed wildly out of the room and down into the willows, bordering on a nearby stream. He paused, sat down, gathered in his wandering thoughts and began to reflect upon the awful tragedy that had ended so seriously, so fatally. He was greatly disturbed in his feelings. Finally he began to realize the exact nature of the act he had committed. He reasoned it out thus: "This man did not come in his own name, or by his own authority. He was a servant of the government and was simply carrying out his instructions. The responsibility of serving the subpoena was not upon him but upon the government. He was therefore in duty bound to serve it. He could not well do otherwise, and I shot him down in cold blood. I am a murderer. The mark of Cain is on me. And even now as a vagabond, I'm fleeing from justice." These reflections, said the bishop, caused him to suffer the torments of the damned—such intense suffering as cannot be described and is known only to those who are guilty of murder. He felt that there was no forgiveness for him in this world or the world to come. At the point where he felt he could not longer endure the torment, he woke up. Realizing at that moment it was but a dream, he shouted for very joy. He was the happiest man on earth. He took his revolver and cast it away as a vile thing, resolving never again to carry firearms, even though his life might be in danger.

After listening to the story with rapt interest, President Snow said: "Bishop Bromley, your dream came from the Lord and was intended as a warning. The Lord knew the firmness of your character and fore-knowing also that you would surely shoot to kill and that no mortal could change your attitude of mind, He sent the dream. And thus you have possibly been saved from the commission of crime. The Lord has truly been merciful to you."

It is with pleasure that I allude again to Abram H. Cannon. He was about my own age and an old acquaintance and schoolfellow, and consequently we were together much of the time. Our friendship for one another was greatly strengthened by a few months intercourse under the peculiar conditions of prison life. I saw much in his character to admire. Strictly moral, temperate, virtuous, and with integrity written on every fiber of his nature, he carried a splendid influence with him and enjoyed great popularity among the prisoners both "Mormon" and non-"Mormon." He mapped out a course of studies and pursued it with untiring diligence during his entire incarceration, thus setting to all his brethren an example that was worthy of imitation. Though young in years, he was a man of considerable experience in the world and took a broad view of life. I think it might be said of him that he was one of that class of men who would meet death with a smile rather than betray the Truth.

To the cohabs, six months incarceration, which was the usual term given to them, seemed a long period. Imagine then how staggering, overwhelming, the prospect of four years was to me. Interminable even as that period seemed, two incidents occurred in the Pen that doubly served to emphasize the slow passing of time. The first was this: Brother Henry W. Naisbitt, a gifted poet and fellow prisoner, wrote a song entitled, "One Day Nearer Home"; and, second, a kind-hearted and sympathetic jeweler of Salt Lake, Brother Amason [Carl C. Amussen], presented us with a handsome, eight-day Calendar Clock. Every night upon entering our cell room, we sang the song and looked at the clock which, with unerring certainty, pointed to the "one day nearer home," but we all without exception felt that we were further away from home than ever, and thus learned by bitter experience that the best way to annihilate time was not to think or ponder over it.

The 13th of May, 1886, will be remembered as a day of unusual interest to the brethren imprisoned in the Utah Penitentiary for conscience sake. Governor Caleb W. West[17] visited the prison for the purpose of making a proposition looking toward their release. He undoubtedly persuaded himself that these men, who had indignantly rejected the proffered leniency of the court at the time of sentence, on condition of making a simple promise to obey the law, would, after having tasted the misery of prison life, eagerly accept of his terms. How the proposition was received will be seen from the following description of his visit, as published in the *Deseret Evening News,* May 14, 1886.

GOVERNOR WEST AT THE PENITENTIARY
He Holds an Interview with the Brethren.
He Makes Overtures that are not Accepted.
Religious Convictions Cannot be Surrendered.

Yesterday afternoon Governor West, accompanied by Marshal Ireland, Secretary [Arthur L.] Thomas, Mr. Adam Patterson (court reporter), Mr. W. C. Hall, and Mr. Webb, drove out to the penitentiary. The object of the visit and what occurred at the prison are fully explained by the following account of the matter, from the pen of Mr. Patterson:

Upon arrival at the penitentiary the party were received by Warden Dow and conducted into one of the apartments of the building outside the wall, and Apostle Lorenzo Snow, at the request of Governor West, was brought into the room, when the following conversation occurred:

Governor West: Mr. Snow, I suppose you are advised of the action of the Supreme Court in your case?

Snow: Yes, sir; I have heard they concluded they have no jurisdiction in my case.

Governor: Of course, you are aware that that determination by that court makes final the decision of that case by the Supreme Court here?

Snow: I suppose so.

Governor: Under those circumstances, of course, that is now the law, because it is the decision of the highest judicial tribunal to which it could be submitted, and I conceived that it would be a very opportune time to call and submit to you a proposition, which, in conjunction with Judge Zane and Mr. [William H.] Dickson, we have thought advisable to make, in order to show you and the people of the Territory that they are mistaken in believing that those charged with the execution of the laws in the Territory are animated by any spirit of malice or vindictiveness towards the people who are in the majority in the Territory; that on the contrary their only wish and only desire, one which is nearest to their hearts, is to have the people of the Territory obey and respect the law. Upon consultation with Judge Zane and Mr. Dickson, and they supporting the view that I have suggested, I have come to say to you and your people here that we would unite in a petition to the Executive to issue his pardon in these cases upon a promise, in good faith, that you will obey and respect the laws, and that you will continue no longer to live in violation of them.

Snow: Well, Governor, so far as I am concerned personally, I am not in conflict with any of the laws of the country. I have obeyed the law as faithfully and conscientiously as I can thus far, and I am not here because of disobedience of any law. I am here wrongfully convicted and wrongfully sentenced.

Governor: Yes, but that is from your standpoint. Of course, that is a question—

Snow: No, no. Perhaps you misunderstand me. I don't mean particularly and exclusively the Edmunds law, I mean the law of the land that I consider supreme—

Governor: The law is actually what the court says it is. If you are here under a conviction of that kind, and your intention was to obey the law, as you say you have done it, then you can sacrifice nothing if you promise and agree to obey the law in the future; you then rid yourself of a conviction which you say is wrongful, and you protect yourself from a future prosecution if you obey the laws.

Snow: Yes, I presume so; but my views are entirely different from that—right directly opposite—the result will not be the one that you anticipate. I speak with knowledge, and you speak with your opinion. I speak in reference to knowledge and am perfectly convinced that the result will be widely different from that which you state. No doubt there will be a great deal of suffering, but I, as one—and I presume it is so with the great majority of this people—am ready to take the consequences. We believe in a certain principle, and that principle is dear to our hearts and we are willing to suffer as the ancients did. We honor the law administered rightfully.

Governor: You have come to the question exactly which I was just going to suggest to you. That being your state of feeling, that being your avowed course of action, you ought then to do the officials in this Territory the justice to say that they are not to blame for this state of affairs; that your own conduct and your own position puts you in disobedience to the laws; that while you suffer, the suffering is incurred by your action and not by any spirit of malice or any desire upon the part of the Government or those who represent it, to do you an injury or to cause this suffering; because you see my object and purpose here now is to unite in an effort to relieve you, but you, by the position you take, preclude any such position being taken; you voluntarily and obdurately place yourselves in this position. Therefore, common fairness should require you not to say and not to publish to the world that you are being persecuted, hounded, maliciously and vindictively pursued by the Federal officials who are entrusted with the administration of the laws.

Snow: Oh, no more so than Jesus Christ and the Apostles. They had these same things to suffer and practiced the same gospel; and we expect that inasmuch as we have espoused the same religion and the same principles that they proclaimed, and for which they lost their lives, that we will have to suffer, and we are willing to do it.

Governor: You are not being prosecuted for opinion's sake.

Snow: Oh, no more than the Roman Empire prosecuted the apostles for opinion's sake. They rendered themselves in obedience to the laws of the country they were in. It was the laws that condemned them to death, and it was the Jewish law that condemned Jesus.

Governor: You are getting off the question and getting upon a question that is so wide that we would have to lengthen our lives to discuss it. I came here with simply one purpose and desire, which was, if I could possibly, by any effort on my part and with the concurrence on your part of obedience to the laws, to receive you from any suffering. You must look at this matter just as it stands. The courts have construed this law, and their construction of it is the law, and we have no right to say anything else. And when you get out, if you continued the course you have pursued, do the same acts again, it will simply be a temporary relief from here—back you will have to come.

Snow: I expect so. I presume that would be the case.

Governor: Well, now you are suffering and you are causing others to suffer, and you are injuring the prosperity of the Territory, and all for no good purpose. You cannot accomplish anything by it. That will not repeal the laws nor will it benefit you in any way; because in prison here you don't enjoy the liberty that is guaranteed by the laws to every law-abiding man; you cannot have the pleasures of home which are protected by the law and you are suffering here without benefit.

Snow: Exactly. But I have no confidence in the courts, even if I was to make a promise I have no idea in the world that the courts would administer us justice. Let them first administer us justice and administer the laws correctly, and then we will see.

Governor: Yes, but that is your own individual opinion, that the laws are not administered correctly.

Snow: Is it your individual opinion that they are?

Governor: I beg your pardon. We must not be too egotistical. I did not make the laws and I do not say what the laws are; on the contrary, I am taking the decision of the courts. I can take the legislative acts and read them and I may think I know what the law is, and go into court and the court says that is not the law. Therefore, I must take the law as decided by the courts, and so must every law-abiding man. It seems to me you cannot say that you have no confidence in the protection of the courts and the officials here—

Snow: I have no confidence whatever.

Governor: You ought not to say that you have no confidence in the protection of the courts and the officials unless you believe that I have come here under false pretenses and that Judge Zane—

Snow: Oh, no.

Governor: That Judge Zane and Mr. Dickson, who have concurred with me, are not doing it in good faith; that is the only way you can say that, because you must have confidence in us or you must believe we are not acting in good faith. You know it is a very unusual thing to see officials who are charged with the execution of the laws, coming as I have done, and with the concurrence of those men, to say that if you will give your promise, in good faith, that you will observe that law, that we will unite to have you relieved from the convictions against you. Ordinarily offenders have suffered for the offenses they have committed and have no chance to promise reformation with the chance of being relieved from punishment, so you must have confidence if you believe in our sincerity.

Snow: I certainly believe in your sincerity, but you are not the court. As to Dickson and as to Zane, I have no confidence in them at all.

Governor: Mr. Snow, I think you are very unjust in that opinion, because I know that this suggestion that I make—

Snow: If you had suffered, you would think differently.

Governor: But you are charging the suffering to them wrongfully, I think. They do not make the laws; they execute them, and the suffering occurs from your disobedience of the laws. You are responsible for the suffering, not Judge Zane nor Mr. Dickson, and I tell you you do them great injustice; because from all the conversations I have had with them and in all their conduct during the short time I have been here, I am sure those men are animated by a good purpose, an earnest desire simply that the people of this Territory obey the law, and they take no pleasure in the suffering which is caused by the disobedience of the laws.

Snow: They send us here without a particle of evidence. It is through the counsel given to the jury by the judge—by Judge Zane, who is influenced by Dickson. I have not a particle of confidence in those men. If you had come entirely alone, without the names of those men, we would have more confidence in the propositions.

Governor: You can have confidence in the propositions, whether I tell you or they, because they are made in entire good faith.

Snow: What did I tell you in the talk we had the other day in reference to the Supreme Court?

Governor: That Supreme Court has a duty to perform. Of course, it could not take jurisdiction of the case, which was not within its jurisdiction.

Snow: They took jurisdiction in the first case that went up there.

Governor: Of course, then, if they were wrong in the first place I would not have so great a respect for them if they did not turn around and rectify it in the other case. Of course, you can have what opinions you please about the courts or the officials, but, as I say, no good citizen can have an opinion which will justify him in violating the law—none. There is no excuse for that.

Snow: All right.

Governor: Of course, I do not know what the result of this would be, but I came with the disposition and to show you and the people here that there is an opportunity for them to escape the punishment they have incurred if they should conform to the law, and escape the misery and trouble they are now enduring in consequence of their violation of the law.

Snow: Well, but Governor, why should this be required of me, inasmuch as I certainly have not as yet disobeyed the law. The law has been wrongfully and illegally administered in the cases of many of us in the Pen.

Governor: But we have to submit to the law as administered by its agents and properly constituted authorities. No one of us, as a citizen, has a right to put his opinion against that determination. We are bound to submit to the construction of the laws which the court gives. We cannot adopt our own construction and follow that, because the decisions of the courts constitute what the law is. You are too intelligent a man to have asked me the question whether you should be required to make such a promise as that, because you know very well you have taught and believed that certain practices are right which the law has put its ban upon. It has been said by our law-making power that it is not right, and not only that it is not right, but that such practices cannot be tolerated in this land, and that punishment will follow a violation of it.

Snow: I defy any man to come forward and testify I have taught any person to disobey the laws. There is no person can come forward and testify to that.

Governor: That has been the teaching of the body that you belong to.

Snow: It has been in the past, but it has not been with me in the present.

Governor: I am not talking about the past. Of course, I don't care to discuss that. I say you are here under a conviction in a court for a past offense, and I come to propose that the Federal officials unite in asking the President for pardon for you and others, to relieve you from any punishment you may have incurred if you, in good faith, for the future submit yourselves to the laws as interpreted and construed by the courts.

Snow: Well, now, Governor, of course, there is no use wasting time on this. If you ask me if I will renounce the principle of plural marriage, I will answer you at once.

Governor: No; that is not the question. The question I ask you is, will you agree, in good faith, sincerely, in the future to respect and obey the laws as interpreted by the courts, which I and every other good citizen ought to do and must do, and failing to do, will incur punishment.

Snow: I was once asked that same question at the First District Court at Ogden, and I expressed to the court my wishes that I should not be required to answer that question. I considered it a question that they had business to ask. I had obeyed the laws and was convicted illegally and wrongfully, and I did not consider it was a personal question as to the future.

Governor: I understand that. That was a question that was asked you in court and you had a right to decline to answer. Now, I come with the earnest desire to save misery and trouble to the people with whom I am to be associated officially, and I have it very near to my heart, if possible, to relieve the people here of a great deal of unnecessary suffering, because I am satisfied that all this suffering, so far as the protection of the peculiar institution which you have established is concerned is useless; that it will do no good whatever—not one particle—and that all the sacrifices which you make and all the suffering that you endure will go for naught. I come with that spirit and with those motives.

Snow: If Judge Zane and Dickson wish to take the course to obtain any proposition from me in this matter, let them first release me and my friends from the penitentiary.

Governor: They could not do it; nobody but the President could.

Snow: Well, we don't ask it.

Apostle Snow then went on at some length to recite the story of their experiences in Illinois and Missouri, claiming that similar persecutions to what they endured there were being inflicted here, and with the same spirit.

The Governor replied that the refutation of that position that it was a persecution for religion's sake lay in the fact that we had hundreds and hundreds of different denominations in the United States and none but the people here had ever any such complaint to make.

To this Snow replied that was because they were man-made Christians, while the Mormons were God's people, and that made all the difference, and started on the subject of modern revelation, which the Governor was not disposed to discuss. Snow also claimed again that he had conformed to the law.

The Governor said he thought that was a mistake; that the court and jury had found otherwise, and that our conduct must be regulated not by the individual's own construction of the law, but by the decisions of the courts.

Snow then repeated what he had formerly said in the court at Ogden in regard to his intention to obey the law in the future, that he thought that it was an improper question, and that he told the judge so.

Governor West then said that Mr. Snow's responsibility, on account of the position he held was much greater than that of many others convicted of the same offense; that by his conduct many a heart would ache and many a tear would flow that he would be responsible for, which might be saved if he would obey the law and use his influence and control among the people to have them do likewise.

Mr. Snow said they had an object in view; that there would be a change eventually, but how much suffering there would be between this time and that period he could not say, but they were prepared to go through it. He would not promise to obey the law even "If you were the President of the United States, although you said the other day he is a better man than you are." He had about the same regard for Dickson's official career that he had for the Jews for killing our Savior.

The Governor then explained to Snow that he had him called out in order that he might first have a talk with him in detail on the matter, but that he was going inside to make the same offer to the other prisoners confined on similar sentences.

Snow said he would not speak a word to them in relation to it, but should leave it to the individual judgment of each person.

The party then entered the enclosure and found the prisoners confined who were not charged with cohabitation had been caused to retire to the east side, and those convicted of the latter offenses were assembled in the large room near the southwest corner of the enclosure. The Governor then spoke to them as follows:

"I have simply come to announce to you something which you probably know. The Supreme Court of the United States has rendered a decision dismissing the appeals in certain cases in which a construction of the law under which you are sentenced is involved, and the tribunal which has the construction and settlement of what the law is having decided it, and you all being aware now of your duty under the law, it occurred to me as a very opportune time to come here and make a proposition to you which had suggested itself to my mind for your relief. That proposition is made after a consultation with Judge Zane and with Mr. Dickson and it is, that we would all concur, in a petition to the President to relieve you from the effect of the sentences which you are now suffering for disobedience of the law if you would, in good faith and sincerity, agree to respect and obey the laws as interpreted by the courts. You know that the effect of the decision which has been rendered and which is the law of the land now beyond question and beyond controversy, is that if you get free here and continue in the same course of life that brought you here, that it is only a question of how long you live, as to how long you will be kept in a place like this. Now it is the desire of the Federal officials here, if possible, to relieve you from past punishment, if in the future you will be subservient and obedient to the laws. That is all I came for, and I came with the honest, earnest, and sincere desire that as many of you as will accept of this opportunity, will relieve yourselves from this punishment, and not incur it in the future. This is all I have to say, except that the proposition is made with all earnestness and sincerity, and with a great desire that some, if not all, will avail themselves of it. It is a matter for you to determine, however, but it is submitted to you in that way. I hope you will take it into consideration, and think about it. I hope that in good faith and sincerity you will try to avail yourselves of our efforts in your behalf. If any of you are disposed to make this agreement in good faith, and you are not prepared to do it now, if you are prepared at any future time you can let the marshal know it, and he will convey the information to me, and I will give the matter such attention as is proper to have you speedily released."

Snow: Would you wish to take a vote on it?

Governor: No, sir. I don't care for any expression now, except that if any parties are willing they can say so now, and if not, I prefer to let it pass until they are willing.

Abram H. Cannon asked the question what they were allowed to do with their wives, and such questions were continued at considerable length and very informally after they were all outside the building.

The Governor said he was not there to expound the law—the only advice he could give them was to obey the law as interpreted by the courts.

Cannon remarked that the interpretations of the courts were various and so conflicting that he would like to be informed how they were to know what the law was.

The Governor replied that he thought with Mr. Cannon's education and intelligence, if he went about it earnestly, he would have very little difficulty in ascertaining what the law was.

The Governor and party then took leave of the brethren and returned to the city.

On the 17th of May 1886, the brethren met in room no. 3 for the purpose of considering the propriety of replying to the proposition made by the Governor. The following is a synopsis of the minutes of the meeting:

> Apostle Lorenzo Snow moved that Rudger Clawson act as chairman of the meeting and that George C. Lambert be secretary. Carried unanimously. The chairman announced that it had been deemed necessary to take some action in regard to the invitation extended to Governor West and called for an expression of the feelings of the brethren. The following brethren spoke: Lorenzo Snow, D. M. Stuart, Robert Morris, James Moyle, Thomas C. Jones, H. W. Naisbitt, Hugh S. Gowans, L. D. Watson, W. G. Saunders, W. W. Willey, John Y. Smith, Amos Maycock, Abram H. Cannon, Rudger Clawson, Henry Dinwoodey, O. F. Due, and John W. Snell. All but two of them expressed the opinion that the proposition called for a reply.
>
> Apostle Snow said it appeared to him that the Governor's action was a matter of policy, although to the superficial observer his proposition might have the appearance of being inspired by the purest motives of friendly interest. Brother Snow called attention to the fact that the Governor had not asked for the united expression of the feelings of the prisoners unless they might be disposed to accede to his proposition.[18] Though a reply such as we would make was not actually called for, it might be best for us to make one and send forth a strong document. If

so, a committee should be appointed who would show plainly and consistently why we declined to make the promise required. The action of the Governor had been unusual and the circumstance would in all probability lead many to read any document we might send forth. There were fifty Mormon men wearing the garb of convicts, sentenced to terms of imprisonment varying from six months to upwards of three years, torn from their families who were in need of their presence and support. And now comes the Governor with authority probably from the President to offer freedom on condition of our making a simple promise that we would obey the law as interpreted by the courts and with a threat of perpetual imprisonment if we should refuse. A wonderful degree of confidence is implied in the request. It is very complimentary to our character for veracity. Our reply might have a telling effect at Washington, but what the result would be ought to be well considered. The people of the nation are watching to see what effect the punishment is having upon us and what we say might influence them to make the pressure harder, again it might cause them to do something magnanimous such as was done when the lawmakers legitimated by law a few years before all the children born of plural marriage. Brother Snow expressed his unbound thankfulness for the feeling of firmness and unity manifested by the brethren. He felt personally willing to make any sacrifice, and if any good could be accomplished by the reply proposed, he was willing to act in the matter.

Elder W. W. Willey moved that a reply be sent. The motion was put and carried.

Apostle Snow moved that a committee of nine be appointed to draft a reply and his motion was afterwards amended by the substitution of eleven for the nine, and carried. Elder Lorenzo Snow, H. S. Gowans, H. W. Naisbitt, Rudger Clawson, L. D. Watson, Abram H. Cannon, Culbert King, D. M. Stuart, George C. Lambert, W. W. Willey, William Grant were nominated by the assembly after which the meeting adjourned *sine die.*

The committee met later and drafted a reply, which was adopted by the brethren at a meeting held on the 24th of May. It was then engrossed by Elder A. H. Cannon and signed by all the brethren, except John W. Keddington, who was to be released from the penitentiary the following morning and preferred not to sign it. Following is the document:[19]

> Utah Penitentiary,
> May 24, 1886.
>
> To His Excellency, Caleb W. West,
>   Governor of Utah,
> Sir:
>   On the 13th instant you honored the inmates of the penitentiary with a visit, and offered to intercede for the pardon of all those enduring

imprisonment under the Edmunds law, if they would but promise obedience to it in the future, as interpreted by the courts. Gratitude for the interest manifested in our behalf claims from us a reply. We trust, however, that this will not be construed into defiance, as our silence already has been. We have no desire to occupy a defiant attitude towards the Government or to be in conflict with the Nation's laws. We have never been even accused of violating any other law than the one under which we were convicted, and that was enacted purposely to oppose a tenet of our religion.

We conscientiously believe in the doctrine of plural marriage, and have practiced it from the first conviction of its being a divine requirement. Of the forty-nine Elders of the Church of Jesus Christ of Latter-day Saints now imprisoned in the penitentiary for alleged violation of the Edmunds law, all but four had plural wives from its passage to thirty-five years prior thereto. We were united to our wives for time and eternity by the most sacred covenants and in many instances numerous children have been born as a result of our union who are endeared to us by the strongest parental ties.

What the promise asked of us implied you declined to explain, just as the courts have done when appeals have been made to them for an explicit and permanent definition of what must be done to comply with the law. The rulings of the courts under this law have been too varied and conflicting, heretofore, for us to know what may be the future interpretations. The simple status of plural marriage is now made under the law, material evidence in securing conviction for unlawful cohabitation, thus, independent of our acts, ruthlessly trespassing upon the sacred domain of our religious belief.

So far as compliance with your proposition requires the sacrifice of honor and manhood, the repudiation of our wives and children, the violation of sacred covenants, heaven forbid that we should be guilty of such perfidy; perpetual imprisonment with which we are threatened, or even death itself, would be preferable. Our wives desire no separation from us and were we to comply with your request, they would regard our action as most cruel, inhuman, and monstrous—our children would blush with shame, and we should deserve the scorn and contempt of all just and honorable men.

The proposition you made, though prompted doubtless by a kind feeling, was not new, for we could all have avoided imprisonment by making the same promise to the courts; in fact the penalties we are now enduring are for declining to so promise rather than for acts committed in the past. Had you offered us unconditional amnesty, it would have been gladly accepted; but dearly as we prize the great boon of liberty, we cannot afford to obtain it by proving untrue to our conscience, our religion, and our God.

As loyal citizens of this great Republic whose Constitution we revere, we not only ask for, but claim our rights as freemen and if from neither local nor national authority we are to receive equity and mercy, we will make our appeal to the Great Arbiter of all human interests, who in due time will grant us the justice hitherto denied.

That you may, as the Governor of our important but afflicted territory, aid us in securing every right to which loyal citizens are entitled and find happiness in so doing, we will ever pray,

As witness our hands,

(signed)

Lorenzo Snow	George C. Lambert
Abram H. Cannon	George H. Taylor
Hugh S. Gowans	Helon H. Tracy
Rudger Clawson	James Moyle
Wm. Wallace	Willey Hyrum Goff
David M. Stuart	H. Dinwoodey
Henry W. Naisbitt	Joseph McMurrin
L. D. Watson	Herbert J. Foulger
Culbert King	Stanley Taylor
William D. Newsom	James H. Nelson
William Grant	Frederick A. Cooper
John Price Ball	James O. Poulsen
Amos Maycock	Robert McKendrick
Oluf F. Due	Robert Morris
John Y. Smith	Samuel F. Ball
John William Snell	S. H. B. Smith
Henry Gale	George B. Bailey
Thomas C. Jones	Nephi J. Bates
John Bowen	John Penman
William G. Saunders	Thomas Burningham
Andrew Jensen	William J. Jenkins
John Bergen	Thomas Porcher
Joseph H. Evans	C. H. Greenwell
James E. Twitchell	William H. Lee

In the early part of June 1886, Marshal E. A. Ireland retired from office and was succeeded by Frank H. Dyer[20] of Park City, Utah. Although little was known of Mr. Dyer, the change was hailed with delight by every prisoner in the penitentiary. Ireland's pusillanimity of character made him an object of derision to all who knew him well. With a genial address and great suavity of demeanor, he was quick to make promises but slow to fulfill them. No prisoner was ever denied a hearing but his wrongs went unredressed and his rights were not respected.

The 4th of July 1886, all things considered, passed off very pleasantly with us. I cannot do better than to introduce here a letter, descriptive of the day, written by one of the brethren and addressed to the editor, *Deseret Evening News*.[21]

INDEPENDENCE DAY AT THE PEN
Marshal Dyer Enables the Prisoners to Relieve
The Monotony of Prison Life.

Utah Penitentiary,
July 5th, 1886.

Editor Deseret News:

Truly this has been "a red-letter day" in the history of the Utah Penitentiary. A resolution having been adopted by the inmates of this institution a couple of weeks since to celebrate Independence Day by getting up a concert and some athletic sports, and word to this effect having reached certain friends in Salt Lake City, they decided upon arranging for our being supplied also with a feast. Contributions in money and edibles sufficient to amply supply our wants in this line for the day were contributed by the following named generous business firms and individuals of Salt Lake City: Z.C.M.I., S. P. Teasdel, Deseret Bank, Woolley, Young, and Hardy Co., Clark, Eldredge, and Co., Z.C.M.I. Shoe Factory, Spencer Clawson, David James, Clerks in the Trustee-in-Trust's Office, John Q. Cannon, John Groesbeck, John W. Snell, Mountain Ice Co., John Beck and Swaner and Co., Bishop H. B. Clawson, and Brother James C. Watson, who, from having each served a term of imprisonment here for conscience sake, know how to feel for their brethren now similarly situated, were chiefly instrumental in collecting and forwarding these contributions, which were made for the benefit exclusively of the Latter-day Saints here confined, but which the brethren on receiving the same decided to share with all their fellow prisoners. The good things provided for our entertainment were received on Saturday evening and since then a force of hands under the direction of a skillful *chef de cuisine* from the interior of the prison, who was pressed into service for the occasion, have been busy preparing to serve them in as good a style as the meager facilities of the institution would allow.

Breakfast being over this morning, preparations were immediately made for the first part of the day's entertainment, a concert, for which a rather elaborate programme consisting of twenty-eight numbers had been arranged. A rude stage made up of the heavy tables from which we eat was arranged in one end of the dining room, and a calico "drop curtain" to work on a sliding principle soon improvised, while all the chairs and benches about the place were called into requisition upon which to seat the auditors.

The performance commenced at 8:30 and was going off with a vim, eleven pieces having already been rendered, when at 9:45 a temporary lull was caused by the arrival of Marshal Dyer and citizens of the 8th Ward to the number of about forty, most of whom were members of the choir, under the direction of Brother John M. Chamberlain. Their visit was not an entire surprise to us, for we had incidentally learned beforehand that the marshal had kindly consented to their coming, promising to accompany them and to kindly allow them to enter the penitentiary and cheer us with some of their sweet music. We were, however, surprised and pleased beyond measure to see so great a number of our friends come among us, and at their being allowed to entertain us by rendering in most delightful style some nine or ten pieces—hymns, choruses, songs, duets, etc.

Our gratitude was not only drawn out in favor of these old acquaintances who had taken this opportunity of giving us an expression of their love, but toward Marshal Dyer in an especial manner for his kindness and liberality in permitting their visit and also for favoring us with his own presence at the entertainment.

A hearty vote of thanks was tendered to the visiting party and also to the marshal, who responded with a brief but appropriate speech, after which a half hour's intermission was taken, during which time our visitors withdrew to the vicinity of the gate, and were there allowed to shake hands with and speak to their particular friends and acquaintances.

The visitors then withdrew and our own programme was resumed. This consisted of an overture, glee, recitations, banjo solo, cornet duet, comic songs, original poem, musical selections, hornpipe dance, character songs, Marseillaise hymn, etc., all of which were rendered in good style. The performance demonstrated the fact that there is a great deal of musical talent among the one hundred and fifty men here incarcerated, and it was displayed to good advantage. The day's amusements concluded with foot racing, hurdle jumping, sack racing, and quoit pitching matches, all of which passed off pleasantly, not a jar or ill-feeling occurring throughout the day.

With two exceptions the inmates of this institution are now enjoying fair health; a man by the name of Moss is suffering from a severe attack of inflammatory rheumatism, and Brother William G. Bickley, of Beaver, is down with the erysipelas.

I am sure I but echo the feelings of all my fellow prisoners as well as my own, in expressing thanks and gratitude to all our friends in the city who, through their kindness and liberality, aided in relieving the monotony of prison life for the day, and also the Marshal Dyer and Warden Dow for the praiseworthy consideration shown by them to us and our friends. A very agreeable feature of our day's pleasure was a surprise in the shape of a visit from the wives of several of the prisoners who live at a distance, whose transportation to the city was kindly arranged for by friends in the city, and who were also permitted to come inside the prison to meet their husbands for a few moments.

Yours with kind regards,
L.

During the summer months the convicts were often taken out in parties of four or five to work on the penitentiary farm, and grub sagebrush for use at the bakery. At such times the temptation to make a break for liberty was very great and was not infrequently yielded to. But during a long series of years there were perhaps only one or two instances where the fleeing convicts made good their escape and it is curious to note also that few if any were ever brought down by gun or pistol shot, although invariably fired at by the guard. At the moment of a break signal is made to the prison wall guards, and almost immediately a half dozen men or more, well armed, some on horse and others afoot, can be seen scouring the country in hot pursuit. Enfeebled by poor and insufficient food and long months of inactivity, the wretched prisoners, puffing and blowing, are soon run down and captured. Chains or the sweatbox, and sometimes both, await all such.

A thrill of excitement invariably sweeps through the yard when it is known that a break has been made. The various activities which engage the prisoners' attention are neglected, and the men, collected in small groups, discuss the probable outcome of the flight and await the result with breathless interest. I have myself partaken of this spirit of enthusiasm and my sympathy and good wishes have generally gone out to the prisoner, independent of previous prejudices. It would be difficult to describe the expression of gloomy disappointment depicted on every face in the yard when a runaway reenters the gate, and languidly strolls up and into the dining room. He is of course immediately surrounded, innumerable questions are put to him, and, as he describes just how it came about the interest deepens. Notwithstanding the many failures to escape, there is generally one or more prisoner in the yard who [is] willing to take the risk of being shot and only await a favorable opportunity to make a dash for liberty.

Two convicts, George Davis and John Watron by name, both serving out a five years' sentence, made several breaks while at work in the field, but always with disastrous results. On the first occasion Davis was soon run down and captured, but Watron, eluded his pursuers and succeeded in reaching Salina, U[tah] T[erritory], in safety, where he hired out to work. A reward of $250.00 was offered for his recapture. Suspicion pointed to this newcomer in Salina and Watron was turned over to the officers of justice by his employer, although he begged piteously for mercy, and offered to serve any length of time without remuneration if his employer would only protect him. He also represented that he had already been confined some two or three years in the penitentiary and had suffered many hardships. It was of no avail, however; his employer needed the money and so Watron was sacrificed. But imagine the chagrin of the winner of the reward, when informed by the marshal that the newspapers had made a mistake; the notice should read, $25.00 and not $250.00. Watron was safely landed in the penitentiary again after an absence of several weeks.

In August 1886 the following prisoners were taken out one day to grub sagebrush, an employment that was looked upon with the most pronounced aversion by every convict in the penitentiary: Davis, Watron, Williamson, Blowers, and Cleveland. [Thomas] Murther, a good-natured, easy-going man, was the guard. His general feebleness, brought on by age, made him an easy prey to the designs of these reckless fellows. Choosing a favorable moment, they jumped upon him, took his gun and pistol, and departed in hot haste toward the mountains. With the object of accelerating their speed, they appropriated a horse and buggy or light wagon that chanced to cross their path. The driver, a lone woman who was almost paralyzed with fright, was unceremoniously ordered to turn over the rig, which she did without delay. Crack, crack, went the whip, and they were soon out of sight.

As soon as word reached the prison the excitement both inside and out became intense. There was a hurrying to and fro of many feet, and soon seven of the eight regular guards were speeding over the country in eager pursuit of the runaways. A message having been sent to Marshal Dyer by telephone, he shortly after appeared at the penitentiary in a buggy and after enquiring the direction the prisoners had taken, he was on the road again immediately. Then came his well-armed deputies in the saddle, one by one, at intervals of about fifteen or twenty minutes. They held hurried interviews with the warden and, in the most dashing style imaginable, galloped out of the yard. Oh, it was an impressive spectacle and reminded one of the knights of old. Five men armed to the teeth with *one* gun and *one* pistol had escaped, and a whole battalion of men, men of undoubted courage, men who were prepared to sell their lives dearly, were charging after them. The remainder of the prisoners were deeply moved by this exhibition of heroism, and awaited the result with the utmost suspense.

Upon reaching Emigration Canyon the fleeing convicts disappeared from view in a large clump of bushes. The pursuers surrounded this spot at a good safe distance, and began shooting into the bushes. After wounding John Watron in the leg, the posse succeeded in capturing them all, and marched them back to the Pen where they were placed in irons. An indictment for grand larceny (stealing government property, represented by the gun and pistol taken from the guard) was afterwards found against the whole party. George Davis pleaded guilty, and was sentenced to an additional three years. In view of the fact that he had already been confined in the penitentiary some four years, this seemed an unnecessarily severe punishment. The cases against the other men were not at the time disposed of.

In the afternoon of the day on which the above break was made, Marshal Dyer, accompanied by Captain [John W.] Greenman, came on to the wall and walked around to the northeast corner. He then had [Samuel L.] Sprague, the guard, call the prisoners to that corner of the yard, when he said: "Gentlemen, you have all doubtless heard that five prisoners have escaped today. I have been disposed to be very lenient in the past, but I think I will have to enforce stricter discipline among you prisoners. I have not been in office long, but I am continually hearing of conspiracies and jobs being put up by men in the pit or yard. I understand there is talk of holding up one of the guards in the pit. I told the guards they would have to take their chances with the men, but I wish to warn you all that should such a thing occur I will kill every man in the yard who does not prevent it. This may seem harsh, but I will do it. There are some good men in this yard, and I hope they, too, heed this warning. There is work to be done here and outside on the farm, and I expect you all to work. I am disposed to treat you well if you behave, but I will have to enforce stricter measures unless this thing is stopped. That is all, gentlemen."

After this speech the prisoners scattered out in various directions, but before they had all passed out of hearing, he stopped again, and said: "Gentlemen, I forgot to mention that there have been fires started three or four times in the bunkhouse. I have instructed the warden not to unlock the door if such a thing ever occurs again. That is all, gentlemen."

The idea of making one prisoner responsible for the conduct of another is rather amusing to those who are at all familiar with the methods of enforcing prison discipline. The terror that these threats carried to the soul of every man present is aptly described by the word "buncombe."

The following brethren joined our ranks during the months of August, September, October, [November,] and December 1886. They were arrested on the prevailing charge, unlawful cohabitation, and sentenced to six months, $300.00 and costs, except as noted: N. H. Groesbeck, nine months, $450.00 and costs, William M. Bromley, ten months, $300.00 and costs, William Felsted, polygamy, three and one half years, $300.00 and costs, Richard Warburton, Jonas Lindberg, eighteen months, $300.00 and costs, W. W. Galbraith, William Y. Jeffs, nineteen months, $400.00 and costs, James Dunn, twelve months, $300.00 and costs, H. P. Folsom, William Robinson, George Hales, Thomas Schofield, James Farrer, R. H. Sudweeks, twelve months, $600.00 and costs, J. H. Dean, Andrew Hansen, eighteen months, $300.00 and costs, Carl Janson, eighteen months, $300.00 and costs, John Gillespie, John B. Furster, Willard L. Snow, eighteen months, $300.00 and costs, T. F. H. Morton, D. W. Leaker, Isaac Pierce, fifteen months, $100.00 and costs, Amos H. Neff, twelve months, $600.00 and costs, James I. Steele, twelve months, $300.00 and costs, O. P. Arnold, fifteen months, $450.00 and costs,[22] James W. Loveless, John Durrant, six months, $100.00 and costs, Hans Jensen, six months, $100.00 and costs, John C. Gray, six months, $50.00 and costs, Timothy Parkinson, six months, $100.00 and no costs, George Dunford, six months, $150.00 and costs, N. V. Jones (alleged bribery), three years,[23] John Stoddard, Lorenzo Stutz, twelve months, $200.00 and costs, M. W. Butler, six months, $100.00 and no costs, Thomas H. Bullock, no fine, George Naylor, William Geddes, six months, $100.00 and no cost, George Chandler, six months, $100.00 and costs, James May, six months, $100.00 and no costs, F. W. Ellis, six months, $100.00 and no costs, Thomas B. Helm, six months, $100.00 and costs, Henry B. Gwilliam, six months, $100.00 and costs, Thomas Allsop, fifteen months, $50.00 and costs, John P. Jones, John L. Jones, Peter Petersen, Joseph Thurber, polygamy, four years and six months, $500.00 and costs.[24]

I shall always consider myself fortunate in having been thrown into the society of such noble men as these "Mormon" prisoners. I was especially pleased to be in association with Apostle Lorenzo Snow. To know him was to love and to admire him. A highly cultivated intellect, a sympathetic heart, gentle and winning manners, gave him great influence over all who had the happiness to be numbered among his friends. He was a man of large and varied experience, both at home and abroad, from which he acquired an extensive knowledge of men and things. Conscientious, energetic, persevering, he had already accomplished much and was revered and honored by the Saints in every quarter of the globe. After having passed through the trials and hardships to which the Church was subjected in the early days, he was called upon at this time, at an advanced age, his hair being silvered with white, to enter a loathsome prison for conscience sake, and he responded with cheerfulness. I would have been ashamed to murmur at my lot in the presence of this venerable man, who had reached the ripe age of seventy-two and who accepted the situation, disagreeable and humiliating as it was, with a smile.

In matters of importance the brethren seldom failed to consult with Brother Snow and he invariably gave them good counsel and helped them to stand up for the few privileges which were theirs. His idea was that people who allow themselves to be trampled upon with impunity, uttering no word of protest, certainly are lacking in moral courage. He was considered an excellent authority on doctrinal points, and his views were frequently sought; as we sat around the table during the long hours of the evening, he often discoursed interestingly upon matters pertaining to the past, present, and future conditions of man. I shall ever look back to those hours—hours passed in prison—as among the most profitable of my life. Many prominent people visited the prison during 1886 and seldom left without an introduction and chat with the "Mormon" Apostle in stripes. If any may judge from observation, I should say that these interviews were productive of good.

In the early part of October Mr. G. N. Dow resigned his position as warden and was succeeded by Otis L. Brown.[25] Just prior to Dow's departure, Brother George C. Lambert prepared a neatly worded paper expressive of our good feelings toward him and best wishes for his future welfare. Nearly every man in the prison was a signer. It will be evident to the reader from this that Mr. Dow's attitude, latterly, toward the prisoners was very different to what it was in 1884 and 1885.

When Warden Dow retired from office to make way for his successor, as already noted, I immediately lost my official position as tutor to his children and also lost the influence I had exerted with the chief officer of the prison in behalf of the "Mormon" prisoners.[26] Anticipating the fate that awaited me, I surrendered my office and gracefully withdrew to the inside several days prior to the installation of the new warden. To satisfy the over-curious, I blandly stated that my resignation had been handed in and was accepted. I took this action for the reason that Mr. Brown had remarked to some of the guards that when he should take charge of the prison, he would send Clawson into the "yard" a "flying." I, with malice aforethought, robbed him of this exquisite pleasure.

As a striking illustration of the influence I had gained with Warden Dow, I submit the following statement. Upon one occasion the warden called me into his private office and said: "Mr. Clawson, I have just received a letter from Marshal Ireland and it concerns you. Would you like to read it?" Somewhat astonished that Mr. Dow would permit a prisoner under his charge to read an order from his superior officer, I replied: "Yes, If you would like me to read it." He handed me the letter. It was in substance to this effect: the marshal had been informed on what he regarded as reliable authority, that Mr. Clawson, the "trusty," was violating a rule of the prison by secretly passing out and receiving correspondence that should go through the prison office and bear the endorsement of the warden. For this purported offense, he now directed the warden to dismiss Clawson as a "trusty" and relegate him once more to the interior of the prison.

After reading it I returned the letter to Mr. Dow, calling his attention to the fact that I had not asked for the appointment of tutor, and was now ready and willing to retire within the prison enclosure. It was at this point that the warden began to apologize for me. He said: "Mr. Clawson, there is Wilford Woodruff, president of your Church, and Mr. Lorenzo Snow, president of the Council of the Twelve, the latter now serving sentence here, who doubtless would desire at times to communicate with each other in a confidential manner on Church matters. If you have been secretly passing communications between these two men, in violation of the prison rule, why it's all right. There is an excuse for it."

I told Mr. Dow that as a matter of fact I had never passed correspondence between these two men. So long as he trusted me with his confidence I would never betray it, by so doing. I told him, however, that if he were to send me into the prison again and I were later under armed guard, called out to see visitors, I would under these circumstances, if opportunity offered, pass letters in and out against the rule of the prison. Upon being asked what he would do in a like situation, he replied that he would do the same. Mr. Dow then added: "Mr. Clawson, you shall not be returned to the 'yard' but shall continue as a 'trusty' as long as I am warden of the prison." And so it was. This decision he made in face of a positive order from his superior officer.

Thanksgiving 1886 was an interesting day to the inmates of the Utah Penitentiary. About 12:00 o'clock the prisoners were ordered into the bunk rooms and locked up. Speculation as to the cause of this strange movement was freely indulged in, but no one could solve the mystery. About 1:00 o'clock the doors were thrown open and we were marshaled into the line for dinner. Imagine our astonishment as we marched into the dining room in beholding the tables covered with beautiful white linen cloths, chinaware, knives and forks (articles not in use at the prison) and fairly loaded down with all the delicacies of the season. Nothing appeared to be lacking that could minister to the appetite. The earnestness and zeal manifested by the prisoners in grappling with the good things were truly marvelous, and if applied to all the concerns of life with equal force would accomplish wonders.

A few ladies were present by permission of the marshal, and supplied the wants of all in a graceful and dignified manner. A smile that indicated the most complete and thorough satisfaction beamed upon every countenance at the close of the meal, and all with one accord pronounced it a grand success. By way of explanation I will state here that this splendid Thanksgiving dinner was tendered as a testimonial to Lorenzo Snow and his fellow prisoners by the women of Brigham City.

Dinner was succeeded by a concert given by a number of well-known artists from Salt Lake City. The program was arranged by father, who acted as chairman. Marshal Dyer and lady, Warden Brown and lady, and several other visitors were present.

PROGRAM

Opening Chorus
Duet from "Pirates of Penzance"............Miss Edith Clawson &
G. D. Pyper
Humorous Reading...Prof. J. H. Paul
Duet, organ and violin...........................Prof. [George] Careless
and Charles H. Burton
Song.. Mr. Thomas
Duet ....Mrs. Agnes Thomas and Professor Stephens
Recitation, "Bernardo del Carpio"....................Rudger Clawson
Song and Accompaniment.................... Professor Evan Stephens
Song, "Moon and I," from *Mikado*............ Miss Edith Clawson
Quartet.................................. Mrs. Thomas, Mrs. Vilate Young
Mr. G. D. Pyper, and Mr. J. G. Midgley
Reading...Prof. J. H. Paul
Song..Mrs. Agnes Thomas
Solo on the Xylophone......................................Mr. A. Beesley
Andersonville Prison Song....................by Miss Edith Clawson,
Mrs. Agnes Thomas, Mrs. Vilate Young, Miss Beesley,
Mr. G. D. Pyper, J. G. Midgley, Prof. Careless,
and Mr. C. H. Burton
Violin Solo .... Prof. Careless
Song..Mrs. Agnes Thomas.

Great enthusiasm was manifested. The applause was loud and frequent and elicited several encores. At the close of the entertainment a hearty vote of thanks was passed to those who had been instrumental in providing us with so rare a musical treat--to Marshal Dyer, H. B. Clawson, and the artists from Salt Lake, also to the women of Brigham City for the dinner. The following acknowledgment was later sent to them.

Utah Penitentiary,
November 26th, 1886.

To the Ladies of Brigham City,
and all others concerned:

Prison life at best presents but a dreary and monotonous aspect. There are not many days in the year when the heart of the prisoner, who is exiled from home and shut out from the world, is made glad. Such an occasion, however, came yesterday, Thanksgiving day, when every man incarcerated in this prison sat down to a sumptuous and elegant dinner, generously furnished and prepared by the ladies of Brigham City. This testimonial of your good feelings came very unexpectedly to us; but the surprise, though great, was by no means equal to the pleasure and delight derived from partaking of the delicious viands.

It is impossible to find language that will fully express our appreciation of this kind act, but we feel to assure you that the remembrance of it will cling to us, and suggest pleasant reflections when other things are forgotten. Thanksgiving 1886 will ever be referred to by us as one of the very, very bright days of our prison life. The kindness of Marshal Dyer and Warden Brown in making it possible for us to enjoy ourselves is also duly appreciated.

Immediately after the close of the musical entertainment which took place in the afternoon, Rudger Clawson arose and moved that a hearty vote of thanks be passed to the ladies of Brigham City and all who had in any way interested themselves in the matter, for the splendid dinner that had been furnished by them. The motion was seconded and carried with a vociferous and unanimous response.

Ladies, we, the inmates of the penitentiary, now have pleasure in tendering to you this vote of thanks, and subscribing ourselves,

Respectfully,
(signed)
Rudger Clawson*
William W. Galbraith*
William M. Bromley,* Committee

Amos H. Neff*	H. T. B. Grey	C. C. Anderson
Lorenzo Snow*	John Bergen*	J. W. Loveless*
John Durrant*	Andrew Hansen*	R. O. Hook
James Higgins*	Jens Hansen*	Hans Jensen*
Peter Wimmer*	Joseph Ladd	J. W. Savage
N. V. Jones*	Harry H. Hawthorne	Hammond P. Pidkin
N. H. Groesbeck*	Thomas Schofield*	W. G. Saunders*
A. Greenwell, Sr.*	Wm. J. Cox*	Timothy Parkinson*
Hyrum P. Folsom*	Joseph H. Evans*	T. F. H. Morton*
Joseph H. Dean*	Wm. H. Pidcock*	Chas. D. Thomas
W. Gustafson	J. E. Raymond	R. H. Sudweeks*
John B. Furster*	E. H. Smith	T. M. Johnson
Charles Denney*	Amos Maycock*	E. G. Darrow
George Hales*	Jas. I. Steele*	James Dunn*
William Stimpson*	O. P. Arnold*	Wm. D. Newsom*
Wm. Robinson*	R. L. Taylor*	R. Warburton*
A. C. Greenwell*	Wm. Y. Jeffs*	J. E. Lindberg*
Royal B. Young*	Francis M. Treseder	Thomas Tidwell
Helon H. Tracy*	S. C. Kinsey	Andy Jones

John C. Gray*	Edward Olsen	E. Williamson
James Farrer*	W. G. Bickley*	P. A. Nelsen
Isaac R. Pierce*	James McDermott	Joshua Sweat
David W. Leaker*	W. H. Orrick	Wm. Felsted*
George Dunford*	Quish (Indian)	James Blowers
George C. Wood*	John Cleveland	Wm. Rose
Willard L. Snow*	Dan Shields	Charles Johnson
John Penman*	John C. Banks	E. Watterson
F. Moss	Pat Rigan	Frank Tidwell
J. Ramirez	Dennis Sullivan	J. Watkins
Louis Ravera	Chas. McDonnell	C. Younger
D. C. Watts	Charles Powers	Frank Stoddard
B. A. Thompson	G. Austin	J. W. Nelson
James Thompson	Frank J. Mitchell	C. W. Bronson
B. F. Marsh	R. R. Rogers	Andrew Pettit
Charles F. Rose	Geo. W. Johnson	T. Scanlon
Perry Decker	Fred Hopt	Leander Wright
Peter Miller	Sam Clements	J. M. Riddle
J. Harrington	George Davis	James Cowley
Fred Smith		

Note: the names appearing with * represent the "Mormon" and those without, the Gentile prisoners.

During this month (November) the facilities for cooking were increased in the culinary department of the prison by the addition of a range costing $700.00. As a result of this change, there was a slight improvement in our diet—not in the quality of the food, but in the cooking of it. It is worthy of note, however, that the warden reduced the number of soup days from three to one a week, and by way of further variety sent in codfish on Friday and beans on Sunday of each week. The beans were usually greatly relished, but the codfish—well, I'll remain silent on that subject.

Christmas of 1886 dawned upon us, but for the first time in many years there was no special dinner for the prisoners. This departure from an old and hitherto popular custom caused great discontent and even though each man was permitted to send out for provisions to the amount of $1.50 to $2.00, the prisoners were not appeased. A large number of turkeys had been reared and fattened on the penitentiary farm, but alas! just as we were fondly anticipating a rich feast, they were dressed and sent to market, much to our disgust.

NOTES

1. Clawson at the first mention of Joe Miller, who tutored the children for a time, stated that their ages were about twelve and five, respectively. At the

time of their graduation exercises on 16 July 1886 George was ten years old (though it was near his next birthday) and Florence had just turned six. See Abraham H. Cannon, Diary, 16 July 1886, Marriott Library, University of Utah, Salt Lake City, and George C. Lambert, Diary, 16 July 1886, Archives, Historical Department, Church of Jesus Christ of Latter-day Saints, Salt Lake City, hereafter cited as LDS Archives.

2. The episode of the graduation of the Dow children is a fifteen-page addition to MS I[3]. Lorenzo Snow was not at this time (16 July 1886) president of the Quorum of the Twelve Apostles, since John Taylor did not die until 25 July 1887 and Wilford Woodruff did not become president of the church until 7 April 1889. Only at this latter date did Lorenzo Snow became president of the Twelve. George H. Taylor indicates that the program in the warden's "parlor" lasted an hour and that "about a dozen of the Mormon prisoners" were allowed to attend. The number twelve is supported by Clawson, for in the part of MS I omitted when MS II was typed, he lists those (other than himself) who attended: Honorable Lorenzo Snow, Henry Dinwoodey, George H. Taylor, Abraham H. Cannon, George C. Lambert, Hyrum Goff, Royal B. Young, Hugh S. Gowans, Robert Morris, C. H. Greenwell, and John W. Snell (the Rudger Clawson Collection, Manuscript 481, Bx 2, Fd 6, MS I, 121, Marriott Library, University of Utah, Salt Lake City; hereafter the Rudger Clawson Collection is cited as RC). Also known to be in attendance were the turnkey, James Curtis, and the prisoner, T. M. Johnson. Henry Dinwoodey sums up the performance of the two children by saying that "they were very good in all the branches" of learning, while George C. Lambert specifies that "the gem of the occasion" was Florence's recitation of "The Charge of the Light Brigade." See George H. Taylor, Diary, 16 July 1886, Utah State Historical Society, Salt Lake City; Henry Dinwoodey, Diary, 16 July 1886, photocopy at the Marriott Library, University of Utah, Salt Lake City, with the original at the LDS Archives; and Lambert, Diary, 16 July 1886.

3. Since T. M. Johnson was the son of a minister in Birmingham, England, he had received a fine education. Johnson, who had been released from prison in August 1885, returned to prison on 2 December 1885 on the charge of burglary, being sentenced twenty days later to a three-year imprisonment, and was released under the Copper Act on 6 June 1888. The prison school was organized in late December 1885 with Johnson as the principal and about a dozen students. The cost for the school was $1 per month or $.50 per month if someone else paid the bill. Beginning in October 1886 the school was run on a different arrangement, with Johnson receiving $20 per month and the school being free to all. The subjects taught included reading, writing, arithmetic, grammar, history, and bookkeeping. See Lambert, Diary, 4 October 1886; David John, Diary, 9 June 1887, Lee Library, Brigham Young University, Provo, Utah; *Millennial Star* 49 (31 Jan. 1887): 70; and Thomas C. Romney, *The Life of Lorenzo Snow, Fifth President of the Church of Jesus Christ of Latter-day Saints* (Salt Lake City: S.U.P. Memorial Foundation, 1955), 382–83.

4. John Penman (1835–96) of Bountiful, having been convicted of polygamy and sentenced to two years' imprisonment and a $25 fine plus costs of

$138.75, entered the penitentiary on 10 February 1886. While still serving this sentence, which would have expired on 13 November 1887, he was sentenced on 12 October 1887 for unlawful cohabitation to a three-month imprisonment and a $25 fine plus costs of $59.65. For attempting to smuggle out a letter written by another cohab, Penman had to remain in prison an extra month, and was finally released on 6 March 1888.

5. While Clawson's reference to the "cruel murder" of Joseph Standing is correct, John Nicholson's use of the term *martyrdom* seems to go beyond the earliest evidence. The intent of the mob on 21 July 1879 was to severely beat the two missionaries. In the first-published newspaper accounts Clawson disclosed that Standing suddenly grabbed a Colt revolver (which had been laid on a tree stump by one of the mob), rose to his feet, leveled the gun at the horsemen, and "demanded them to remain quiet and listen to him or he would shoot." This unexpected confrontation precipitated the deadly reaction of the mob member seated nearby, who just as quickly raised his own pistol and shot Standing in the face. (*Denver Tribune*, 31 July 1879, as quoted in Ken Driggs, " 'There Is No Law in Georgia for Mormons': The Joseph Standing Murder Case of 1879," *Georgia Historical Quarterly* 73 [Winter 1989]: 759). Another contemporary account, which is preserved in Clawson's 1879 scrapbook, confirms the existence of the pistol in the following words: "At this moment Standing secured a pistol, whether he had picked it up or wrenched it from one of the party, Mr. Clawson being unable to state" (*Salt Lake Daily Herald*, 1 August 1879, in RC, Bx 17, Bk 2). Immediately after talking to his church leaders in Salt Lake City, Clawson's story was significantly different. In Clawson's own memoirs he claims that Joseph Standing "'jumped to his feet, turned to face the horsemen, clasped his hands firmly together, and with an overture as if he were ready to fire (and yet he was unarmed to my certain knowledge) said in a commanding voice, 'Surrender.' " (RC, Bx 1, Fd 2). In the 1886 published version, which is the form of the story that is most often retold, Clawson related that after waiting near a spring for about an hour Standing tried to bluff the mob when he suddenly "leaped to his feet with a bound, instantly wheeled so as to face them [the three horsemen], brought his two hands together with a sudden slap, and shouted in a loud, clear, resolute voice— 'Surrender' " (John Nicholson, *The Martyrdom of Joseph Standing* [Salt Lake City: Deseret News, 1886], 27). When Nicholson visited the prison after the publication of the book, Clawson (who had supplied the information for the Standing narrative both in interviews and in his 1879 scrapbook) and Nicholson got "into an altercation over the former expressing a feeling that he ought to have a pecuniary interest in the book" (Lambert, Diary, 27 July 1886). See RC, Bx 16, Fd 4, Letter to Lydia Clawson [after mid-October 1885].

6. Clawson could not remember the exact date that the shout occurred and the closest he could pinpoint the time was the "Summer of 1886" (see marginal notation in MS IV^2). Truman G. Madsen assigns the date of 8 April, but this Thursday date conflicts with his own previous statement that the shout occurred on a Sabbath and it is based upon a misinterpretation of the repetition of a triple "amen" after the prisoners heard on that date the report of the

recent general conference (Truman G. Madsen, *Defender of the Faith: The B. H. Roberts Story* [Salt Lake City: Bookcraft, 1980], 197). Steven H. Heath, in "The Sacred Shout," *Dialogue: A Journal of Mormon Thought* 19 (Fall 1986): 119, follows Madsen's misdating; cf. Abraham H. Cannon, Diary, 8 April and 24 July 1886. That the Hosanna Shout really occurred on 24 July 1886 is supported by the diaries of Abraham H. Cannon, Herbert J. Foulger, James Moyle, George H. Taylor, Helon H. Tracy, and George C. Wood.

7. Not all the Mormon prisoners in the bunkhouse were "heartily in favor" with giving the sacred shout. George H. Taylor records that "some doubted the wisdom of it. But as Br. Snow led off, I felt that it was right" (Diary, 24 July 1886). Abraham H. Cannon is more specific and relates: "Into this latter [the Hosanna Shout] I could not enter with spirit and I felt badly about it because I thought my heart was wrong, until on speaking with Geo. Lambert, Royal Young, and others I found their feelings were like mine in this matter. This comforted me" (Diary, 24 July 1886). Similarly, George C. Lambert expresses his dissatisfaction: "I did not feel any enthusiasm, for while I felt to praise God in my heart, it seemed to me a very inappropriate place for such shouting. I did not, however, feel to demur and fancied that I was probably the only one who felt so, until I afterwards talked with A. H. Cannon, Rudger Clawson, & R. B. Young, and found they felt the same" (Diary, 24 July 1886). If Lambert is correct that Clawson also felt that the Hosanna Shout was inappropriate, then this is another instance in which the passage of time has altered Clawson's memory.

8. Clawson has not recorded the exact words of the shout, since the terms *hosanna* and *amen* were thrice repeated. Accordingly, the form actually shouted in the prison in 1886 was most likely a triple recitation of the following: "Hosanna, Hosanna, Hosanna, Glory to God and the Lamb, for ever and ever, Amen, Amen, and Amen!" Herbert J. Foulger records precisely this form, while George H. Taylor does not have the word glory (Herbert J. Foulger, Diary, 24 July 1886, photocopy at Marriott Library, University of Utah, Salt Lake City, with the original at LDS Archives; Taylor, Diary, 24 July 1886). The earliest use of a triple hosanna repeated three times was at the dedication of the Kirtland Temple on 27 March 1836. Joseph Smith's history reports that "we sealed the proceedings of the day by shouting hosanna, hosanna, hosanna to God and the Lamb, three times, sealing it each time with amen, amen, and amen" (B. H. Roberts, ed., *History of the Church of Jesus Christ of Latter-day Saints: Period I, History of Joseph Smith, the Prophet* [Salt Lake City: Deseret News, 1948], 2: 427–28).

9. Clarence Horace Montgomerie y Agramonte (1830–1929) was a soldier of fortune, an editor, a photographer, a deputy marshal, and a salesman of mining machinery. In 1879 he married Clara F. Stenhouse Young, the daughter of T. B. H. and Fanny Stenhouse and the widow of Brigham Young's son, Joseph Angell Young. They had three children from 1880 to 1884, but were divorced in 1887. See Carolyn Young Hunsaker, " 'Dear Father . . .': The Life of Clara Fedarata Stenhouse Young Agramonte, 1850–1893," in the Clara Agramonte Collection, Marriott Library, University of Utah, Salt Lake City.

10. Abraham H. Cannon not only dates this episode to 25 March 1886 but also corrects Clawson by indicating that John Riddle issued the initial shout and James Cowley gave the response. The following is Cannon's account: "A short time before noon Agramonte a photographer came to the 'Pen' by orders of Marshal Ireland and began taking pictures of the prisoners who were called outside the gate by ones or twos. These are evidently to place in the rogues' gallery, so that prisoners, if they escape, can more easily be found. Just after dinner, Agramonte got on the wall with his instrument to take a picture of the yard. Just then a prisoner named Riddle shouted 'wife-beater,' which Agramonte has been proven to be, and Cowley shouted immediately 'Agramonte.' Just then the guard Parker happened to come around a corner of the building, he being in the yard. He doubtless reported to the Warden and then came and placed the two men in sweat-boxes—one in each" (Diary, 25 March 1886).

11. The term of Nephi J. Bates (1848–1921) of Monroe was only three months (not four months) and the fine was $1 (not $100), which was the smallest fine imposed on any of the Mormon polygamists. The $99 error occurred in the manuscripts in the following manner. The reading of MS I* was "no fine," which was properly corrected in MS I² to "$1.00," with the two underlined zeros being slightly raised and smaller than the digit one (RC, Bx 2, Fd 6, MS I, 134). The typist of MS II misread the amount as $100, and this error went unnoticed in MSS III-V. Bates entered on 14 April 1886 and was released on 29 June 1886 after paying his $1 fine and court costs of $293.20.

12. John Bergen and Clara Matilda Lundstedt (the woman he was seen in bed with by deputy E. A. Franks) were arrested at eleven o'clock in the evening on Saturday, 17 April 1886, and were brought to the prison at one o'clock in the morning. On Monday, 19 April, their bonds were set at $5,000 and $1,000, and since they were unable to pay it they were returned to the penitentiary. They remained in prison awaiting Bergen's trial, and on 25 April it was reported of Bergen that he "obtained this last woman [as a plural wife] by fraud, as his Bishop would only give him a recommend to the temple on his saying that all he wanted to do was to get his son adopted to him. Should it be proved that he then went and got this woman he will most likely lose his standing in the Church" (Abraham H. Cannon, Diary, 17, 19, and 25 April 1886). There was quite a difference between what was said by his wives at the grand jury hearing and the trial, but Bergen seems to have married Matilda without his bishop's consent (*Salt Lake Herald*, 27 April 1886). John Bergen was convicted of unlawful cohabitation on 26 April 1886 and released on 24 March 1887.

13. Ambrose C. Greenwell, Sr. (1833–97) of West Weber entered the penitentiary on 26 May 1886. Because he was convicted of two counts of unlawful cohabitation, his sentence was for two six-month periods. The next day Abraham H. Cannon observed that Greenwell "has undoubtedly been accustomed to tippling for many years, and now that he is prevented from obtaining the least drop of intoxicants, he is very nervous and can scarcely eat anything,"

while Henry Dinwoodey noted that "he feels very bad for the want of a little Liquor; he trembles all over" (Abraham H. Cannon, Diary, 27 May 1887, and Dinwoodey, Diary, 27 May 1886).

14. In the list for April, May, and June 1886 William Grant (1838–1916) of American Fork has been accidentally omitted. He entered the penitentiary on 14 April 1886 for a four-month sentence. There is no reason why Clawson would intentionally eliminate William Grant since he is twice mentioned in these memoirs, serving on the 17 May 1886 committee to draft a reply to Governor Caleb W. West and signing the reply of 24 May 1886. Grant was released at 5:00 A.M. on 24 July 1886, but he returned for a second term on 20 April 1889 and remained until 20 August 1890. See William Grant, Diary, 13 April 1886, Lee Library, Brigham Young University, Provo, Utah, and Helon H. Tracy, Diary, 15 April and 24 July 1886, Marriott Library, University of Utah, Salt Lake City.

15. A cohab diary dates the introduction of the calisthenics to 2 July 1886: "A number of the prisoners in the yard have commenced to take calisthenic exercises twice a day with R. Clawson as teacher. This does me good" (Abraham H. Cannon, Diary, 2 July 1886).

16. The sixty lessons in double-entry bookkeeping each lasted one hour. In 1923 Clawson suggested that his installation in the church auditing committee may have been because "President Snow got the impression I could do the work from having attended, as a visitor, a number of my bookkeeping class sessions at the Utah Penitentiary" (Rudger Clawson, "Reorganization of Financial System at President's Office, under Administration of Presidents Lorenzo Snow and Joseph F. Smith," Ms 5322, which document is restricted at the LDS Archives, but a carbon copy is available in RC, Bx 23, Fd 9). He was proud that during the time he was in prison he earned $500 teaching bookkeeping, which is an excellent return for the $45 he spent on a series of forty bookkeeping lessons taken in New York in the mid-1870s ("President Rudger Clawson's Seventieth Birthday Celebration Held at His Home, Sunday, March 13, 1927," 5, in RC, Bx 1, Fd 15).

17. Caleb W. West (1844–1909), who was born in Kentucky, was the thirteenth and fifteenth governor of the Territory of Utah, serving from 1886 to 1889 and again from 1893 to 1895. He joined the Southern army during the Civil War and was captured and confined in military prisons at Camp Chase, Ohio, and Johnson's Island, Lake Erie. After the war West worked in the circuit clerk's office in Kentucky and also began to practice law. President Grover Cleveland appointed West as territorial governor in April 1886 and he arrived in Utah in the next month. See Kate B. Carter, comp., *Heart Throbs of the West* (Salt Lake City: Daughters of Utah Pioneers, 1945), 6:62–64.

18. The following remarks by Lorenzo Snow were deleted from MS I before MS II was typed: "He [Governor Caleb W. West] would probably not refuse to accept such a document as we might send him and let it go before the world. There are times for us to speak and there are times for us to keep silent. The question is in which category the present action should be placed. Before receiving his sentence, he [Lorenzo Snow] had felt that it would be better for

him not to say anything, and that the silence of other brethren when sentenced had preached a louder sermon to the world than anything they could say. But as the time approached, he decided that it would be an opportune occasion to present to the world the testimony of an Apostle, and so in the present instance" (RC, Bx 2, Fd 6, MS I, 142–43). Also, the same wording is found in the diary of George C. Lambert, who served as secretary for this meeting.

19. See "Response of the 'Mormon' Prisoners," *Deseret News* (weekly), 2 June 1886, and Edward W. Tullidge, *Tullidge's Histories* (Salt Lake City: Edward W. Tullidge, 1889), 2, part 2: 23–24, for printings of this letter, which was in response to the governor's offer of a conditional amnesty. Clawson suggests that John W. Keddington did not sign the reply because he was being released the next day. However, Thomas Porcher, who entered the penitentiary the same day (21 November 1885) and left with Keddington on the same day (25 May 1886), did sign the reply, so Clawson's explanation is not adequate. Evidently, Keddington was already hesitant about signing the reply, and then Abraham H. Cannon's warning that he would some day regret it "ruffled him and he declared he would not sign it" (Lambert, Diary, 24 May 1886).

20. Francis H. Dyer (1854–92) was made a deputy sheriff in his native Mississippi at the age of sixteen, continuing until he was twenty years old. Dyer came to Utah in 1876 and worked in the mining industry in the Bingham Canyon and the Little Cottonwood Canyon. He also hauled ore from the Crescent mine and built its tramway. President Grover Cleveland appointed Dyer as U.S. marshal in April 1886. The Senate approved his appointment on 28 May and he started his duties on 16 June 1886, serving for three years. See Vernal A. Brown, "The United States Marshals in Utah Territory to 1896" (M.S. thesis, Utah State University, 1970), 154–63.

21. The celebration for the Fourth of July actually took place on Monday, 5 July 1886, and the quotation from the *Deseret Evening News* describes the activities of the latter day. Though Clawson identifies the author of the account only as "one of the brethren," the "L" at the end of the article refers to the Mormon journalist George C. Lambert. In his diary Lambert, who entered the penitentiary on 11 May 1886 and was released on 11 November 1886, discloses that he "wrote a letter to the 'News' in the evening giving an account of our celebration" (Lambert, Diary, 5 July 1886).

22. On 13 April 1885 Orson P. Arnold promised that in the future he would obey the law of the land (referring to the Edmunds Act of 1882), as presently interpreted by the courts. Judge Zane, based on this promise, only fined him the usual $300 and did not impose a prison sentence. The next year Arnold was caught visiting his plural wife, and on 21 October 1886 he was convicted of unlawful cohabitation and sentenced to fifteen months and fined $450 and $101.80 for court costs. He was released on 20 March 1887, after serving five months. Others who promised to obey the law, thus avoiding a prison sentence and receiving only a fine, were Truman O. Angel, Jr., John Daynes, John H. Rumel, Septimus W. Sears, Bishop John Sharp, and James Taylor. John Aird, George Harmon, and Joseph H. Sisam received no prison sentences, but had to serve a month in prison because they could not afford

to pay the fine. For Clawson's reaction when Bishop John Sharp made his promise to the judge, see RC, Bx 16, Fd 4, Letter to Lydia Clawson, 23 September 1885, which is reproduced in this volume. In 1885 President Wilford Woodruff described the two sides taken when Mormon polygamists were brought to trial: some have "Deserted their wives & Children, Broaken their Coven[an]ts Denyed their religion & dishonored God," while others "prefer to go to prision with Honor than to have *Liberty* with *Dishonor* and this is now the test which is to try all the Elders of Israel who have obeyed the Celestial Law of Marriage" (Scott G. Kenney, ed., *Wilford Woodruff's Journal: 1833–1898, Typescript* [Midvale, Utah: Signature Books, 1985], 8:337). See James B. Allen, " 'Good Guys' vs. 'Good Guys': Rudger Clawson, John Sharp, and Civil Disobedience in Nineteenth-Century Utah," *Utah Historical Quarterly* 48 (Spring 1980): 164–72.

23. Nathaniel V. Jones, Jr. (1850–1921) was not imprisoned for both unlawful cohabitation and bribery, but simply for the latter offense, in spite of the fact that his name is included with polygamous Mormons. Jones was sentenced to three years' imprisonment on 13 November 1886, along with Frank Treseder, for attempting to bribe U.S. Deputy Marshal Franks to receive information about prospective arrests of Mormon polygamists. This is to be contrasted with the Treseder family tradition, which has reversed the bribery to refusing "to take a bribe to tell on some of those living in polygamy." Jones was discharged by the Third District Court on 3 May 1888. See Roselyn W. Slade, "Francis (Frank) McKay Treseder—An Early Artist of Utah," unpublished paper, Utah State Historical Society, Salt Lake City; Joseph H. Dean, Diary, 13 November 1886, LDS Archives; and Charles R. Bailey, Diary, 131, Merrill Library, Utah State University, Logan, Utah.

24. The name of James Higgins (1820–1904) of West Jordan has been accidentally omitted from this list. Having been charged with unlawful cohabitation, sentenced for eighteen months, and fined $400 and costs of $99.20, he entered the penitentiary on 30 September 1886 and was released early by decision of the court on 28 February 1887.

25. Otis L. Brown was appointed by his friend, Marshal Frank H. Dyer, to be the new warden early in October 1886. Previous to this appointment Brown was weighmaster and storekeeper at the Crescent mine. See George C. Wood, Diary, 1 October 1886, and *Salt Lake Daily Tribune,* 2 October 1886.

26. The four following paragraphs about Warden Dow are a late addition of nine pages to MS I³ (RC, Bx 2, Fd 7). Lorenzo Snow was in prison from 12 March 1886 to 8 February 1887, but since George N. Dow resigned as warden in October of 1886, this statement must have preceded that date. Also, the titles used by Clawson are anachronistic, for Wilford Woodruff and Lorenzo Snow did not assume these positions until 7 April 1889.

CHAPTER 4

1887

Eighteen and eighty-seven found matters here in Utah still in an unsettled condition. The crusade against our people had lost none of its rigor. There were some sixty-five or seventy of the brethren serving out terms of imprisonment in the penitentiary for conscience sake, and there was a prospect of many convictions for unlawful cohabitation in the near future. Notwithstanding there was an opportunity to escape imprisonment by making a simple promise to obey the law, as interpreted by the courts, very few of the brethren took advantage of it. Those who came to prison were prepared to suffer hardships rather than surrender. I do not remember having heard a single murmur from any of the brethren against the Lord, although of course they felt extremely indignant at times toward their persecutors. I cannot but think that the Lord was well pleased with the cheerfulness, patience, and resignation exhibited by those who were called upon to suffer bonds and imprisonment because of their devotion to principle.

The following is a list of the brethren who were added to our numbers during the months of January, February, March, and April 1887. They were sentenced as follows:[1]

To six months, $300.00, and costs for unlawful cohabitation: Ishmael Phillips, Hy. Reiser, Isaac Brockbank, L. H. Mousley, Henry Whittaker, J. P. Mortensen, Rasmus Nielsen, A. G. Driggs, William H. Foster, Bedson Eardley, John Adams, Ezra T. Clark, Peter S. Barkdull, Joseph Hogan, Joseph Blunt, Herman Grether, W. H. Watson, Matthew Pickett, William J. Hooper, Levi North, Hyrum B. North, Harrison Sperry, A. W. Winberg, Thomas Butler, William R. Webb, R. C. Kirkwood, David John, Albert Singleton.

The following were sentenced to six months, $100.00, and no costs for unlawful cohabitation: Robert Henderson, Thomas McNeil, Hugh

Adams, William Palmer, Peter Anderson, Charles Frank, Abraham Chadwick, John Marriott, Thomas W. Kirby, William Dalley, James Dalley,[2] Don C. Snow, J. T. Arrowsmith, John L. Gibbs, Sanford Fuller. The following were sentenced to six months, $300.00, and no costs for unlawful cohabitation: Joseph Parry, Niels C. Mortensen. The following were sentenced to six months, $25.00, and costs for unlawful cohabitation: A. W. Cooley, H. F. F. Thorup. The following were sentenced to six months and no costs for unlawful cohabitation: Soren Peterson, C. P. Christiansen, and Edward Peay.

Harvey Murdock was sentenced to five years, $500.00, and no costs for polygamy. George Crismon was sentenced to six months, $150.00, and costs for unlawful cohabitation. Henry Grow was sentenced to five months, $50.00, and no costs for unlawful cohabitation.[3] The following were sentenced to six months, $50.00, and no costs for unlawful cohabitation: George Kirkham, James Kirkham, and Edwin L. Whiting. John England was sentenced to six months, $150.00, and costs for unlawful cohabitation. William Unthank was sentenced to six months, $300.00, and no costs for unlawful cohabitation. Edwin Standring was sentenced to six months, $200.00, and no costs for unlawful cohabitation. George D. Snell was sentenced to six months, $200.00, and no costs for unlawful cohabitation.[4]

The following were sentenced to six months, $100.00, and costs for unlawful cohabitation: Solomon Wixom, Alex. Edwards, Richard Collett. Richard Collett was the 205th man sentenced for violation of the Edmunds-Tucker Law. William Harrison was sentenced to six months, $100.00, and no costs for unlawful cohabitation. This man was severed from the Church about ten years ago, but has come to prison with apparent good intentions.[5]

One of the brethren who was convicted of unlawful cohabitation and numbered with the foregoing company, upon entering the prison inquired for me, saying, "I'm anxious to see Brother Rudger Clawson, the first man convicted and sentenced under the Edmunds-Tucker Law." He hunted me up, and striking me familiarly upon the shoulder, addressed me about as follows: "Brother Clawson, I'm awfully glad to see you and to be with you in prison." His countenance beaming with a captivating smile, he further said: "I brought my violin with me—we'll sing and we'll dance and have a jolly good time, won't we?" With a tone of sadness in my voice I replied: "Yes, dear Brother ____, we certainly will have a jolly good time" (?). However, I did not grow enthusiastic over the prospect, for I had already spent two and a half years behind the bars. In chatting with the brother a week later I noticed that the spirit of jollification had entirely left him, and the expression on his face gave him the appearance of a man who had discovered something rather unpleasant.

A few months subsequent to Brother Snow's advent into the prison, his case was taken upon appeal to the Supreme Court of the United States, the point at issue being segregation of the offense. As to the outcome, it was not only a matter of absorbing interest to him personally, but also to many of the brethren similarly involved, both inside and outside the penitentiary, for in the event of a favorable decision in his case, these others under the same circumstances might be benefitted. A careful estimate showed the saving of imprisonment to the brethren to be some two hundred years. It would be impossible to describe the feelings of joy and thankfulness that took possession of each anxious heart on receipt of a favorable decision of the Supreme Court, February 7, 1887. The next day Brother Snow, after wearing a convict's garb some eleven months, took his departure. He was met at the gate by a large number of relatives and friends. It is but truth to say that we rejoiced at his going while realizing the greatness of our loss. Not a few of the brethren were released, under this decision, within thirty days.

Although matters at the penitentiary under the Dyer and Brown administrations moved along quite satisfactorily to the prisoners in many respects, yet there were some things that invited criticism. The practice of shaving and clipping the convicts once a week, which was inaugurated by ex-Marshal Ireland, but lightly enforced by ex-Warden Dow during the last few months of his term, was revived by the new officials. Aged and feeble brethren, men who had grown grey in the battle of life, were required to pass under the barber's razor at an inclement season of the year, thus endangering their health. Severe colds, rheumatism, neuralgia, etc., made their appearance among the prisoners in consequence of this treatment. Dr. Hamilton, the prison physician, made many fair promises to the more aged ones, but he willfully neglected to mention the matter to Warden Brown or else his orders were ignored, and so the evil was not remedied.[6] After a time, however, there was a slight relaxation in favor of the infirm, who escaped the razor, but were pretty thoroughly stripped of hair and beard by the scissors.

On February 2nd, 1887, Brother Nathaniel V. Jones was put in the sweatbox. When informed that Joe Bush, appropriately called by some of the prisoners, "Ruffian Joe," was inside guard at the time, the reader will not be seriously shocked. It seems that Brother Jones accosted Bush and very justly reproached him with having taken advantage of every opportunity to vent his spleen upon him. This Bush denied, and further stated that in ordering Jones out of the dining room that morning after breakfast to make way for the waiters who swept the room and washed the dishes, he simply spoke to him as he had done to others. Brother Jones disputed this statement, said it was not true, and reiterated his accusation. "Have a care, Jones," said Bush, "how you talk to me or you'll get into trouble."

It would seem from what subsequently followed that Brother Jones failed to "have a care," although very little more was said. Bush withdrew to the outside for a few moments, presumably to consult with the warden, and returning again with a malicious and savage smile playing upon his repulsive features, he conducted Brother Jones to the sweatbox, who, as he entered, asked to see the warden. The guard glared at him a moment, then slammed the door in his face. This was the first case, so far as I know, in which an inmate of the prison was denied a hearing before being subjected to punishment.

Although the box was scarcely large enough for the accommodation of one, yet a coarse, brutal negro who had been thrust into this vile retreat a few hours before, was forced upon Jones as a companion—how great the indignity to Brother Jones! Owing to the absence of ventilation, a foul and sickening stench pervaded the enclosure, thus making it utterly impossible for one within to breathe with any degree of comfort. When night came the weather turned extremely cold, so that sleep was out of the question. Altogether it was a night such as seldom comes to a man of refined and sensitive feelings.

Shortly after Brother Jones went into the box, a remonstrance, as given below, was addressed to the warden:

> Utah Penitentiary,
> February 2nd, 1887.
>
> O. L. Brown, Warden
> Sir:
> One of our fellow prisoners, N. V. Jones, is now in the sweatbox. We very respectfully desire to call your attention to the fact that he is in a delicate physical condition, only having partially recovered from a severe attack of sickness. He was complaining of a sore throat but a few hours since. In our opinion, it would greatly endanger his health, if not his life, to keep him in the box at this inclement season of the year, especially when it is known that the box is extremely damp.
>
> Respectfully,
> (signed)

Dr. Wm. H. Pidcock	Rudger Clawson	Amos Neff
J. H. Dean	W. W. Galbraith	George Dunford
	George Naylor	N. H. Groesbeck

At the expiration of about twenty-four hours, which to Jones must have seemed an age, he was permitted to part company with the negro and once more join his brethren.[7]

On February 14th I organized a third class in bookkeeping, composed of the following brethren: Isaac Brockbank, George Naylor, John Lee Jones, Henry Reiser, and John Riddle (non-"Mormon"). The results attained in this course, which was completed in fifty-seven lessons, were gratifying.

The following is a copy of a letter mailed to President Cleveland, February 24th. Comment is unnecessary.

> Utah Penitentiary,
> February 24, 1887.
>
> To the Hon. Grover Cleveland,
> President of the United States,
> Sir:
>
> I herewith respectfully submit for your consideration the following facts. I am twenty-nine years of age. In November 1884, I was convicted of polygamy and unlawful cohabitation, and sentenced by Judge Charles S. Zane to four years imprisonment and to pay a fine of $800.00. I have now served out two years and three months of this term. That to which I particularly desire to draw your attention is this. When I entered the prison, *fourteen* of its inmates were undergoing punishment for *murder,* five having been sentenced to life, and the remainder with two exceptions to a long term of years. Of this number, *ten* have gone out on a full and free pardon, two have been released and two only remain, one of whom is a life man. The immediate outgrowth of my alleged crime is life, of their crime, death.
>
> A proposition has been made to me, as also to others of my faith, that if I would promise to obey the law in the future, *as construed by the courts,* I should receive a pardon; while, on the other hand, no such requirement whatever was made of the parties mentioned. Why, then, I respectfully ask, should a promise be required of me and not of them? And what, Mr. President, will justify a leniency extended to one class of criminals—those who are guilty of *murder,* as against another class— those who are guilty of a misdemeanor only?
>
> Respectfully,
> (signed) Rudger Clawson

Suffice it to say that the President did not deign to favor me with a response to this letter.

Up to about March the first of this year, the brethren had been confined in bunk rooms no. 2 and no. 3 almost exclusively. They were, therefore, as comfortably situated as it was possible for them to be in the Utah Penitentiary. The "toughs" on the other hand were assigned to room no. 1, where they made night hideous with the most astounding noises. Coarse and brutal laughter, profanity, vulgarity, dancing, singing, sparring, and quarreling were freely indulged in. The three most degraded characters among these men, at this time, were a negro by the name of [James] Epps, commonly called "Honey" Epps; Louie Ravera, an Italian; and Pete Miller, the latter of American extraction. They were just a trifle above the animal, the negro being a little in advance of the other two.

It seemed but just that the better and more refined class of prisoners should be kept separate from the others, and be allowed to mingle together during the long hours of the night. But for some reason not given (I attributed it to prejudice), the prison officials saw fit about this time to make a radical change. Dyer, the guard, stepped into bunk room no. 3 just after dinner one day and rather startled those present by ordering the following brethren to take their bedding and move into no. 1: N. V. Jones, W. H. Watson, Ezra T. Clark,[8] A. G. Driggs, L. H. Mousley, Timothy Parkinson, James I. Steele, George Chandler, William Palmer, John Gray, P. Andersen, John Durrant, Joseph H. Dean, and Rudger Clawson. He then stepped into no. 2 and issued a similar order to those whose names are given below: Joseph Parry, Harvey Murdock, F. W. Ellis, Abraham Chadwick, Joseph H. Thurber, William Felsted, Thomas Allsop, Henry B. Gwilliam, Rasmus Nielsen, and John Penman.

An equal number of "toughs" from room no. 1 was distributed in no. 2 and no. 3. This was mixing things up with a vengeance. Whereas up to this time, rooms no. 2 and no. 3 had been tolerably free from the evils existing in no. 1, they were now very much lowered in tone. The "toughs" screamed with delight as they took possession of their new quarters, while the brethren who made way for them were correspondingly depressed. I observed that two of the guards, viz., Doyle and Dyer, rejoiced exceedingly over this incident. Anything that militated against the brethren appeared to inspire these small-souled creatures with a sort of fiendish joy.

The change was far from being agreeable to our feelings. It seemed as if we had descended into the very bowels of hell. Nothing could exceed the noise and confusion that held sway until bedtime, while a great cloud of tobacco smoke—dense, strong, and nauseating—filled the rooms. Last of all, the consciousness of being associated with a class of men, some of whom had grown feeble from venereal disease, and were constantly but secretly committing the most flagrant crimes against nature, was revolting in the extreme.[9]

One of the brethren, Rasmus Nielsen, was compelled to sleep with "Honey" Epps, the negro, who maintained a filthiness in his personal habits not often met with. In complaining to Joe Bush of such treatment and asking to be removed to another bunk, he not only received a sharp rebuff but was threatened with the sweatbox. At the expiration of two weeks, Joseph H. Dean and I were moved back into no. 3 and, owing to the crowded condition of the prison, four or five of the brethren in no. 1, with others, were permitted to sleep in the dining room.

The following is a list of the brethren who constituted my fourth class in bookkeeping, which was organized March 14th, 1887: George Crismon, Edward Schoenfeld, A. W. Winberg, L. H. Mousley, Thomas Butler, Joseph Parry, and James Kirkham. I was well satisfied with the progress made by this class.

The advent into the penitentiary of McDonald and Slade, pugilists, who were convicted of prize fighting April 22nd, and sentenced to thirty days imprisonment, created a perfect furor.[10] The news spread through the yard like wild fire and these two worthies were soon surrounded by a great crowd of convicts who literally stared them out of countenance. The idea of having real live professional pugilists in their midst was almost more than human nature could comprehend, so they gazed at them with increasing admiration again, and again, and again. This silent homage must have been very gratifying to the two fighting men, although at first it seemed to startle them a good deal. They were hardly prepared for so odd a reception. However, it was not long before they had become hail-fellows-well-met with the "toughs," who conversed with them in the most familiar manner. McDonald evinced a most daring but enterprising spirit by organizing without delay a select class in sparring composed of Mat. Casey and Paddy Grant, who were apt and close students in the art of self-defense. Mat. Casey, a thorough "tough," in his turn instructed [Joseph] Curtis, a boy of about fourteen years who had been placed in his charge, in the "manly" art. Truly, the penitentiary is no place for children.

Sunday morning McDonald and "Honey" Epps engaged in a sparring match on the penitentiary "Boulevard." When it was known what was going on the convicts came flying in posthaste from every quarter of the yard and immediately formed a ring around the combatants. Then the fun began. Of course the negro, although a powerfully built fellow, stood no chance with the professional, who pummeled him in a most thorough and artistic manner. It is due the negro to say that owing to the hardness of his skull, he took the punishment with becoming fortitude.

Words are not sufficiently expressive to paint the enthusiasm that prevailed during the contest. Even the attention of the guards was secured and held fast, improbable as the statement may appear. It is perhaps worthy of note that Marshal Dyer, Warden Brown, ex-Governor [Eli H.] Murray, the famous mathematician, and a number of other visitors witnessed the gladiatorial struggle from the wall, and seemed to enter fully into the spirit of it. I fancied that if the brethren had been engaged in any such conduct on the Sabbath Day, while visitors were on the wall, they would have met with a prompt and stinging rebuke if not punishment. McDonald and Slade were pardoned out after a few days only of incarceration.

In the early part of May, the following rule was tacked against the south side of bunk room no. 1, opposite the dining room:

Notice.
Do not congregate in this alley and stare at
visitors on the wall. Any violation will be
misdemeanor. Warden.

So far as I know, this rule was pretty strictly observed. I think it not unlikely, however, that many of the brethren while passing in and out of the dining room, often paused a moment and looked up to where visitors stand on the wall. A few days after the new order was issued, Brother Edward Schoenfeld and Thomas Butler each received a note from the warden, as follows:

Utah Penitentiary,
Warden's Office,
May 2, 1887

Mr. _____
You are hereby notified that I have taken five (5) days from your copper for violation of printed notice concerning staring at persons on the wall.

(signed) O. L. Brown,
Warden.

The brethren were not a little amazed at such treatment as the offense was committed, if at all, unconsciously. They were given no opportunity of speaking in their own behalf. I do not think it would be generally considered a very serious breach of etiquette for prisoners to look at visitors on the wall who came, many of them, to see relatives and friends, and to be recognized by them.

During the summer of 1887 a number of prisoners made attempts to escape. Among them were Smith and Wheeler. They, being employed in the kitchen, were accustomed to being called out early. One morning while it was still dark, when the turnkey's back was turned, they made a sudden break for liberty, and were soon out of sight. At 10:00 p.m. the next night they were recaptured in Salt Lake City and brought back to the "Pen." Both were loaded with chains, and for many a long week thereafter were compelled to carry all the water used at the prison for culinary purposes—a duty that previously devolved upon all prisoners, turn and turn about. Their punishment was exceptionally severe, as, in cases of this kind, the chains had heretofore been thought to be sufficient. The chains consist of shackles or ball and chain, weighing 25 to 30 pounds.

The third break was made by Thomas and Ladd who were employed in the "bake" house. Detained by work one evening a little later than usual, they took advantage of a favorable chance and decamped, leaving the Territory with the utmost precipitation. At the expiration of a few days, however, they were recaptured in Idaho and sent back to the penitentiary. After passing a night and a day in the sweatbox, without food or water, they were taken out and heavily chained. For many a weary day succeeding their return, they were required to labor in the hot sun at various employments to atone for the past.

The warden's confidence in the "toughs" was completely shattered and he now looked upon them with a distrustful eye. A certain number of "trusties," however, were indispensable to the welfare of the prison, so the brethren were sought after and a few of them were elevated to that lofty distinction. Their well-known trustworthiness had no little influence in deciding this choice. It was an established fact that under the most favorable circumstances for escape the "Mormon" prisoners invariably clung to the prison with a tenacity that was truly remarkable. I am not aware that Warden Brown ever gave them credit for being the most reliable prisoners in the "Pen," but he certainly showed his appreciation of their general behavior by permitting them to go and come at will, unaccompanied by guards. Thus, in spite of the bitter prejudice existing in his mind towards them, they gradually but surely gravitated to the top.

In the latter part of July, a fight occurred in room no. 1 in which "Honey" Epps, the negro, Harry Hawthorne, the bigamist, and two Irish prisoners took part. Epps was the originator of the trouble, and but for the interference of the guard would doubtless have come out with a broken head. Notwithstanding the fact that Epps was principally at fault, all were punished alike. Epps and Hawthorne were put into one sweatbox and the two Irishmen into the other. After 48 hours confinement, they were released.

During the progress of the fight, one of the men picked up a chair and handled it in a rather threatening manner, but struck no one. This little circumstance, though unimportant in itself, led to the removal of all the chairs and tables from the bunk rooms at night, which resulted in great discomfort to the brethren, who were obliged thereafter to use the hard wooden benches that had been provided. I sought an interview with the warden and protested against such treatment, stating that there had been no fighting in no. 2 and no. 3 and that it would be unjust to punish the occupants of those rooms for something that others had done. It was of no avail. The order had been issued, and, like the law of the Medes and Persians, it stood. In all matters that affected the welfare of the brethren unfavorably, as in this case, I observed that Doyle, the guard, seemed to wield a potent influence. Punishments meted out to the "toughs" were not as a rule deemed sufficient until made to reach the "Mormon" prisoners in some way or another. "No innocent man shall escape" describes the situation clearly.

An example of the extent to which punishment was sometimes carried in the Utah Penitentiary was the case of Pete Miller. Having refused to work he was taken out, after a two or three days' confinement in the sweatbox, and hung up by the wrists, his toes barely touching the ground, in the hot sun, and kept in that position until he promised obedience to the warden's behests. He was then loaded with the chains. There seemed to be no question as to the warden's right to punish refractory prisoners, but that he was justified in torturing them was gravely doubted by the prisoners.

August 11th, 1887, was an eventful day. Fred Hopt was executed—shot—for the murder of John F. Turner in 1880. He had been under arrest some seven years, a part of the time in close confinement. There was a strong feeling against him in Salt Lake City and throughout the Territory, but he enjoyed the confidence and sympathy of the U.S. marshal, Warden Brown, the guards, and a large number of the prisoners at the "Pen." This was partly due, no doubt, to his long imprisonment and general good behavior. Strenuous efforts were made by some of his friends to have the sentence commuted to life imprisonment, but without success. No one could conceive the mental anxiety he suffered during the forty-five days he was under death sentence, but it must have been very great. He looked for relief almost up to the last moment.

The fatal day at last arrived. The weather was clear but warm. Death was in the air, as was evidenced by an awful feeling of gloom that seemed to have taken possession of everybody in the prison. Breakfast over, the guard announced that all those who wished to shake hands with the doomed man and say good-bye to him might do so. The prisoners, thereupon, in a body passed before his cell, and shook hands with him one by one in a most sympathetic manner. Hopt, who stood in the door, was deeply affected by this mark of friendly feeling and had the utmost difficulty in preserving his hitherto calm demeanor. His voice, however, as he uttered the oft repeated word "good-bye" occasionally betrayed the powerful emotions that were working within him.

During the long hours of the forenoon the prisoners collected in groups, some in one corner, some in another, and discussed in a quiet and subdued tone the approaching event, while preparations for the execution were silently going on. When, at last, a large white tent, from which the messengers of death would issue, had been placed in position and an ordinary house chair put opposite about one hundred feet, all was ready. A Catholic priest was in attendance upon Hopt during the last few hours of his life.

At 12:00 o'clock the prisoners were remanded to the bunk rooms and locked up, the windows having been previously covered with blankets to shut off the view. It would be difficult to describe the feeling of suspense and gloom that settled down upon those bunk rooms. About fifty men were gathered together in room no. 3 where I was confined, many of whom were boisterous characters—men who ordinarily cursed and swore, who quarreled and fought, who danced and sang, not a little of the time, and yet the awful stillness that prevailed during that period of three quarters of an hour was so intense as to be painful. For the time being the "toughs" were completely overwhelmed. I say for the time being, because an hour after the execution, they had resumed their previous mode of life. When the presence of death itself—death in a violent form—has not lasting power to turn men from their evil ways, what will?

At about quarter to one o'clock the doomed man was conducted to the fatal chair. He maintained a superb calmness to the last, as evidenced by the fact that he quietly smoked a cigar while proceeding from his cell to his death. A sharp ringing report, which fairly startled us, indicated that all was over. I do not remember to have passed a more unpleasant day during my long imprisonment.[11]

In the afternoon of August 20th, Bishop Harrison Sperry, ex-convict, was seen standing on the wall. Immediately after the supper bell rang, the prisoners formed into line, as usual, and, as we marched into the dining room, I thoughtlessly shook my fist at the Bishop, who smiled in reply. This very trifling incident was observed by Mr. Norrell, the guard, who reported it to the warden. The following afternoon, August 21, I was called to the gate. "Is there any truth in the report that you waved your hand at visitors on the wall yesterday?" asked the warden. "Yes, sir," I replied. "Did you not know that you were violating the rules?" "Yes, sir. I did it rather thoughtlessly, but still I knew it was in violation of the rules." "That will be sufficient," he said, and I came back into the yard. Shortly after supper, Ed Jenny, the guard, notified me that I must go into the box, and in I went.

When the day of the month (August 21) is mentioned in connection with the very expressive compound word sweatbox, it will readily be seen that my situation was far from being pleasant. The ventilation was extremely defective, and owing to the heated condition of the air, I perspired freely all the evening, although partially disrobed. There was an entire absence of furniture and bedding in the box, so that in seeking repose, I was obliged to stretch myself along the hard bare floor of the box with nothing but my striped "con" coat for a pillow. Under circumstances so unfavorable one might suppose that sleep would be impossible, and yet—I remember the fact with astonishment—I slept soundly six or seven hours during the night. At last the dawn of another day broke in upon us—not for me, however, for it could not get at me. Considering the extraordinary severity of the sweatbox punishment and the mildness of my offence, I naturally anticipated a release during the early morning, but in this I was sorely disappointed. I was not only not released, but received no breakfast— not even a cup of cold water. I ruminated much during the long hours of the day of "man's inhumanity to man"; and did not fail to note with what avidity cohabs were snatched up and severely punished for slight infractions of the rules, while on the other hand the toughs fairly "mutilated" the rule prohibiting obscene and profane language without being called to account. I was released from "durance vile" about one o'clock, having been in confinement some eighteen hours.

Apropos of this subject, I will state that on two separate occasions, once when Jack Emerson "ex-con" and once when Billy Brennan "ex-con" were on the wall, signs of recognition were exchanged between the visitors and some of the toughs, the guard standing by and permitting it.

In September preparations were made for the building of a new penitentiary—Congress having appropriated $50,000.00 for that purpose. To make room for the new building, room no. 3 was moved into the southeast corner of the yard, and rooms no. 1 and no. 2 were moved back to where no. 3 stood. By this change, ample room was made for the new prison. Work was begun and pushed ahead with great vigor. Owing to the necessity of keeping the entrance to the yard constantly open, it was deemed unsafe to allow the toughs and the long-timers the freedom of the yard, as heretofore, so that they were all transferred to room no. 3 and kept under lock and key both day and night, except at meal times. The cohabs and short-timers were confined in no. 1 and no. 2—the latter being my bunk room—but were not locked up during the day. This arrangement, as will be seen, was somewhat favorable to the cohabs. However, Brothers Jones, Thurber, Murdock, Penman, and Wood, being long-timers, were confined in no. 3 with the toughs. The record made by these "Mormon" prisoners in the Utah Pen by no means justified such treatment. One can easily surmise how very unpleasant the situation in no. 3 must have been. In a room hardly large enough to accommodate thirty, sixty men were kept huddled together like wild beasts, both day and night. The ventilation was very defective. What with tobacco smoke spreading in volumes throughout the room, tobacco spittle trickling in small streams over the floor, and shocking profanity constantly offending the ear, one used to finer things could almost look with favor upon the suicide theory.

After some weeks of close confinement, the brethren named were permitted to remain out in the yard during the day and finally Brothers Jones and Thurber succeeded in getting a transfer to room no. 2. The others were later given a like privilege.

The deduction for good conduct, or "copper," that was allowed prisoners when I entered the prison was quite liberal. On a term of 4 years, it amounted to about 14 months, but in 1885 a new construction was given to the copper act by W. H. Dickson, the District Attorney, and sustained by the court, which reduced the copper on a 4 years sentence to about 9 months. By this change I lost 5 months "copper," which, had I served my time out, would have been a grievous hardship. In March 1886, a new copper act was passed by the Legislature, which was even more liberal in its provision than the one of 1880, as first applied. This latter was repealed. On the 20th of October, I made an application to the Supreme Court of the Territory for discharge, but with what result will be seen by reference to the following excerpt from the [23 October] *Salt Lake Herald*. Of course I did not ask for the new "copper" from November 3, 1884, but only from March 11, 1886, the date of its passage:

THE SUPREME BENCH.
The Rudger Clawson Writ of Habeas Corpus Refused.

A brief session of the Supreme Court was held yesterday morning, when the application for a writ of *habeas corpus* in the case of Rudger

Clawson was argued. The applicant was represented by Col. [James O.] Broadhead, Judge [Jabez G.] Sutherland, and Mr. [James H.] Moyle. The motion was made to secure credit for Mr. Clawson under the new copper act for good behavior, instead of under the old law, which provides for more commutation for prisoners confined in the penitentiary.

The statement of the case was presented in a clear and logical manner by Judge Sutherland, in which he claimed that the new law should be applied to Mr. Clawson's case, and that under it his term of three and a half years should be held to expire on the 18th of last May, and the six months' term in addition thereto should have ended last Tuesday, the 16th.

The Judge argued that the court's decisions in former cases that the law could not affect prisoners then in custody, related only to Territorial prisoners, it could not be extended to United States prisoners, but under the law of Congress of 1875, the commutation act in force at the time the prisoner's sentence expired was the only one applicable. The act which existed at the time the sentence was pronounced could not be followed, for it had ceased to be a law, but the provision that should be made to apply was that which was operative at the time the prisoner was entitled to claim the credit of commutation for good behavior.

District Attorney Peters opposed the application in a brief argument, holding that the present copper act, having gone into effect since the passing of sentence, could not be made operative on that sentence without interfering with the judiciary.

Colonel Broadhead claimed that the application of the new act did not impair an existing legal judgment. The act of Congress was made by its own provision to apply to "all prisoners who have been or shall hereafter be convicted," and said that they should have the benefit of the local commutative laws. The right of reduction of time for good behavior was fixed by Congress, not by the Territorial Legislature, and it was under the action of the former that the applicant made this claim. That law had been in force before the passage of the judgment. The prisoner could not claim a discharge as a United States prisoner under the old Copper law, because it was not in force at the time that he could present his claim. The only commutation which he could ask under the Congressional Act of 1875, was that allowed by the local statute at the time he was eligible to apply for it, and no other, because no other was in force. The applicant claimed his rights under existing statutes. The proposition was plain that Mr. Clawson was entitled to his discharge. The district attorney had read from two authorities in opposition to their claim, but both those authorities had been reviewed and their bad reasoning shown in a subsequent and more careful decision rendered by the Supreme Court of Ohio.

Judge Sutherland here suggested to the Court the fact that the Ohio decision, changing those quoted by the district attorney in support of his present position, had been procured through the efforts of Mr. Peters himself.

The Court took the matter under advisement until 4:00 P.M., to which time recess was taken. At 4:00 o'clock in the afternoon the Court refused to grant the application.

In view of the above action of the Supreme Court, I made an application to President Cleveland, as follows, for a pardon:

To His Excellency,
Grover Cleveland,
President of the United States,
    Rudger Clawson in the Utah Penitentiary of Utah [Territory] respectfully represents:

That, on the 3rd day of November, 1884, having been convicted on an indictment for polygamy and for unlawful cohabitation under the act of Congress approved March 22nd, 1882, he was sentenced for the former to pay a fine of $500.00 and to be imprisoned in the Utah Penitentiary for a term of 3 years and 6 months, and for the latter offence to pay a fine of $300.00 and to be imprisoned for a further term of 6 months, that he has been confined in said penitentiary under this sentence ever since it was pronounced.

He further respectfully represents that during this said imprisonment he has demeaned himself according to the rules of discipline of the said prison, and been guilty of no misconduct, as appears by the certificate of the United States marshal hereto annexed. That as he is advised by his counsel and respectfully represents he is not entitled to the credits of time for good conduct under the laws of the United States, except according to the territorial system of commutation. On this point he respectfully refers to,

Rev. St. U. S. [part 1], p. 1080 [1073], sections 5542, 5543; 18 U. S. St. at Large, Part 3, p. 479.

That the act now in force in the territory providing for deductions for good conduct is one approved March 11, 1886, (Laws of Utah, 1886, pp. 5–8) by the 3rd and 4th sections of which his imprisonment would have ended on the 18th day of October 1887. That by the 7th section of said act, a previous statute on the same subject enacted 1880, and in force at the time of said sentence, was repealed; that on the 24th day of October 1887, on petitioner's application for discharge, it was held by the Supreme Court of said Utah Territory that the petitioner is not entitled to credit for good conduct under the said Territorial Statutes and the Utah Act of March 11, 1886, but only under the Territorial (repealed) Act of 1880. That with the meager credits provided by that statute, if it can now have effect since it is repealed, the petitioner will not be entitled to discharge until April 1888.

In consideration of the premises, the petitioner respectfully asks that he be granted a pardon of said offenses.

(signed) Rudger Clawson

Dated, November 10, 1887.
To His Excellency
Grover Cleveland, President United States
I hereby certify that Rudger Clawson, an inmate of the Utah Penitentiary, has demeaned himself during his imprisonment from November 1884 to date, according to the prison rules and discipline, and has been guilty of no misconduct. That he is entitled to such deduction from his term as the laws allow for good conduct in the prison.

(signed) Frank H. Dyer, U.S. Marshal

Dated, November 10, 1887.

The following is a list of the brethren who were sent to the penitentiary during the months of July, August, September, and October.[12] Each was sentenced to 6 months, $100.00 and costs, except as noted: James A. Woods, Thomas H. Smart, 6 months, $300.00 and costs, Alex. Bills, George Wilding, Sr., James Smith, 6 months, $300.00 and costs, Joseph Clark, 6 months, $300.00 and costs, J. H. Ridges, 6 months, $25.00 and costs, Henry Beckstead, John Cottam, 6 months, $50.00 and costs, James M. Fisher, David [Daniel] Harvey, 6 months, $150.00 and costs, Isaac Riddle, 6 months, $300.00 and costs, Levi Savage, 6 months, $300.00 and costs, William Blood, 6 months, $150.00 and costs, John A. Marchant, John P. Wright, 6 months, $50.00 and costs, Joseph C. Perry, 6 months, $50.00 and costs, Edwin Rushton, 4 months, $50.00 and costs, Hyrum H. Evans, 6 months, $50.00 and costs, Frederick Petersen, Thomas G. Labrum, 3 months, $25.00 and costs, John Oborn, 6 months, $50.00 and costs, Charles Burgess, 6 months, $25.00 and costs, James C. Watson, 6 months, $300.00 and costs, 2nd term,[13] John T. Gerber, Wm. S. Muir, Nathan Hanson, James Loynd, 6 months, $50.00 and costs, Samuel Anderson, 6 months, $50.00 and costs, Lars Jacobsen, 6 months, $50.00, William Yates, 6 months, $50.00, Charles McCarty, 6 months, $300.00 and costs, Victor Sandgren, Aaron Hardy, 6 months and costs, John T. Lambert, 6 months and costs, Edward Cliff, 6 months, $200.00 and costs, A. Homer, 5 months, $100.00 and costs, N. P. Madsen, 3 months, $200.00 and costs, Jesse R. Turpin, Charles Livingston (pardoned),[14] James Welsh, 6 months, $50.00 and costs.[15] These and the other brethren maintained throughout the fall cheerful and contented spirits.

About this time the following rule was posted against the bunkhouse:

To guard against the admission of articles of contraband, prisoners are notified that in future no article of merchandise will be permitted to enter the prison unless ordered through the warden.

It was evidently the intention of the warden to compel the brethren to trade with him instead of getting supplies through their relatives and friends. There would have been no objection to this, only his prices were unusually high and the brethren as a rule extremely poor.

A prisoner by the name of [William] Comus, Canadian, was put into the sweatbox at one time and kept there for thirteen days. He was deprived of food and received but a scanty supply of water for two and three days in a stretch. Being without bedding, he also suffered greatly from the cold. Barbarous! The commission of a serious breach of the prison discipline would hardly justify such severe punishment, but the sum and substance of his offence, as related to me by himself, was this. After some little conversation with the warden about a letter addressed to the Canadian government relative to his case, but which had been detained at the gate, he remarked. "They (meaning district attorney and others) have bulldogged me into prison, but when released *I will have satisfaction*, if I have to go to Washington for it."

Brother Joseph H. Ridges, the builder of the famous Tabernacle organ at Salt Lake City, came to me one day highly elated and said: "Brother Clawson, I have discovered the secret of perpetual motion. I shall proceed at once to construct a model," he said, "that in its operation on a small scale will amply prove the claim I'm making. But first, Brother Clawson, inasmuch as I have taken into copartnership a gentile prisoner by the name of G. H. Carney, I would kindly ask you to draw up a paper for our signature setting forth our joint interest in this new invention." With a twinkle in his eye he said: "Brother Clawson, there are millions in it." "Millions in it, you say? Why, yes, I will gladly draw up the desired agreement and since there are to be such tremendous riches in it, surely you'll remember your brethren in bonds. Can you not spare me a small interest in the discovery?" "I'm sorry," he said, "but I really cannot favor you in this matter." I drew up the paper for him which was duly signed by both parties and witnessed.[16]

Later with permission of Warden Dow, Brother Ridges proceeded to construct his model.[17] He obtained the necessary materials from Salt Lake City. He explained that the principle upon which he sought to develop the new energy was that of the waterwheel. Instead of using water he purposed using bird shot for the motive power. The shot after going over the wheel would be brought back perpetually by a system of belts and pulleys and cups used again and again. Thus power, which is so necessary and valuable in the industrial world could be perpetually developed by the same motive force at a minimum cost—in the mountains, on the desert, in the city—almost anywhere. The model was built in a small room within the prison walls under the greatest secrecy. Day after day passed slowly by for two months while the inventor, now a recluse, molded into shape the creation of his mind. All this time the prisoners in the yard, the guards on the wall, the warden and his family were talking about the great discovery which Brother Ridges claimed to have made, and were eagerly awaiting the hour when he would give the demonstration.

At last the long expected day arrived. The model was brought forth, and a thrill of admiration stirred the excited crowd of prison officials and prisoners who gazed upon it in awe, for it was a thing of beauty and of mystery, complete in every detail. The builder of the great organ had put into the model the skill and experience of a lifetime. The look of admiration in the faces of the bystanders must have awakened in him a feeling of exultation and joy. There was in the model the great power wheel, the lesser wheels, the pulleys, belts, and cups, and there, just over the wheel, was the shot—such a combination as inspired in the inventor and I may say in all who stood around, the most extravagant and highest hopes of success.

And now the critical moment had arrived. The crowd under great nervous strain stood silent and expectant. Brother Ridges opened the head gate—the shot rolled down into the cups on the belting. The great wheel revolved on its axis, the lesser wheels turned, and while the machinery was in motion the cups that brought the shot down took it up again, and again brought it on to the wheels, giving them a continuous motion. Great excitement prevailed in that little prison group for at last it appeared that perpetual motion was a demonstrated fact. A buzz of satisfaction was heard on every side. Admiring glances were bestowed upon the organ-builder. Some were on the point of offering heartiest congratulations. At this moment of signal success, one of the onlookers drew attention to the alarming fact, till then unnoticed, that every time the shot came down and was returned and came down again, the great wheel moved a little slower, the lesser wheels moved slower also and in fact, the whole machinery was visibly slowing down. A look of desperate foreboding crept over the inventor's face. Could it be possible the model was losing power, or was it a mere optical illusion?

The crowd watched these developments with profound interest. Slower and slower the wheels moved until at the end of twenty minutes, they came to a dead stop, and Joseph H. Ridges' dream of perpetual motion, which was to make him a millionaire, came to a dead stop, too. It was then that he acutely sensed the fact that he was merely a poor, unhappy cohab. The toughs stood silent and dejected for a moment and then gave a shout of derision. Disappointed, chagrined, the inventor put the model, though a thing of beauty, away and never referred to it again. Perpetual motion exists in the sun, moon, and the stars, but was not found in the Utah Penitentiary.

In addition to two or three studies, I had during the autumn two classes in bookkeeping, making my fifth and sixth classes. They included the following named brethren: Charles Livingston, James C. Watson, William Blood, Alex. Bills, Aaron Hardy, Charles McCarty, and Joseph H. Thurber. During my imprisonment I earned, in teaching bookkeeping, the sum of $500.00, which was of material benefit to my family.

During my incarceration at the penitentiary, no special effort was made by the prison officials to encourage studious habits on the part of the prisoners. Aside from police duty, there was little for them to do, and so a great deal of valuable time was wasted which might have been profitably employed in reading and study if only they had had access to a good library. The cohabs were individually furnished with reading matter by friends from the outside. It would seem to be the part of wisdom to supply criminals with good books, for the purpose, if possible, of weaning them from a life of wrong-doing. A provision of this kind would certainly supplement the work of the gospel ministers who held divine services weekly at the penitentiary.

On November 3, 1887, I wrote as follows: "Three years have dragged their slow length along since I first entered the penitentiary as a convict. These thirty-six months, measured by the rate at which time seems to travel on the outside, were equivalent to about eight years."

I found it no easy matter at times to separate my early life from life in the penitentiary, not because of any similarity between the two conditions, but because of the difficulty experienced in going back in my mind to a time when I was not in prison. Then too, the monotonous aspect of prison life was simply terrible to contemplate. Variety, which is so necessary to the well-being of every individual, is unknown to the convict; one day so nearly resembles another in every particular as almost to create confusion in the mind. It might be said of an extended term in prison, that it is one long, tedious, never-ending day— a living death. Ordinarily a few years confinement breaks down the constitution and unfits a man for the duties of everyday life. The following lines from one of George Eliot's works so aptly describe the situation in a general way, that I venture to place them before the reader:

> There is something sustaining in the very agitation that accompanies the first shocks of trouble, just as an acute pain is often a stimulus, and produces an excitement which is transient strength. *It is in the slow, changed life that follows—in the time when sorrow has become stale, and has no longer an emotive intensity that counteracts its pain—in the time when day follows day in dull unexpectant sameness, and trial is a dreary routine;*—it is then that despair threatens; it is then that the peremptory hunger of the soul is felt, and eye and ear are strained after some unlearned secret of our existence, which shall give to endurance the nature of satisfaction.[18]

While walking the prison yard in solitary and thoughtful meditation, I often was profoundly impressed with the truth of a clause to be found in Theo. Parker's works, as follows:

> Every new truth of morals or religion which blesses the world conflicts with old notions, binds a new burden on the men who first accept it; demands of them to lay aside old comforts, accept a new name, endure the coldness of their friends, *and feel the iron of the world.* [19]

On the 1st of December, 1887, word came by wire from Washington that President Cleveland had acted favorably upon my application for pardon, but it was several days before I was released. On December 13, 1887, after a confinement of three years, one month, and ten days, I was released and came forth from the Utah Penitentiary a free man.[20] I will not attempt to describe the sensation that crept over me at the moment of release, but will merely say it was *glorious.*

Rudger Clawson

Aftermath

A little incident that transpired the day I left the prison might be of interest to the reader. Warden Brown, observing on several different occasions that I was engaged in writing up my journal, sent in word to me by way of warning that it was a waste of my time, a useless employment. He intended, he said, to seize the manuscript when I should be released from prison, and would surely destroy it. He hoped I would take the hint and discontinue my effort in that direction.

Thus was I put on my guard. From that day on until I completed the work in hand, as appears in this writing, I made a careful copy of every third or fourth page of the notebooks. I filed these duplicates away in the bottom of my trunk. The notebooks when filled were stripped of their covers, rolled up, and tied with a string. In this shape I passed them to my visiting folks from time to time as opportunity offered.[21] They were concealed in my trousers at the back just under the suspenders and, as the guard on duty in searching the prisoners simply felt of their side pockets, these rolls escaped notice. True, it was against the rule of the prison to pass my writings in this manner, and in the event of detection, exposed me to punishment, but the arbitrary attitude of Warden Brown furnished my justification. A sigh of relief passed my lips as, finally, the last roll went safely out.

When the day and hour arrived for my departure from prison, a guard stepped up to me and said, "The warden wants the key to your trunk as he finds it locked." I replied, "Tell the warden he cannot have it. I am sending this word to him because my time of imprisonment has expired." A little later I was ushered into the warden's presence. He said, "Mr. Clawson, give me the key to your trunk." I said, "What do you want with it?" "I propose to examine the contents carefully to see if there is anything contraband in it," he replied. I then said, "If that be your purpose, you do not need the key, for I tell you there is nothing contraband in it." The warden was growing angry and said in rather a vehement tone, "If you refuse to give me the key, I shall order the guard to break open the trunk."

"Mr. Brown," I said, "I know what you want. It is my journal. That is something that belongs to me individually, and is of little value to others. I think it would be unkind and unfair on your part to forcibly take possession of it. You are not legally entitled to it, and I warn you not to take it from me."

With increasing impatience the warden made another demand for the key, and I gave it to him. He opened the trunk and eagerly examined the contents. His eye finally rested upon the journal leaves I had purposely deposited there for him, and he seized them with great avidity. "I am sorry, Mr. Clawson," he said, returning the key, "but it becomes my duty to take over your journal." I again expostulated with him against this high-handed proceeding and left the prison.

It may be interesting to the reader to know that after Warden Brown was relieved of his official position, I met him one day on the street. "Mr. Brown," I said, "you are just the man I have greatly desired to meet, inasmuch as I have a special communication to make." "Yes, Mr. Clawson," said he, "what is it?"

"You will remember, Mr. Brown, my last hour at the 'Pen,' when you insisted upon taking forcible possession of my journal. Now, don't you think, Mr. Brown, really, that that was a contemptible thing to do, quite unworthy of the warden of an important prison?

"Mr. Clawson," he answered, "I very much regretted it but I felt it was my duty to confiscate your journal."

"Well, Mr. Brown," said I, "I wanted particularly to say to you that you didn't get my journal at all. The leaves you did get were prepared for you and you were, therefore, entitled to them. Furthermore, let me tell you, my journal is at home and if you will call in now or later I shall be delighted to show it to you."

Mr. Brown, chagrined and embarrassed, hastily walked away without further comment. Suffice it to say that had my journal been captured by the prison officials, I would have felt it to be a distinct loss to my library.

NOTES

1. In compiling the lists of the Mormon cohabs for the first quarter of 1887, Clawson accidentally omitted the following five individuals: Edward Schoenfeld was sentenced on 1 March 1887, for unlawful cohabitation, to six months' imprisonment and a fine of $50 and costs of $47.70 and was released on 31 July 1887; William H. Tovey was sentenced on 1 March 1887, for unlawful cohabitation, to six months' imprisonment and a fine of $25 and costs of $68.45 and was released on 2 August 1887; Thomas H. Morrison was sentenced on 1 March 1887, for unlawful cohabitation, to six months' imprisonment and a fine of $25 and costs of $30.40 and was released on 31 July 1887; R. M. Rogers of Pleasant Grove was sentenced on 21 March 1887, for unlawful cohabitation, to three months' imprisonment and released on 6 June 1887; and George Peay of Provo was sentenced on 30 April 1887, for unlawful cohabitation, to six months' imprisonment and a fine of $100 and costs of $75 and was released on 29 September 1887.

2. William Dalley and James Dalley, who entered the penitentiary on 22 March 1887 and left on 21 September 1887, both had fines of $300 and court costs of $59.90 and $114.45, respectively. Consequently, Clawson should have placed their names in the previous paragraph.

3. Henry Grow (1817–91) entered the penitentiary on 19 March 1887 and was released on 24 July 1887, but he did have to pay court costs of $117.10. Consequently, Clawson should have placed his name two paragraphs earlier.

4. George D. Snell (1836–1911) of Spanish Fork entered the penitentiary on 12 April 1887 and was released on 11 September 1887, but he did have to pay court costs of $50. Consequently, Clawson should also have placed his name two paragraphs earlier.

5. William Harrison (1828–95), who was the owner of a large hardware business in Salt Lake City, had three wives. He was excommunicated from the church about 1878 or early 1879 and with his three families moved from Salt Lake City to Provo in February 1879. He received a second patriarchal blessing in Provo on 6 February 1883, which probably indicates that he had recently been rebaptized into the church. Harrison entered the penitentiary on 21 March 1887 and was released on 20 August 1887. See *Deseret Evening News,* 7 January 1895.

6. John F. Hamilton (1830–92) had been in the service of the U.S. Army at Camp Douglas and then with several others organized St. Mark's Hospital in April 1872. See Ralph T. Richards, *Of Medicine, Hospitals, and Doctors* (Salt Lake City: University of Utah Press, 1953), 32–33.

7. Peter Wimmer (1842–1930) of Parowan was sentenced on 27 May 1886 to six months and a $300 fine plus costs of $191.10 for unlawful cohabitation. He entered the penitentiary on the next day and was released on 29 November 1886. Wimmer also served a second term in prison for adultery from 25 March to 25 April 1890. An account about Wimmer was included in MS I* after the 2 February 1887 account of Nathaniel V. Jones in the sweatbox, but because Clawson could not remember the exact date it was later crossed out. The following quotation about Wimmer is derived from MS I*: "While writing the above, I was reminded of an incident that occurred last fall. Peter Wimmer, a brother from Southern Utah, passed a night in the 'box' for what, in my opinion, will be considered a very trifling thing. One noon on filing into the dining room for dinner, bro. Wimmer, seeing no rations at his place, quite innocently appropriated one of two plates of meat and potatoes that were within reaching distance. The prisoner who sat next to him reported to the guard—the 'Earl' of Richmond—that he (Wimmer) had stolen his dinner. Protestation and denial were of little avail, so bro. Wimmer went into the 'Sweat' box, and came not forth again until the dawn of another day" (RC, Bx 2, Fd 7, MS I, 182–83). Clawson's memory is not quite right, since this episode occurred at breakfast on 2 November 1886 with Wimmer and the black prisoner next to him sharing what appeared to be an extra plate of food. When the new prisoner, James McDermott, protested, the head waiter came to the table and the disturbance was heard by the guard, Richmond. As a result at one o'clock they were both put into the two sweatboxes, making two in each box since that morning two prisoners had already been put there for fighting. Wimmer and the black man were taken out the next morning at 8:30 or 9 o'clock. See George C. Wood, Diary, 2 and 3 November 1886, Archives, Historical Department, Church of Jesus Christ of Latter-day Saints, Salt Lake City, hereafter cited as LDS Archives; George C. Lambert, Diary, 2 November 1886, LDS Archives; Joseph H. Dean, Diary, 2 and 3 November 1886, LDS Archives; and Helon H. Tracy, Diary, 2 and 3 November 1886, Marriott Library, University of Utah, Salt Lake City.

8. Ezra T. Clark (1823–1901) of Farmington was convicted of unlawful cohabitation on 17 February 1887 and entered the penitentiary on 21 February 1887, the day of his sentence. This change to the rougher conditions of bunk-

house number 1 would have occurred just a little over a week after his arrival. Clark paid his $300 fine and costs of $117.20 and was released on 20 July 1887. For newspaper reports of his trial, see Annie Clark Tanner, *A Mormon Mother: An Autobiography*, 3d ed. (Salt Lake City: Tanner Trust Fund, University of Utah Library, 1976), 85–92. Cf. Annie Clark Tanner, *A Biography of Ezra Thompson Clark* (Salt Lake City: Tanner Trust Fund, University of Utah Library, 1975), 35.

9. The following material from MS I* (which was later crossed out) continues Clawson's discussion of homosexual practices among the convicts: "Great blotches on a man's face ordinarily tell a tale to[o] horrible to contemplate with complacency. An evidence that some of them were guilty of practices that I shrink from naming may be drawn from the fact that one man was placed in solitary confinement on a very serious charge, viz., that of Sy" (the Rudger Clawson Collection, Manuscript 481, Bx 2, Fd 7, MS I, 188, Marriott Library, University of Utah, Salt Lake City, hereafter the Rudger Clawson Collection is cited as RC). Clawson here abbreviates the term *sodomy*.

10. Duncan McDonald from Butte, Montana, and Herbert A. Slade, a Maori from New Zealand, were brought before Judge Charles S. Zane on 23 April (not 22 April) 1887, and for the offense of "prize fighting" on the previous evening he sentenced them each to an imprisonment of thirty days and court costs of $36.35. They entered the prison that day, but were pardoned by Governor Caleb W. West seven days later. See *Salt Lake Tribune*, 24 April 1887; Wood, Diary, 23 April 1887; and Henry Reiser, Diary, 23 and 30 April 1887, LDS Archives.

11. While it may not exhibit good grammar or spelling, the following account provides another inmate's portrayal of the execution of Frederick Welcome (also known by his alias, Fred Hopt): "I felt as I never felt in my life. My feeling was So Depressed that I could not Eat My Breakfast. I walked the Yard. Soon after we were told if we Wished to Go and Speak to Welcome to be Brief. Most all went by his Door where he Stood and Shook hands with him. I went and he said Good by. That was the first time I ever Shook hand with a perso[n] that was going to the World of Spirits. All was prepared and at 1 o'clock we were looking up and wile we were Siting in our bunks with the Iron Bars Windows covered up with Blankets all at once Bang went the Guns and all was over" (George Kirkham, Diary, 11 August 1887, LDS Archives). Welcome was executed a few minutes before one o'clock with the five executioners using four live rounds. After his body was removed, John Adams "examined the place of execution and saw the fresh blood upon the ground and four ball holes in the adobie wall where they had struck after passing through the body of Welcome" (Adams, Diary, 11 August 1887, in private possession). See L. Kay Gillespie, *The Unforgiven: Utah's Executed Men* (Salt Lake City: Signature Books, 1991).

12. Clawson accidentally omitted the list of prisoners who were admitted to the Utah Territorial Penitentiary from May to June 1887: Gustav Anderson, Joseph P. Barton, Willard Bingham, James W. Burton, William Butler, Elisha Campbell, Samuel Carter, Ralph Douglas, William Douglas, John J. Dunn,

Kanute Emmertsen, Jens Frandsen, Hans Hegsted, Allen Hunsaker, Hans Jensen, Jens P. Jensen, William E. Jones, Peter J. Lammers, Peter Madson, Lars Nielsen, Alexander Orton, Hans J. Peterson, Lars C. Peterson, Daniel B. Rawson, Albert G. Slater, Levi J. Taylor, Joseph W. Wadsworth, William L. Walters, Jens P. C. Winter, and Samuel Worthen.

13. James C. Watson (1844–1906) worked as a guard on Main Street. His first prison term was from 9 May 1885 to 12 December 1885. The second term was from 11 October 1887 to 11 March 1888.

14. Charles Livingston (1835–1908) was sentenced on 14 October 1887 to six months' imprisonment and a fine of $100 plus costs of $75 for unlawful cohabitation. However, after sixty days he was pardoned by President Grover Cleveland and released on 15 December 1887.

15. James Welsh, who entered prison on 15 October 1887, is the last cohab listed by Clawson. The following thirty-five names need to be added to complete the list up to 12 December 1887 when Rudger Clawson was released: Rodney C. Badger, Peter S. Barson, Henry Beal, Andrew C. Berlin, Isaac Bullock, David B. Bybee, Charles O. Dunn, German Ellsworth, Isaac Farley, Richard Fry, Hans Funk, Nils Gyllenskog, Christian Hansen, Hans C. Hansen, Jens Hansen, Oluf Hansen, Peter C. Hansen, Thomas Henderson, Orlando F. Herrin, Rudolf Hochstrasser, Henry Hughes, John Jenkins, Fred Jensen, John L. Jones, Byron W. King, Ferdinand Oberhansli, Christian Petersen, Fred A. Petersen, Jens Petersen, Peter M. Petersen, Ralph Smith, Andrew Stromberg, John Warwood, William Willie, and Thomas Young. Thus, with the names given in the text of Clawson's memoirs and the associated notes, this makes a complete listing of the Mormon cohabs at the Utah Territorial Penitentiary during Clawson's incarceration.

16. Originally the account of the construction of a perpetual motion machine was the following single paragraph in MS I*: "Brother Jos. H. Ridges and a gentile prisoner by name of G. H. Carney are searching after the secret of perpetual motion and claim they have found it. The new power will be applied to the ordinary water wheel, under the title of the 'Self Power Machine.' At present (Novr. 15, '87) they are engaged in the construction of a model which will illustrate the new theory, and we await the results" (RC, Bx 26, Fd 1, MS I, 227b). This earliest account is significant because it contains the contemporary title for their waterwheel invention (the "Self Power Machine") and because it implies an equal partnership between Joseph H. Ridges and the non-Mormon George H. Carney. A marginal notation by Clawson in MS II[2] to "develop further" led to the more extended account of MS II[3]. In the present memoirs Clawson attributes to Ridges the announcement of the discovery of perpetual motion and uses the term *inventor* in reference to him. However, the actual 15 November 1887 "Article of Agreement" between Ridges and Carney, which was written up by Clawson, signed by both men, and witnessed by Clawson and Nathaniel V. Jones, clarifies their relationship. In this document the invention is called "The Self Power Machine," Carney is the inventor, Ridges is the builder of the model, and both parties to the agreement were to share any profits equally. The day of the trial run of the machine

occurred on 25 November 1887, according to a statement signed by George C. Wood and Francis M. Treseder (RC, Bx 15, Fd 1).

17. Since Joseph H. Ridges entered prison on 26 September 1887 and since Warden George N. Dow retired in October of 1886, it must have been Warden Otis L. Brown who gave Ridges permission to construct a model of his perpetual motion machine.

18. George Eliot (1819–80) is the pseudonym of Mary Ann Evans. The italic has been added by Clawson since it was so appropriate to his incarceration. This quotation is the opening paragraph of the second chapter of the fourth book of *The Mill on the Floss*, which was first published in 1860. Numerous English and American editions of this work have been published, though the best critical text is Gordon S. Haight, ed., *George Eliot: The Mill on the Floss* (Oxford: Clarendon Press, 1980), 241.

19. Theodore Parker (1810–60) was an American Unitarian theologian. His popular *Ten Sermons of Religion* was first published in 1853 and by 1867 had gone through five printings in the second edition. The italic has been added by Clawson. The quotation is taken from the chapter "Of Truth and the Intellect" in *Ten Sermons of Religion*, 2d ed. (Boston: Horace B. Fuller, 1867), 56; and in volume 3 of the Centenary Edition of his works edited by Samuel A. Eliot, *Sermons on Religion* (Boston: American Unitarian Association, 1908), 43. In 1886 Helon H. Tracy read aloud from Theodore Parker's works, while Clawson practiced his shorthand (Diary, 30 October 1886, Marriott Library, University of Utah, Salt Lake City). The 393-page second edition was read in 1887 by David John, who refers to the volume as the "Discourses" or the "Lectures" of Theodore Parker (Diary, 20 and 24 June 1887, Lee Library, Brigham Young University, Provo, Utah). There is no evidence that Clawson had any further contact with Unitarianism, even though Unitarians established their society in Salt Lake City in 1891 and Clawson lived until 1943. See Stan Larson and Lorille Horne Miller, *Unitarianism in Utah: A Gentile Religion in Salt Lake City, 1891–1991* (Salt Lake City: Freethinker Press, 1991).

20. Clawson gives 13 December 1887 for his release from prison instead of the correct time—one o'clock in the afternoon of Monday, 12 December 1887. He gives this wrong date both here and at the beginning of his large diary, which he began in May of 1891. The reason for this error seems to be that what was correctly riveted into his memory was the exact length of his incarceration and not the precise day of his release. Clawson added his total time—three years, one month, and ten days—to the date of his imprisonment (3 November 1884) and arrived at a date one day too much. That his release was on the twelfth is confirmed by the *Deseret Evening News* of 12 December 1887, the *Salt Lake Daily Herald,* 13 December 1887 (which was published each morning and refers to his release the previous afternoon), and the contemporary diaries of George C. Wood and his half brother, Hiram B. Clawson, Jr. William Yates, who had seen Clawson leave, reminisced: "I was really pleased to See Brother Clawson leave that old pen and once more enjoy his liberty" (Journal, LDS Archives).

21. Others used different methods to get their diaries out of prison. Thomas W. Kirby explains that the reason his diary ceases nine days before his release is that he had it smuggled out through the help of George Crismon (Diary, after entry for 30 June 1887, LDS Archives; cf. Dale Z. Kirby, "From the Pen of a Cohab," *Sunstone* 6 [May–June 1981]: 39). Other cohabs mailed their diary pages in letters to home and then wrote them up when they were released (Tracy, Diary, 20 March and 25 May 1886).

Rudger Clawson, age 7–8. (Courtesy of Special Collections, University of Utah Library)

Florence Dinwoodey. (Courtesy of the Utah State Historical Society)

Rudger Clawson and Joseph Standing (*seated*), 1879. (Courtesy of David S. Hoopes)

Lydia Spencer, about the time of her marriage, 1883. (Courtesy of Roy Hoopes)

Pearl Udall, about the time of her post-Manifesto marriage, 1904. (Courtesy of Elma Udall)

Rudger Clawson, early 1880s. (Courtesy of Roy Hoopes)

F. M. Treseder's painting of the territorial penitentiary, 1886. (Courtesy of the Springville Museum of Art, Springville, Utah)

C. R. Savage's photo of the territorial penitentiary. (Courtesy of the Utah State Historical Society)

F. M. Treseder's painting of the territorial penitentiary, 1886. (Courtesy of the Springville Museum of Art, Springville, Utah)

C. R. Savage's photo of the territorial penitentiary. (Courtesy of the Utah State Historical Society)

Prisoners in their uniforms, 1885. *Left to right*: Francis A. Brown, Freddy Self (non-Mormon), Moroni Brown, A. Milton Musser, Parley P. Pratt, Jr., Rudger Clawson, and Job Pingree. Someone has cut the head and shoulders of George H. Kellog out of the photo because he was a non-Mormon, but his feet and legs are still visible between Musser and Pratt. (Courtesy of the Utah State Historical Society)

C. R. Savage's photo of inmates in the territorial penitentiary. (Courtesy of the Utah State Historical Society)

Cohabs in the territorial penitentiary, 1888. *Standing, left to right:* Sylvester F. Jones, Simon T. Topham, Joseph S. Barney, Lorenzo D. Watson, Thomas Chamberlain, George Q. Cannon (*seated*), James H. Langford, Samuel W. Woolley, Samuel Bateman, Francis Webster, Cornelius McReavey, and John T. Covington. *Seated, center bottom:* Benjamin Perkin, William R. Butler, and Francis M. Lyman. (Courtesy of Special Collections, University of Utah Library)

Rudger Clawson, 1898. (Courtesy of Special Collections, University of Utah Library)

Rudger Clawson, 1912. (Courtesy of Special Collections, University of Utah Library)

PART TWO

Love Letters to Lydia:
A Selection of Letters from Prison

[3 November 1884]

I embrace you affectionately and say good-bye for a brief season. In haste, your loving husband,

Rud.

P.S. I am anxious to know how things are going at home both as regards yourself and Flo[rence], and if anything unusual occurs you must try and get word to me. Do not fail to give my *love* to mother and tell her that I am well and cheerful.

R.

[after 25 March 1885]

My dearest Lydia:

Another chance has offered itself, so I write you a few lines. How very much disappointed I was in not seeing you on Thursday, I do not care to say. It is certainly a very great hardship for a man's family to be denied the privilege of visiting him, but when the wicked rule the people mourn [cf. Proverbs 29:2]. Possess thy soul in patience, however, my dearest sweetheart, for this cannot last forever. We have no reason to be sorrowful and unhappy, but should rejoice continually, for it must not be forgotten that we are struggling to introduce and maintain, in opposition to the whole world, one of the most glorious principles ever revealed from heaven.

Two or three years imprisonment is nothing compared to the wretchedness that would result from dishonoring God in the least degree. Happy are we whether in prison or out of prison, whether in life or in death, so long as we are true and faithful to the Great Jehovah, and magnify His Holy Name in every act of our lives. Under existing circumstances two or three years appear to be a very long time, but when we remember that there is an eternity before us, they dwindle down to insignificance. Fret not thy soul, therefore, but lift up thy head and rejoice in the thought that up to this time we have been faithful to the great principle which will exalt us in the presence of God.

Those who denied you the privilege of coming to see me will receive a just reward. The measure they have measured to you will be measured to them again, pressed down and running over [cf. Luke 7:38]. When they are thrust into Hell and see their wives and children given to men more worthy than they, how then think you they will feel. Will not their torment be almost more than they can bear? I think so. This is undoubtedly their fate, lest they speedily repent and make restitution for the great wrongs they have done.

This present brief separation will knit our hearts firmly together in the bonds of affection and will cause us to look forward in anticipation to the joy and pleasure of our reunion. My love is *thine,* and thine is mine, and the thought comforts me. How very much I long to clasp thee in my arms and press thee to my heart. Can greater happiness be derived from any source than from the fond embraces of pure love? Not the love of the world, but love that springs from a pure heart.

And when our thoughts turn to little Remus, so pure, so innocent, so lovely, who has been sent from heaven to bless and cement our union, what reason have we to grieve and worry over a short separation? Hug and kiss him a thousand times for me, and may heaven watch over and bless you both.

Whenever you feel disposed to give way to sorrowful thoughts and feelings of unhappiness, read this and my other letter and know that I love you.

July 8, 1885
Utah Pen

My dearest Lydia:
Your note came duly to hand. I was surprised as well as pleased to receive it, for I did not suppose from the strictness of the rules that it would come through in the way you sent it. Our religious services Sunday were extremely interesting and you may be certain that we were delighted to see the folks from Salt Lake. I only wish it could be arranged for you to come out with them occasionally, but I very much fear they would refuse you admittance on the ground of relationship. They have the power, as we already know by sad experience, to keep us from seeing and visiting each other, but they cannot chain our

thoughts, which are free to roam the wide world over, and you may feel assured that mine are often hovering about you and darling little Remus, whom I love dearly. I regret to hear that he is not very well and pray kind heaven to bless and strengthen him that he may grow in grace and understanding, as well as large in stature, and become a shining light in Zion. He must take my place during our brief separation, and whenever your thoughts turn to me caress him fondly and affectionately, remembering always that if he is not his father, he is nevertheless the very next thing to him. His picture, which is as perfect a likeness as could well be taken, pleases me beyond expression, and evinces your thoughtfulness. I shall wear it constantly next [to] my heart, and in lieu of seeing him shall prize it very highly.

Sometime when you are feeling at your best, if your own picture were taken and sent to me, I should be very glad. If I cannot see and visit with you, if I cannot embrace and kiss you and if I cannot manifest my love for you in the *various other ways* which marriage admits and sanctifies, had I your likeness I could at least look upon those features which are so dear to me. I was very much disappointed in not seeing you on Thursday, but trust you may succeed in getting a pass before long. However, be of good cheer for whether present or absent I shall not forget thee. Send with my clean clothes a bottle of Insect Powder, some clean sheets and a pillow case.

With fond love and many warm embraces, I remain,

Ever thine,
Rud.

P.S.: It is reported here by some of the guards that Flo has had a divorce, but as you mentioned nothing of the kind, I presume there is no truth in it. You must keep me posted in this matter. I shall be glad to hear from you whenever you get a chance to write: I think it would be safe to send notes as you did the picture, which I did not discover until I went to put my shirt on and would have missed it then only could not get my arm through sleeves.

R.

July 24, [18]85

My dearest Lydia:

If I cannot see you and tenderly and affectionately embrace you on this a day of general rejoicing in the midst of the Saints, I can at least write you a few lines expressive of the love, the ardent love, I bear you. There is sweet consolation in the thought that this separation, so cruel, so hard to bear, cannot last forever; time inexorable time defies the power of man and swiftly and noiselessly speeds on, bringing nearer, still nearer, the day when we shall again be reunited in all the tender and fascinating associations of married life, in the fond look, the burning kiss, the fervent embrace—all sanctified by love, pure and noble.

This life would present but a dreary aspect without love, that mighty engine which curbs the passions of the human heart and ennobles, purifies, and exalts the soul of man. It is that mysterious power, which draws men and women to each other and binds them together in bonds the most pleasing and joyous, the most firm and enduring known to mortal beings. I cannot conceive of a more blissful and truly happy condition than where a man and woman dwell together in perfect love, and we have reason to believe that true and lasting happiness can only be attained by a permanent union of the sexes. The scriptures say: "The man is not without the woman, nor the woman without the man, in the Lord" [cf. 1 Corinthians 11:11]. Exaltation and eternal increase can never be secured, except by marriage in the New and Everlasting Covenant.

There are very many young people in Salt Lake, doubtless, who, when they see my condition congratulate themselves in not taking a course that would lead them into the penitentiary, but I have no regret whatever. If I shall remain faithful, I will inherit wives and children both in and out of the world, where others who rejected plural marriage because of the fear of imprisonment will be left wifeless and childless. It is true we are separated and the separation is painful, but if by this and other sacrifices made from time to time, we can secure an eternal association together, happy indeed are we. We should rejoice all the day long that such a prospect is held out to us. I do; the thought gives me much comfort, and should console you. I have already written so much about love that little space is left for other matters, but before leaving the subject I will say you little know how very much I should like to clasp you in my arms at this moment. I do not think I have forgotten how to manifest the love I feel for one who is dear to me.

Do not think I have forgotten the baby; my thoughts often turn to him and to his charming picture. I love him and pray for him and you constantly. Mrs. [Angus M.] Cannon brought word that he had been sick but is now better. I do hope that he will have good health in future.

My health is good. I was in the sweatbox a couple of days but am not injured a particle by the experience. It was unjust, but am on good terms with the warden now. I should love to hear from you and to know how everything is moving along. I wrote Stan [Clawson] a letter sometime ago; ask him if he received it. I would like an answer from him. Jim Watson has become a "trustie" and works on the outside. I think you could get a letter to me through his folks. See Hugh Watson about it. If Stan should write, send his letter that way.

I embrace and kiss you many, many times and also the baby and remain,

Truly and ever thine,
Rud.

Utah Pen
August 1885

My dearest Lydia:

I saw thee on the wall yesterday, and as I looked I *loved* thee, Aye! with all the tenderness and passion of a fond and devoted heart. Had my arms been long enough, I would have reached up, encircled you about with them and given you one of those warm and fervent embraces, with an ardent, glowing kiss such as thrills the very soul. My dearly beloved Lydia, your own heart will tell you that the love I bear thee is deep, broad, inexhaustible, and overwhelming, and when we are again united in those joys and pleasures of other days, you will be the recipient of more substantial tokens of my affection than anything that can be communicated by letter.

The joy and happiness growing out of the pure association of kindred spirits are indescribable, for they are only to be felt and comprehended by the inner soul. You know them and so do I; we are kindred spirits. Thou lovest me and I love thee, and in our mutual love we may expect to pass many quiet, happy peaceful days yet. Yea, as you stood on the wall with our darling baby in your arms, I fancied I could trace in the features of my own beloved sweetheart and wife the evidences of that love and enduring affection which I know burns in your heart for him who is thy husband.

Our separation is painful and full of anguish, but be of good cheer and ever remember that we are still young in years and full of life and animation. Time will roll swiftly away, and in our reunion, we will make our enemies to realize that they have utterly failed to crush out the love which burns in our hearts for each other and to separate and destroy us. Be humble, be prayerful, be patient, and all will be well with thee and me. When you come on the wall again and look down into mine eyes, call to mind the tender and overflowing love contained in this missive, and with the [opera] glasses, I will pierce thee through and through, lay bare thy heart and read there the affectionate and enduring love that I claim as my own. You may be a little surprised that I remained in the house so long yesterday, but I was not aware of your presence. I shall keep my eye open another time.

If I remove my hat from the head, it is a token of my desire to clasp you in my arms, to embrace you passionately and fondly, and to impress a dozen warm kisses on your lips. If you place your right hand to your throat as if in the act of buttoning your dress, I shall know that your heart swells with love and that you also greatly desire to be in *my arms* and to be *hugged and kissed fondly and passionately*. If my left hand goes into my left coat pocket, you will know that a very strong wish concerning you and myself burns in my heart—but I will not tell it; and if your right hand is carelessly placed on the wall just in front of you, I shall know that you have guessed my wish and share it with me. When I wave my handkerchief in the air, you will know that I often think of you in the silent hours of the night and wish that you could be with me. And if you transfer the baby from one arm to another, it will be an evidence that your thoughts also often turn to me and that my desire is your desire. A kiss thrown by the hand denotes my love for you but will not reveal one half or third part of that ardent passion. The kiss in return will be a slight manifestation of your affection for me.

And now my thoughts turn to the baby. He looked quite well from where I stood and appears to be growing rapidly. I must confess I love him dearly, and derive much pleasure from seeing him. Heaven bless and preserve you both. You must not expect to get many letters from me as I must necessarily act with caution and prudence. What I do not write, I will endeavor to make you understand by the signs and tokens mentioned above. Those slight movements of the hands and arms, while they may mean nothing to the guard, will mean *much— very much*—to you and to me, and will convey to each of us a volume of tenderness, love, and affection. Therefore, do not forget the *tokens*.

And now, my dearly beloved wife, I must draw this letter to a close, and say good-bye, but not until I have given you a hug and a kiss that you will remember for many a long day to come.

Ever thine,
Rud.

You can send me a letter through [James] Watson's folks with safety. I should love to hear from you.

R.

[on separate slip of paper]

An idea has struck me relative to the best method of communicating with you in the future. Get a valise to send my clean clothes in and have a secret pocket put in it somewhere, either under the lining on the inside or under the flap on the outside or wherever it would go unnoticed. In this way we can often get word to each other with safety. I have a valise at home but don't know just where it is, although I think Fred [Clawson] has it.

[August 1885?]

My dearest Lydia:

Thursday is past and gone and I did not see you. If you knew how much, how very much, my own beloved sweetheart, I missed your face and that of the baby's, you never for a moment could doubt my love. I was delighted and pleased to see the folks and enjoyed their visit immensely. That they refuse you a pass is the unkindest cut of all, but I do not and cannot reconcile myself to the suggestion made by mother (namely, that of remarriage), as it would undoubtedly be displeasing in the sight of Heaven. Your feelings, of course, are the same as mine on this point. There is nothing of a legitimate and proper nature that I would not do for the privilege of seeing you occasionally and oh! what would I not give for another such a visit as we had when last I was in the city.

Notwithstanding several miles intervene between us, I draw thee to me and embrace and kiss thee with all the fervor and passion of a fond heart. No matter what comes, know that I love thee and also know that I have not forgotten and cannot forget how to love. Could you be with me for an hour, a day, or month, a year, aye! forever, I would make thee to realize this confession as you never can realize it while we are separated. This is written in great haste but is nevertheless true.

I think you had better carry out my idea in relation to the valise; but be very careful. My own beloved Lydia, one fond and affectionate embrace, a passionate kiss, and then good-bye.

Ever thine,
Rud.

Do not fail [to] hug and kiss baby for me.

Utah Pen
September 9, [18]85

My Dearest Lydia:

I deeply regret to learn of baby's sickness and truly hope this note will find him altogether recovered. I also trust you are feeling better. You both have my constant faith and prayers. If what you say about yourself is true, it will be necessary to wean the baby before a great while, say in December, but above all things you must not worry, as that will make the baby sick if anything will. No matter what people may say or think so long as I am satisfied; I shall know that the *little darling* belongs to me, for how can I forget the circumstances which brought about such a state of affairs. I was there and you were there, and did I not fold you in my arms, and did I not press you closely to my heart, and did I not kiss you with all the ardor and passion of a pure and vigorous love? You may be sure that, if heaven blesses those fond embraces with a little stranger, I shall welcome him or her with open arms and a thankful heart. So do not worry *one particle,* but always remember that *we know what we know.* I must further caution you to be very careful of your health for, if you are in that condition, I would not lose it for the world.

In relation to the other matter, [I] must say that I do not and cannot feel that it is right we should be remarried by the law. It is a step that would bring reproach upon the Priesthood and, consequently, ought not to be taken. You seem to think that unless it is done, you cannot come to see me. A very offensive petition for better food, signed by most of the prisoners, was sent out to the warden recently. My name was not on it and as a result there is not so strong a feeling against me as formerly. By applying to the marshal yourself for a pass, I think you will be able to get one once, if not *twice,* a month. Try it anyway every two weeks.

Father and mother were just here, and I had a very pleasant visit with them. You speak of mother in your letter; she appeared to be feeling very kindly towards you and mentioned your visit at the house yesterday.

And now in closing I will say, my own beloved sweetheart and wife, that thine image is often in my mind. Yes, I think of thee most constantly and as I think I love thee. Were you in my arms at this moment, I would make you to know by warm embraces and passionate kisses what it is to be loved by one who loves as few men love. When I retire at night to my lonely couch, oh! how I miss thee. I have not forgotten and never can forget what a pleasant bed-fellow thou art and how delightful it is to sink into a sweet and peaceful slumber with thee, my dearest Lydia, in my arms. When thou retirest tonight, think of me and know of a surety that, were it possible, I should be with you and would bestow upon you all those tender endearments that can only be appreciated and enjoyed by those who keep sacred the marriage covenant. Know that I love thee and be happy. Drive grief and sorrow away and cultivate a spirit of calm resignation, for the time will soon come when we shall rejoin each other, and I will cause you to feel that you have lost nothing by the separation in a way and manner to thrill your very soul.

Kiss and hug the baby for me as you would hug and kiss me were I at home, and believe me I shall embrace and kiss you both in my mind's eye most tenderly and affectionately. God bless you.

Ever thine, thine forever,
Rud.

P.S. By the way, who is the young lady that is waiting for me? You have excited my curiosity and must gratify it. You say she is nice; your judgment is good. I believe you. Write her name on the inside of my shirt bosom next time. *Don't fail.*

Utah Pen
September 23, [18]85

My Dearest Lydia,

Time is rolling swiftly on. Why, just think of it, nearly a whole year has dragged its length along since I was admitted to this Paradise. Ere you realize it, my beloved sweetheart, I shall be a free man, full of life and vigor and all the fire of an ardent and overwhelming love. Ah! you can afford to wait with patience and cheerfulness for there are doubtless many happy, happy days ahead of us yet. And when we are again re-united, oh! I will show you what it is to be beloved. Will I clasp thee in my arms, will I draw thee very, very close to my heart, will I impress a hundred warm and passionate kisses upon thy lips? Will I do all this? Yes, I will, and not only once, twice, or thrice, but many times ere life ends.

We have great reason to rejoice, for has not the Lord greatly blessed us? We are now on the right track and He has preserved me from falling into the errors that some have committed since this crusade was instituted, and enabled me to endure with cheerfulness my confinement up to the present moment. I am happy in the thought and so ought you to be. If we shall but continue faithful, our future and eternal happiness is secured. Then away with mournful and gloomy thoughts and tears of sorrow and pain.

I cannot tell you how much I regretted to learn of the course taken by Bp. [John] Sharp. He was a man I always greatly admired, but it appears to me that he has made a serious blunder. I say this, too, after having been myself nearly a year in prison, being thereby competent to judge of the matter. Six months behind the bars is not a drop in the bucket compared with the unhappiness that must inevitably follow such a step. Rather than that Father should assume a similar position, I would prefer to hear of his death. These are my feelings, and I will not for one moment do Father the injustice to think that he will seek by any pretext whatever to evade the issue.

The marshal seems determined to humiliate us, if possible. I am today wearing stripes with a prospect of having my hair cut short and my moustache removed. They have, however, mistaken their man, if they think it annoys me one whit, why I rather like it. I laugh, oh! how heartily I laugh at them, and inwardly say: what fools these mortals be. The very thing they consider a disgrace is in reality a distinguished honor. So three cheers for the stripes! You will find that my heart beats just as regularly and just as warmly under convict clothes as under broadcloth and that I can and do love you with all the tenderness, affection, and passion that fired my soul a month ago. This may all seem impossible but only procure a *private* interview with me, my own beloved wife, and I will prove it to you in a manner to remove all doubt. Ah! you know I would, that merry twinkle in your eye tells me that you know I would.

How is dear little Remus, the pride of our hearts? He looked so charming from the wall Thursday. I felt that I must reach out and take him in my arms and kiss him a thousand times. He is the outgrowth of our love, and how pure and innocent he is. So is our love for each other.

And now I come to a close. As an evidence of my love, I throw my arms around you, and in doing so I place my lips against your lips and softly whisper,

Ever thine, thine forever,
Rud.

P.S. If you were to make a very small pocket on the inside of one of my garment legs down very near to the end, I think we could write each other with safety. I got the letter referred to in your last note, and this leads me to think they do not examine the clothes very closely. You did not tell me [the] name of young lady mentioned. Write it on the *inner bosom* of my shirt. How is it you have not been to visit me lately? Can you not get a pass? With many fond embraces and one fierce and overpowering kiss, I stop short.

R.

Utah Pen
November 12, 1885

My Darling Lydia,

I fancy you would like to hear from me, so I take this opportunity to write you a few words of love and affection. My health is good, hopes for the future bright, and spirits cheerful. But not withstanding all this, a shade of sadness sometimes—it might be said often—settles down upon my face. Now, you are curious, very curious, to know the cause of it, aren't you? If it were not so, your name would not be woman. I am half inclined not to tell you, as it is not absolutely necessary that you should know; still, upon second thought, if you will draw very near to my lips, I will whisper the secret into your ear. The shades of sadness appear, when I realize that you, my own beloved sweetheart, cannot be with me to receive all those deep, unbounded, and far-reaching manifestations of the tender passion, to which your own pure and enduring love justly entitles you, and which, as you well know, I so much delight to bestow upon you.

What, think you, is the wish of my heart at this moment? It is this, my darling, that you might spend one good solid month in my society. If the time did not pass away as a pleasant but fleeting dream, then indeed has love lost all its virtue and ravishing charms. But love is as grand, beautiful, and attractive as it ever has been; so you can safely trust yourself and baby to my keeping for thirty days. It is true, the accommodations are not very elaborate, the diet is modest, the weather is cold, and my cot is exceedingly narrow, but I promise to hug you so close to my heart and kiss *you* so often and so passionately that your whole body will be in a constant glow of warmth and you will never once think of the weather and will almost forget being crowded for room. As to the diet, I shall say nothing, if what has already been said is not sufficient. Only get permission to come and you [may] look for a right royal reception—just such a reception as a lover might look for from a lover, or, which would doubtless suit you a thousand times better, such as a fond loving wife might expect from an equally affectionate and amiable husband. I see you are delighted with the idea, but if you are compelled to decline the invitation, think of me occasionally and ever bear in mind, that, if I cannot have you with me, I at least have it in my heart to bestow upon you all the tender and exquisite love, accompanied with fond and gentle caresses, that your nature is capable of receiving in which is by no means insignificant.

I hope to see you and darling baby soon. Can you not work it to get a pass twice a month? At all events, be sure and have it plainly written on the pass that you are to see me alone. This is a very important feature of your visits. You know and I know that we cannot be ourselves and act natural towards each other with a guard present. An interview between a man and his wife *and a third party!* The idea is ridiculous, if not extremely absurd. Now you know how annoyed I shall be and I can imagine how very much disappointed you will be, if we shall be compelled to endure the presence of a third person, when next you call. A half hour's visit with you alone is worth more to me than a whole day with you in the company of others. My darling, I imagine I hear you say, "Those are my sentiments exactly." Then I say, woe unto him who shall step between man and wife even for so brief a period as thirty short minutes. However, lose not thy courage for the time draweth nigh—who knows how close it may be—when we shall again be to each other as we have heretofore been. You will then be the better prepared to enjoy and appreciate all those tender and melting endearments, which the law, stern and cruel as it is, deprives you of at present.

If you fail to kiss the baby again and again and again for me, you needn't look for a single kind word, a pleasant smile, or a fond caress from me when next we meet, for I shall deny you all these.

As is thy love for me, pure, strong, and constant, so is mine for thee. Be thou, therefore, happy and look to the future, which looms up bright and glorious. Good night and pleasant be thy dreams. As I retire to my lonely couch, know this, dearly beloved wife, that my thoughts are of thee.

Both now and forever, truly thine.

Rud.

P.S. This letter is not for publication. I shall be angry if it appears in the paper.

Utah Penitentiary
November 30, [18]85

My darling Lydia:

I now propose to write you a few lines in reply to your affectionate letter of last Thursday, which came safely to hand. It is always extremely gratifying to me to hear from you and our little darling, and to know that everything at home is moving along as smoothly as could be expected under present circumstances. There is nothing, I must confess, which would give me greater pleasure and happiness than to be certain that you, my darling, are in the condition referred to. If I love thee, dearest sweetheart, and who has the audacity to dispute it, what is more natural than that that love should be consummated by reproducing ourselves in children—heaven's most precious gift.

And when you say, Rud, I really and truly believe I am "enceinte," why if time and place were favorable, I would bestow upon you such demonstrations of love and tenderness as would entirely convince and satisfy you that all is right. I can well believe that you have not altogether forgotten the happy circumstances which brought about your supposed present state. It was at our last private interview. Oh! blissful remembrance! I bestowed upon you then, as I always feel to do, the melting endearments which pure affection invariably suggests. The fond and passionate kiss, the rapturous embrace—these were thine and thine by right, and if kind Providence should crown that love scene with another human life, no one in this wide world will be more delighted, and overjoyed, and grateful than myself.

And I can readily imagine what your feelings are outside of this vague fear of what some one may say or think about it. Beloved darling, I wish you would let this matter trouble you no longer, for if we are satisfied and happy in the reflection, that is surely sufficient. And in the auspicious event of a birth, I shall not be slow in claiming the little stranger, and in giving him or her a reception worthy of his or her parentage. Children are blessings of inestimable value, so I say by all means let them come along and be partakers of our all-absorbing love. And now while my thoughts are busy picturing the joy a new arrival would bring into our little home circle, if you will draw near and gently throw your arms around my neck, I promise that you will not regret it, for in the twinkling of an eye my burning lips would press against thine and speak in language tender and more affectionate than words: *I love thee, sweetheart, I love thee.*

You tell me that Millie is with you at present. I am very glad to hear it and trust you will keep her as long as possible. It appears to me that the extra work which could be done in this way would justify you in paying her a little something, and yet remove a good deal of hardship from your own shoulders. You really ought not to use the [sewing] machine at all under existing circumstances, as, providing you are in the family way, who can tell what the result might be?

You ask me if I would remarry Flo should she desire it. That is certainly a strange question to ask. Whatever put it into your head. You might have known that I could not answer it, for who knows what the future will develop. I can truthfully say this much, however, that I shall endeavor to do right—whatever that may be.

We have heard of the shooting of young Jos. McMurrin, and a frightful occurrence it was. [Henry] Collin, as you are doubtless aware, was brought to the Pen for safekeeping. Great excitement prevailed here this morning. The prison authorities evidently anticipated trouble, as the men were all locked up in the bunkhouses, and soldiers stationed just outside of the wall. The scare appears to be over, for all is quiet now.

One word more and I close. As you stood upon the wall Friday, I am sure you could see and understand how very much I desired to reach forth and clasp you in my arms and kiss you with all the fervency of my nature—just as I have kissed you many, many times in the past and just as I hope to kiss you again and again in the future. But alas! there was an impassable gulf between us—a gulf which will one day entirely disappear and then, and then—I will not tell you what is in my heart. The baby looked lovely from where I stood. I do not remember to have seen him act so positively cute. When you come again I shall take him from you and keep him here, I care not what you say. Good night, dearly beloved wife, and as you sink into peaceful slumbers this night think of him, who if it were possible, would be so near you that he could feel your heart throb against his.

As before so now and forever thine,

Rud.

Write the first chance you get, not in pencil but ink.

Utah Pen
December 3, [18]85

My darling Lydia:

It was a matter of great surprise and annoyance to me that you should take the position you did this morning. I was little prepared for it in one whom I love so dearly. Flo came here one day some months ago and asked what I proposed to do in the future. Of course, I could not say. She then continued: if you will not promise to do so and so, you must choose between us. I made my choice, and you well know the result. Today, like Flo, you asked, what do you propose to do after being released. Of course I could not say. You then said: if you do so and so, you must choose between us—almost Flo's exact words.

I had supposed that my course up to date would give ample evidence to you that I intended to do about right. And my letters of recent [time] have certainly exhibited the profound love and affection I bear you. But it seems I have not secured your confidence: you cannot trust me. I greatly regret it. And another thing, it is not at all pleasant to be threatened with what you will do under certain circumstances. It appears to me that it would be much better and a great deal more effective to bring love and affection to bear in seeking to obtain what you think are your rights rather than to use threats. I should have spoken a little more freely this morning only there were others present.

I close with love,
Rud.

Utah Penitentiary
April 16, 1886

My own dearest Lydia:

Bro. Lorenzo Snow, for whom I entertain the highest regard, desires me to convey to you his very best respects, and to say that language is inadequate to express his admiration of the course you have taken during the present crusade. Your devotion to principle and faithfulness to the marriage vow are, in his opinion, worthy of our "Mormon" women and a credit to the nation.

Ever thine, thine forever,
Rud.

Utah Pen
May 31, 1887

My dearly beloved Sweetheart:

The sun rises and sets, day follows day in slow but sure succession, and so the time will come when I shall be with you again, when our interviews shall partake of the utmost privacy. No guards will be present to check the natural outflow of affection. How sweet and precious is that thought! I can then bestow upon you those evidences of love—tender, thrilling, overpowering love, that your heart yearns after both day and night, and which is so well calculated to satisfy a woman's nature. What is wealth, what is fame, what is power compared to pure and unselfish love? Take love from the earth and life is robbed of half its value—yea more.

Dearest sweetheart, I fancy we are alone together: as you turn your eyes toward me with an expression of passionate love and gentle invitation, my arms steal around your waist, our lips meet, and you know the strength of a man's affection by the warm kisses and fond embraces that are showered upon you. Do you think this picture is overdrawn? Well, all I can say is only wait a little, be patient, and you shall see how completely I can satisfy your love. I know it is great, I know it requires a wonderful amount of affection, constant caresses, and tender endearments, but if your heart were as big as a mountain I believe that I could meet all of its demands.

I never could have believed that the time would drag as it does now [that] the time of my imprisonment draws to a close. The days seem to lengthen out beyond all endurance. And after all my invitations, you still decline to come and live with me. Why, you know not what you lose by living the life of a maiden. Were you to come, I would give you a reception such as you would scarcely forget in a lifetime. The past would soon be forgotten in the happiness of the present. Well, this much I will say that our present separation will only be a temporary loss to you, for I am holding in reserve for you such an outflow of love as will well nigh overwhelm you. You will then be ready to acknowledge that you hardly knew what it was to be *hugged and kissed* by him who has stolen your heart, and that if he doesn't know how to arouse a woman's love and secure her affections, no man ever did. I tell you all this that you may be prepared for those joyous moments that shall soon come to you, and which shall more than compensate for my long absence. Methinks I hear you say, "I am satisfied."

Love cannot altogether be expressed in words, so I close for the present, but not without throwing my arms around you and kissing you again and again.

Thine, yes *thine*, both now and forever,
Rud.

P.S. Whenever you feel unhappy, read this letter and look to the future. *After I have been home one month to a day, put this letter in my hands.*

A Love Message
Utah Pen
July 17, 1887

My darling Sweetheart:

Today is Sunday. The weather is pleasant. I am sitting out in the yard under the blue canopy of heaven, breathing the fresh and invigorating mountain air that comes sweeping down Parley's Canyon. My attention is first attracted by one thing and then another—by the convicts who are promenading on the Boulevard, by the magpies that hang in cages against the bunkhouse, by a young deer, an interesting and docile animal, that was brought into the prison a few days since, and then my thoughts turn to thee, beloved one! I say to myself, "So near and yet so far."

All that separates us from each other's society are the prison walls, and yet what an effectual barrier they present—an impassable gulf. Thou art mine and I am thine, but from all outward appearances we have no claim on each other. It is true, my darling, that I can see you occasionally, but not as a beloved wife, who is entitled to all the endearments that grow out of true love. No, I must treat you with comparative coldness, must act towards you in all respects like a mere acquaintance. Now this is certainly very trying to one's feelings, but the lesson is not without its good effect. Our experience of the last two and half years, though singularly difficult to endure, will be invaluable to us. We have learned to know ourselves and each other better, far better, than we possibly could have done, if things had always gone on smoothly.

Tests that have been applied to you and me and others of late tend to develop traits of character which inspire love and confidence, but which otherwise might never appear on the surface. Oh! what a great thing it is to find one to whom you can give your heart and feel that it is in safekeeping. Have we not succeeded in finding such one? Were we not born for each other? I think we were. Darling sweetheart, I looked upon thee Thursday afternoon in that neat white dress and stylish hat, and loved thee—aye, loved thee with all the intensity and fervor of true love. Was I contented to sit there, as I did, and simply converse with you on the common topics of the day? No, a thousand times no, but I longed to take you in my arms and smother your lips with kisses—burning, glowing, loving kisses. Not such kisses as are passed in friendship, but kisses full of fire, and magnetism. Such kisses, and only such, as would satisfy a woman's nature.

Do not I read your heart rightly when I say that a woman is by no means satisfied with a love that is tame and insipid, a love that manifests itself in polite and studied gestures, a love that lacks feeling and spirit? Yes, I know I do, and I venture to say that the only love which would fully meet the demands of your nature and disposition must be intense and fervid—full of vim, full of energy, full of ardor, full of fire and full of magnetism. If a man has not love such as this to give you, there remains a void in your heart and you are not satisfied. Ah! my darling! how well I can read you. You cannot keep your secrets from me. I will search them out. Write, sweetheart, and tell me if I have not laid your heart bare.

My love for you is all that I have just described, as you shall soon know. You will say, "I could not have guessed half the happiness that was in store for me." Only think—a few months hence, and we can enjoy each other's society in all the privacy that belongs to a quiet home, and then you shall know the strength of my love, and I shall know that of yours. You will then partake of all the joys peculiar to married life, and which are doubly dear to those who sanctify them by an upright life. Wretched and unhappy is that man or woman who seeks outside of wedlock for those joys and pleasures that rightly belong to it. Nothing is purer and holier than the relationship of man and wife when true love is the binding link, and nothing brings greater happiness to man or woman than such a union. The man without the woman or the woman without the man is incomplete. How often have we felt this to be true during the last 2½ years. Darling, "I need thee, every hour I need thee."

This letter is long but it don't tell half the story of my love for you, time only will do that. Keep a brave heart and be patient. The clouds will soon roll away and be succeeded by sunshine—bright and beautiful. Know this and be happy, that my heart beats for you constantly. I embrace and kiss thee and say, good-bye, sweetheart, good-bye.

Thine,
Rud.

P.S. Kiss the baby for me and write. I love to hear from you as well as to see you on visiting day. As an evidence that you have received this letter, and that you love me with all the intensity and fervor that a woman is capable of feeling for a man, wear a *black velvet bracelet* on your left wrist when you come to see me next Thursday. I shall be quick to notice if you have observed my request.

R.

Utah Pen
August 22, [18]87

Darling Lydia:

I fancy you hardly looked for a letter from me today. Nevertheless, here is one come to take you by surprise. You must not think, however, that I write merely for the sake of writing. No, I have something to tell you—something which, if it does not greatly astonish, will at least please you. I pause—hesitate—doubtful as to the propriety of confiding the secret to you. Can I, should I, trust you? Yes, I will, so listen: *Darling there is a good time coming.* It is not very far away, and you and I shall be there. The awful gulf that now separates us will have passed away like a dream, leaving us free to enjoy each other's society in all the privacy and sanctity of home. Then will follow, as time rolls on, those little love scenes so dear to your heart, and which you remember and which I remember with such pleasurable emotions.

What can be more precious to the young lover—and surely we are young lovers—than the fond embrace, the passionate kiss, and the whispered avowal of love. And then there is the thrilling language of the eye, which stirs the soul to its very depths and reveals the secrets of the heart. Well, when I speak of these things, when I tell you that only a few months separate you from such joys as those only can feel who are inspired by an intense, ardent, and pure love, can you any longer doubt that there is a good time coming?

Now, my darling, what shall we do until this good time comes? Why, do the best we can. You will come to see me occasionally, and I shall put my arm around you and kiss you; while the guard, as he stands there glaring at us, knows nothing of the love—the burning, glowing, liquid love—that lies beneath the surface of such cold formality. How very unsatisfactory in many respects these 30-minute visits are, and yet I know not how we could get along without them. The thought of having a guard present at our interviews—an intruder who steps between man and wife—annoys me at times almost beyond endurance. I feel as if I could pick him up bodily and fire him out of the window. This, however, is one of the many trials of prison life which must be patiently borne. Notwithstanding this disagreeable feature of my imprisonment, I love to have you come, I love to see you, especially when you look neat and chaste and modest as you most always do, I love to look into your face, every feature of which is so familiar to me, I love to kiss your lips, but just how much I love to kiss them I will not tell you, and I love to look into those eyes which fairly glitter and sparkle and beam with love for one who, I fancy, is not entirely unknown to me.

Now, dearest sweetheart, you will know when you come again, why it is I love to see you. I don't know that I ever told you before. I might go on and write volumes on the subject of love, which is inexhaustible, but I forbear. I clasp you to my heart, and kiss you with such ardor that you can scarcely catch your breath, and then I whisper in your ear the charming words, *I am thine and thou art mine*, good-bye.

Rud.

P.S. When you come again, and sometime during our visit, look me square in the eye and say "Pineapple," which will be equivalent to saying: Rud, my heart yearns with an intense yearning, for the caresses and endearments which thou hast promised me. I shall then say "Peach," which will be equivalent to this: Loved one, they shall yet be thine. Do not forget the meaning of the words; I shall not.

R.

Important
[the following postscript is written in shorthand]
After January we shall lie down on the sofa and go to sleep. At the end of a [quarter] [hour] you will come to wake me, dear, by kissing and caressing me.

Rudger Clawson.

[after 22 August 1887]

Lydia:

An opportunity offers and so I write you a few lines. The object of this letter is to call your attention to a matter of some importance. Read and consider attentively the postscript to my note of Aug 22nd. In that P.S. I made a simple request of you, asked you to do a certain thing and *you failed to do it*. You may be sure that I looked at you closely several times during our last visit and wondered if you would remember to carry out the request I had made—but you did not. Now, what am I to think? Shall I say that it was due to indifference on your part or that you simply forgot it? And yet how can I accept the latter view. In matters pertaining to the affections, to the heart, I had been led to think that you were never forgetful. Why, you have yourself told me so time and again. All the little commissions I have given you of late were attended to with the utmost decision and dispatch, but when it comes to a matter of vastly greater importance you actually forget. Ah! Lydia! Lydia! I don't think I should have forgotten; in fact I did not forget, but was ready to make the answer as indicated in the P.S. The two words that were to have passed between us were very simple in and of themselves, but they had a *significant meaning*. Well, well, let it pass, we'll say no more about it; it's a small matter anyway.

You remember I said to you a short time ago that I wondered if you would forget the many little suggestions made in my letters. I believe you replied by saying: Do I ever forget? At that time, I could not say that you did—but now—well, well, never mind. Of course, it would be unreasonable to suppose that one could remember every little suggestion that is made in a letter, and I have already made so many that I shall not blame you if you fail to carry them out. Good-bye sweetheart.

Thine,
Rud.

A Message of Love
Utah Penitentiary
September 7, 1887

My darling little wife:

Once more I sit down to write you a few lines of love and tender regard. I shall begin by saying that I read your last letter once, twice, thrice, yes, and more than that. Did it interest me? Yes, it did, because I knew that every word of it came from your heart, and when a woman speaks from her heart it counts for something. Yes, darling, I know that you love me; why, you could not conceal it from me if you would! Every glance of the eye, every movement of the head, every tone of the voice, every quiver of the lips, and every motion of the body reveals the secret. You are a little amazed at this statement, but why should you be? When a woman's heart swells with love—pure, chaste, and womanly love—her whole nature partakes of the emotion, and uses the eye, the voice, the lips, and the arms to give expression to it. If I should ask you, sweetheart, why you love me, you would doubtless say, "I cannot tell, I do not know, I am sure, but I love you." If you were to ask me the same question, I would say, "I love you, my darling, because I love you." We can give a reason for most things, but not for love. It is spontaneous.

You meet—by chance perhaps—a kindred spirit, and your very soul is drawn out to that spirit. There is something in his nature—a something indefinable—which responds to your own. His presence thrills your whole being with sweet and pleasurable emotions. Do what you will, you cannot resist the peculiar, yet to you fascinating and subduing, influence that emanates from him. He seems to be necessary to your very existence. You know not why, but you feel that you cannot live without him. Your love for him—an all-absorbing and overwhelming love—cannot be described by words, but is shown in a thousand little ways that a woman of tact has at her command. This, I take it, is *true love*, a love that dies not but lives forever, and as time rolls on grows into a bright and glorious flame. You tell me, dearest sweetheart, and I doubt it not, that yours is true love. Consequently, it must be similar to what I have just described.

And now, if we were together, I fancy that you would turn to me, and, with a most penetrating and searching glance, ask the question: "Rud, is not your love for me, also, true love?" I should then take you in my arms, and, after kissing you a dozen times with the most tender and passionate violence, whisper in your ear: "Yes, darling, it is true love." With love such as this, what can keep us apart? Naught, but the cruel hand of injustice.

For three long years the hateful walls of Utah's gloomy penitentiary have divided us, but the happy moment of our reunion draws near. Only a little while and we shall be together again, husband and wife, and then will I bestow upon you those loving endearments that fairly melt the soul with quiet and peaceful joy. The fond embrace, the thrilling kiss, and the whispered confession of love—of tender but vehement love—these, yes all these, shall be thine. Now, what excuse can you have for getting the blues? Think of the future and be cheerful, light-hearted, and gay. When you come again, let your face be wreathed in smiles and your eyes sparkle with joyousness; then shall I know that this letter has made you happy.

I do not propose to tell you how very much pleased and charmed I was with your visit time before last—the day Ida Smith was up. But this much I will say. You looked so sweet and attractive, all dressed in white, emblem of purity, that I felt like taking you in my arms and devouring you with kisses. I verily believe I should have done so had not we been so well guarded. You owe your escape to Warden Brown, whom you must thank for this act of heroism. If I could see you two or three times a week, I should be better satisfied than I am. Marshal Dyer would probably say: "Well! Well! I declare, one can never do enough for these convicts," but love is very exacting, you know.

Darling, I close this letter and say "good-bye," but ere we part I embrace and kiss thee again and again.

Though absent, yet ever thine,
Rud.

P.S. If you wear a black velvet ribbon around your neck on your next visit, I shall view it as a mark of that abiding love which you entertain for me. That which follows is not the least interesting part of this letter:

[the following postscript is written in shorthand]

My dearest sweetheart, as soon as I make love to you [so much] and so then you will have the opportunity to make love to me after January. And I doubt not that you will be equal to the occasion and allow my love in a way that will [gratify] me.

Rudger Clawson.

APPENDIX 1

The Families
of Rudger Clawson

Rudger Clawson
b. 12 Mar. 1857
d. 21 June 1943

1st wife	2d wife	3d wife
Florence Ann Dinwoodey	Lydia Spencer	Pearl Udall
b. 12 Aug. 1864	b. 13 Nov. 1860	b. 20 June 1880
m. 12 Aug. 1882	m. 29 Mar. 1883	m. Aug. 1904
div. July 1885	d. 1 Feb. 1941	released about 1913
d. 20 Sep. 1947		d. 7 Apr. 1950

Rudger Elmo	Rudger Remus	no children
b. 3 Jan. 1884	b. 25 Mar. 1885	
d. 19 Apr. 1898	d. 18 Nov. 1904	
	Hiram Bradley	
	b. 6 Nov. 1888	
	d. 10 Dec. 1975	
	Margaret Gay	
	b. 1 Sep. 1890	
	d. 25 Jan. 1985	
	Daniel Spencer	
	b. 26 Aug. 1892	
	d. 4 May 1893	
	Vera Mary	
	b. 28 May 1894	
	d. 13 Mar. 1897	
	Samuel George	
	b. 25 Sep. 1896	
	d. 16 Dec. 1942	

Lorenzo Snow
b. 21 Aug. 1898
d. 18 Apr. 1962
Francis Marion
b. 11 Aug. 1900
d. 28 Apr. 1901
Lydia
b. 11 Mar. 1903
d. 31 Mar. 1980

APPENDIX 2

The 1884 Prison Journal of Rudger Clawson

The Utah Penitentiary, which is situated at the base of the Wasatch Mountains about five miles south-east of Salt Lake City, will at present accommodate one hundred men. The prison proper is enclosed by massive adobe walls, not less than twenty feet high, which give a commanding view of every spot on the interior. The enclosure is large and spacious, and admirably adapted to the sports indulged in by the inmates. The walls are constantly patrolled by guards, both night and day, who are required to pass back and forth from the sentry rooms at least every fifteen minutes. They carry rifles of the latest improved pattern and keep a vigilant eye upon every movement that is going on below. At the slightest indication of revolt or attempt to escape, these guns are levelled at the convicts with telling effect, as it seldom becomes necessary to fire. Nevertheless, these men, many of whom are of a daring and desperate character, are almost constantly devising some scheme to effect an escape, of which fact I shall take occasion to speak hereafter.

At the west end of the enclosure, just outside of the walls and attached to them, is a two-story adobe building, which is occupied by the warden and family, and in which is located the kitchen, where all the cooking for the prisoners is done.

The prison proper consists of a lumber one-story building, rectangular in shape, divided into two rooms, with a door leading into each, one facing east, the other, west. Immediately attached to the west door is a small room occupied by a number of night guards, who are called on duty in addition to those on the walls.

The yard is illuminated after dark by three large lamps with reflectors, attached to the west wall at equal distances apart; darkness favors escape, while light acts as a detective. In both rooms, a bright light hangs from the ceiling during the long hours of the night and enables the guards, who, being heavily armed, are required to make a circuit of the building every fifteen minutes, to gaze in through the bars and see that peace and quiet reigns among the inmates. This precaution seems necessary and wise, as, in some instances, these desperate men have endeavored by digging under the foundation of the building, to escape the iron grasp of the law. Not a great while since, a number of the convicts had actually succeeded in effecting an underground passage from the building, and were on the point of making an opening through the surface on the outside, when, much to their dismay and horror, they learned that the guards had discovered all and were anxiously and impatiently waiting for the first man to show his head above the ground, when, it is strongly believed and with good reason too, he would have been instantly shot dead. Suffice it to say that no head ever appeared.

The west room is a little larger than the east, and will hold (I'll not infringe upon the truth by using the word accommodate) about sixty men, who are crowded together, when standing on the floor, like so many cattle in a box car. The beds in both rooms are arranged pretty much the same as on board a ship in the steerage department; viz., there is a tier of bunks constructed of rough lumber, standing about two feet from the floor and running around three sides of the room. Immediately above this, there are two other tiers situated at equal distances, but not allowing sufficient room to stand erect. Mattresses of straw are placed in these bunks, and two men throughout are delegated to occupy the same bed, each man being allowed two pair of light blankets by the Government.

It might not be amiss to remark that in the winter season the prisoners, being denied the use of a stove, in many instances suffer extremely from the inclemency of the weather. In one corner of the room is located what in prison parlance is termed the "Dunnigan," which is kept in a filthy condition, and constantly emits odors rank as death. It might be said, with strict deference to the truth, that there is a degree of filth and a general air of uncleanliness connected with this prison that is positively revolting to a person of refined habits. Winter life in the Utah Penitentiary, it is generally conceded, is far preferable to summer; in the latter season the place fairly swarms with vermin. It is marvelous but nevertheless true, that bedbugs may be gathered up from the bedclothes by the handsful, and some of the men have actually written their names on the wall in blood extracted from these pests. The constant scratching indulged in by the convicts indicates fully that bedbugs are the least of two evils. "Truth is stranger than fiction."

All of the most desperate and depraved characters are confined in the west room, and comprise: ten or twelve murderers, numerous horse thieves, highway robbers, burglars, one or two rape cases, petty thieves &c.; such a company, at least, as one would scarcely care to mingle with for any length of time.

Having been convicted of the alleged crime of Polygamy, I was brought to the Utah Penitentiary Nov. 3, 1884, arriving here shortly after dark. Partaking of a few mouthfuls of supper, I was at once conducted (and as I believe by special order of Marshal Ireland) to the west room of the prison. Upon reaching the door and while the guard was busily engaged in unlocking it, my ears were saluted with the most appalling noises, such as it has not been my misfortune to hear in a great while past. They were evidently intended as a sort of intimidation; I caught such expressions as, "a fresh fish," "bring him along," "we have been waiting for him," "will someone get a rope," "lynch him, lynch him!" The bolt dropped, the door swung on its hinges, and I was ruthlessly pushed into this motley crowd. The scene that met my curious gaze, time will not efface. Here crowded closely together, with barely room to pass one another, were about sixty men and boys of the roughest and most degraded character, smoking, chewing and spitting tobacco juice, swearing and cursing in a loud and boisterous manner, and ripping out such shocking oaths as to cause the blood to curdle in one's veins. Many of the men were heavily ironed, and what with the clanking of chains as they walked to and fro and the general uproar and confusion, such a feeling of horror and dismay was fastened upon me as the pen cannot describe.

After I had grown somewhat familiar with my surroundings, one of the fellows approached and rudely asked if I could sing. Upon answering in the negative, he further asked if [I] could dance. Again answering no, he asked if I would put on the gloves and take a turn with one of the boys. This I consented to do, but the gloves having been left outside, it was suggested that I be thrown up in a blanket. This proposition seemed to meet with considerable favor until one of the boys judiciously remarked that there was no occasion for such haste, that there would be plenty of time to initiate him, and favored the idea of letting it go until the following evening, which was accordingly agreed to. The following evening, so far as my presence in that room was concerned, never arrived; good fortune favored me, and I was moved into the east room, thus narrowly escaping some pretty rough treatment and successfully eluding those who had set their hearts upon the joys to be derived from initiating a "fresh fish." The cursing and swearing that occurred in the west room, when evening came, and I was found missing, is unparalleled I think in the history of Utah.

Nine o'clock having arrived, the time for retiring, I slipped into bed with a fellow from Ogden, whose every movement and appearance and even language indicated that my companion was a tramp of the purest breed. The room was full of noxious tobacco smoke, having but little chance to escape; many of the prisoners were hawking and spitting from their bunks out on to the floor all night long, and an odor issued from the "Dunnigan" almost sufficient to induce strangulation. Such surroundings as these did not, it may justly be said, bring many moments of rest to my weary soul this first long night in prison.

The east room is occupied by about thirty convicts who indulge in all the habits of vice which characterize the west room, but are not considered dangerous. In this room I spent the best part of a week, a portion of the time occupying the same bed with Bro. Joseph H. Evans. I at present pass my nights in the room formerly used by Belle Harris, and latterly by Nellie White, and just opposite to the apartment in which Lydia Spencer was confined.

It is a small room (perhaps 10 x 13) attached to the building occupied by the warden, with one window heavily ironed facing the north, thus forever excluding the sunlight. The door which is made of lumber is secured by a long iron bar, running horizontal with the floor and fastened by a padlock. The furniture consists of an iron cot, table, carpet, rocking chair, and stove, all supplied by myself. After undergoing the hardships incidental to life in a dungeon, the ease and comfort experienced in my new quarters have a salutary and benign effect upon the soul. I retire to this apartment at six o'clock in the evening and emerge at six in the morning; during the day, I mingle with the convicts within the walls, studying character, reflecting upon the vicissitudes of life, conversing with Bro. Evans, reading, &c., &c.

One of the vicissitudes of life, which has made a lasting impression upon my mind and which strikes me as being extremely inconsistent, is this: I am sent here to endure all the horrors of prison life, because, as it is claimed, I have entered into the practice of plural marriage, which consists in simply taking the same course as did old father Abraham, Isaac, and Jacob, and, as I firmly believe, the Lord Jesus Christ himself, viz.: the marrying [of] more than one woman, acknowledging and treating them as honorable wives, rearing and educating the children that spring from such unions, and otherwise conducting oneself as an upright husband should do. If this be crime, what then is virtue? On the other hand, those who sent me here, many of them, are guilty of the gravest sexual crimes, among which illicit intercourse is not the least. A case of abortion recently occurred in Salt Lake City; the party who committed this heinous offence, violating the laws both of God and nature, is today walking the streets, breathing the air of freedom, the grand jury having totally ignored the whole affair.

The dining room will next engage my attention. This is a one-story frame building, about 40 x 15 ft. in dimensions. It is arranged with a sort of table, or shelf, attached to the inside wall and extending around the entire room, with a stationary bench just below. There is a large circular heating stove in [the] center of [the] room, as also two long rectangular tables. It is here where the convicts take their daily meals, three in summer and two in winter season.

To see one hundred rough, rude men gathered together, as in this place, and eating with a vehemence that is startling, is a rare and unusual sight. Every seat is occupied, while those who eat at the long tables are obliged to stand. The utmost confusion prevails at every meal, and while some quietly and uncomplainingly partake of their daily rations, others indulge in the most boisterous and profane language, finding fault with the food and severely criticizing the cook.

At the beginning of each month, eight or ten men are delegated to act as waiters; just prior to a meal, the room is cleared of any loiterers who may be hanging around the stove, whereupon the waiters at once proceed to the outer gate, through which the food is passed, and returning with same, dish out to each prisoner a given quantity, a tin plate, knife and fork, spoon and tin cup being allotted to each. It is amusing to watch the movements of the boys outside, while the waiters are busily engaged within. They gather around the closed door like a pack of famished wolves, impatiently awaiting the moment when they may be allowed to rush in and devour the steaming victuals. When that moment arrives, the pushing, the surging of the crowd, the tramp of many feet as they stream into the building are indeed strange and bewildering to a newcomer.

The food comprises boiled beef and gravy with potatoes, vegetable soup of a thin and weakly nature, hash endowed with great strength, dry bread, tea and coffee of the blackest hue; hash and soup being served every alternate day. This diet continues throughout the year, except at Christmas time when a good dinner is provided. A tub of meat or soup and one of potatoes, a bushel basket of bread, sliced, and two very large cans of tea or coffee suffice for a meal, and will feed one hundred men. I am informed that about eighty large loaves of bread and eighty pounds of meat are consumed each day.

A fact perhaps not unworthy of notice is this. At every meal each man is entitled to three or four large slices of bread, a supply which is seldom all eaten at one sitting. Whatever remains is reserved for future use during the day, and that brings me to the point. Scarcely a moment passes between meals, but there may be seen a large number of convicts, gathered around the stove, engaged in toasting bread, as follows. Each man has one or more slices in his hand, which, after being thoroughly moistened with hot water, is plastered upon the stove, which is circular in shape, bulging at the center. The water cements the bread to the stove, and in this way it is thoroughly fried on one side, then turned over. I leave the reader to picture in his mind the scene that is presented to the eye, while this process is going on. It might here be added that bread cooked in this style is held to be a great delicacy among the prisoners.

The convenience and comfort that may be derived from the use of a knife and fork at meals were suddenly denied us a short time since. It is a rule of the place, that, immediately after each meal, the knives and forks must be returned to the warden by whom they are carefully counted. This precaution is taken that none of the prisoners may be provided with the means of possible escape. Suffice it to say that a knife and fork were recently retained by an unknown person, and as a result we are now (Nov. 24, [18]84) and have been for some time past deprived of these very desirable and in fact indispensable culinary articles.

It is a great hardship, as every person of taste and culture will readily admit, to sit down to a meal without knife or fork, especially when a large tough piece of boiled meat is to be eaten. There is a grim satisfaction, however, in the circumstance that we are still permitted the use of a spoon. I learn that the missing knife and fork, which had evidently been buried in the earth with evil intent, have been recovered, but this fact has not as yet in any way benefitted the convicts at large, who are still obliged to eat with their fingers. It seems highly unjust that all should be made to suffer for the misconduct of one, but such is life in the Utah Penitentiary.

The dining room is not only devoted to eating purposes, but also serves as a sort of workshop. A number of the men are industrious and studious, while others, and by far the greater number, are extremely indolent, and, as it appears, good for nothing. While some are diligently pouring over their books, others again are engaged in the manufacture of hair bridles and riding whips; one man devotes a good deal of his time to making miniature ships; another, carved photograph frames; and still another aspires to be an artist, as may be witnessed by the numerous landscape scenes that adorn the walls, and has, it must be admitted, achieved some little excellence in this direction. But, after all, hair work seems to be the specialty that characterizes this prison. While the convicts are engaged in their various occupations, there [is] a constant noise and uproar, caused by loud and boisterous talking and the shuffling of feet, that is extremely harsh and painful to the ear.

The amusements indulged in are many and various in their nature, such as baseball, marbles, checkers, chess, and last but not least card playing. The day that appears in the eyes of the prisoners best suited to ball playing is the Sabbath. This fact I have gathered from observation. The game is entered into with a great deal of vim, and as a result is accompanied with much noise and confusion. The distinguishing feature of this, as well as all other amusements, is profanity and low vulgar language.

Men of thirty and thirty-five years of age seem to derive a vast amount of pleasure from the simplest games in marbles, such, in fact, as would ordinarily entertain a boy twelve or thirteen years old. This is indeed singular but true. The aspirations of such characters, it will be justly perceived, cannot be very exalted; their thoughts do not soar high, but are of a low and groveling nature. More than this, many of those with whom I am compelled to associate or mingle are so steeped in crime, as at this moment to be suffering from severe private diseases.

I will here remark in a general way that those who are not secretly devising some means of escape are actually perfecting plans for further depredations when released; quite a number might be mentioned who are even now serving second and third terms. Upon mature reflection I feel justified in saying that, in nine cases out of ten if one term in prison fails to show a man the error of his ways and lead him back to a virtuous life, he will eventually be laid in a criminal's grave.

One of the most popular amusements of the place, however, is card playing, and in this connection gambling is freely indulged in; consequently, considerable money and large quantities of tobacco pass from hand to hand. It is but natural, after all, to look for such vices here as may be found in our large cities and which are by custom made fashionable.

It might be very properly asked, what means are employed to keep the large numbers of convicts confined here, in subjection? There are many ways by which this end is attained. A special object of terror to all is the sweatbox, appropriately so named. It is a sort of cell, standing alone from the main prison, and exposed to the scorching heat of summer and chilling blasts of winter; [it] is constructed of lumber, with an iron cage inside, being about six feet in height, six in length, and three in width. Men guilty of offenses are often thrust into this cage, and there confined sometimes twenty-five or thirty days, according to the enormity of the misdemeanor. I am credibly informed by those who have undergone this punishment, that in the summer the heat is so stifling and oppressive as to be almost unendurable; while in the winter the cold pierces one's limbs through and through, not admitting of a moment's rest. Those who are unfortunate enough to get into the "box" are allowed no bedding whatever and subsist entirely upon bread and water. In fact a man but just recently emerged from this place of punishment, who had passed ten solitary days and nights therein, shivering with the cold; and I draw the conclusion that, as he is now burdened with a ball and chain weighing 18 to 20 lbs., he must necessarily be regarded as a dangerous case. He left his companions strong and robust, but returned alas! pale and emaciated. His general demeanor, however, denotes a man of stubborn and unbending will, and in this respect he manifests characteristics worthy of a better cause.

Another and later case is that of a man by name of Jno. Smith, who passed two days and nights in the "box"; but, if all I hear is true, he has had ample opportunity heretofore of becoming familiar with this sort of experience. It is generally admitted in the yard, and my observation confirms the fact, that he is extremely unruly and hard to handle. Being strong and active, it required the strength of four powerful guards on one occasion to incarcerate him. While in confinement his chief delight, apparently, is to make all sorts of unearthly noises, such as attend cursing and swearing, boisterous laughter, singing on a high key, bellowing in imitation of cattle, barking like a dog, and striking the cage with the chains that adorn his ankles, which, as indeed they well might, greatly disturb and exasperate the guards. By way of correction, the night being quite chilly and the air being rent with the usual noises from the sweatbox, the door was suddenly thrown open and eight or ten buckets of ice cold water were dashed in upon him, completely drenching his body and clothing, and wetting the floor sufficiently to require his standing up all night. At the thought of such treatment, a shudder creeps over my whole frame, and I instinctively open the stove door, stir up the fire, and add more fuel.

I am witness of the startling fact that this fellow actually emerged from the "box" with a cheerful and smiling countenance, thoroughly unconquered, thus exhibiting an interesting phase of human nature.

Men will sometimes endure the greatest hardships with a stubbornness and defiance that are indeed surprising.

A few words relative to Smith's crimes. It is said that he is here now awaiting trial on a charge of having "held up" and robbed a passenger train on the Utah and Northern R[ailwa]y. He was the only one, it appears, engaged in the undertaking and displayed considerable personal bravery. Suffice it to say that he met with admirable success in every respect, except in the trifling matter of eluding the officers of justice. It now turns out that, notwithstanding the fact of his having exhibited an unusual degree of intelligence in robbing the train, he is hopelessly insane. It must be remembered, however, that this man is awaiting trial for an offense, which carries with it a severe penalty; and it is believed by many of the guards, if not the warden himself, that insanity has simply been assumed to evade the stringent punishment following conviction. My first impression of the man was that he must undoubtedly be crazy, but, after close and careful observation, I have discovered what appears to be a sort of "method in his madness." At least it may be said that the general characteristics of insanity are not visible in this man's face. It is admitted on all sides that, if he be indeed sane, he is a sharp, shrewd fellow. He is now, and has for a long time been, heavily ironed, but has succeeded a number of times, I am told, in cutting them off, which in itself is no small undertaking.

The facilities for bathing here are very limited, so limited indeed that, if one should desire to indulge in the pleasures of a bath, he must do so in the open air, thus becoming subject to the curious gaze of the "crowd." The so-called pleasures are conspicuous for their absence, and it might be added that, cold weather interfering, bathing has become somewhat unpopular in the Utah Penitentiary, and consequently is not freely and generously indulged in at this season of the year. It is indeed a curious spectacle to see a man in the open air floundering around in a tub of water, sitting down, standing up, leaning over and introducing all the movements that accompany a bath. So much for cleanliness behind the bars.

Men, upon whom the death penalty has been passed, are confined in what is termed the "condemned cell," which resembles the sweatbox, being however considerably larger. Just prior to execution the condemned passes his time in the presence of two or more guards, who keep a vigilant watch over him night and day, and is denied nothing except liberty. It is a standing rule, I believe, that his every desire must be gratified until within a few hours of the end. In this place of retirement Fred Welcome passed the weary hours away, while recently under the death sentence. It will be remembered how very nearly he approached the grave in expiation of his terrible crime; the reprieve, which has delayed the execution for a few short months perhaps, arrived just forty minutes before the fatal moment. The time had gone so far in fact that all his prison companions had passed through the cell, one by one, shaking hands with and bidding him a last farewell. I am informed that he was calm and collected, betraying not the slightest sign of nervousness.

This man, who from the first expressed a strong disbelief in a future life or punishment after death, when brought face to face with the grim monster, freely acknowledged that he thought there must be a hereafter and that he would be required to appear before his Maker. But, strange to say, immediately after the reprieve arrived, he took his former position and is now as atheistical as ever. After some thought, I am led to the conclusion that men who are guilty of heinous crimes and who fear the vengeance of a just God, very often persuade themselves, against the will, that with death one becomes extinct, vanishes away. But alas! such a mild fate awaits not the man who sheds innocent blood.

Fred Welcome bitterly denounces the whole "Mormon" people, who, he claims, are using their means and influence to have him executed. His general demeanor and actual statements indicate that an opportunity to slay the "Mormons" in wholesale lots would afford him an infinite amount of happiness. This feeling doubtless arises from the fact that the father of the man whom he slew in cold blood is a "Mormon." However, the "Mormon" people, and I might add the world at large, will not seriously regret the departure from this earth of such men as Fred Welcome.

"Honor among thieves" is an old and familiar saying, but a few weeks experience in the Utah Penitentiary has demonstrated to my entire satisfaction that this expression was never intended to apply to my companions in misery. Honor in any sense seems to be entirely unknown here. If in unity there is strength, in division there is weakness. A hundred men, united together and working to the same end, could accomplish wonders towards effecting an escape from within these walls, but, strange to say, there are many tale-bearers among the convicts, who, to gain favor with the guards and the warden, constantly betray one another; and such characters, as is too often the case, seldom adhere strictly to the truth. The base treachery daily exhibited among these fellows is extremely repugnant to one's feelings. It would be very unwise and imprudent, and I will add wrong, to encourage or assist in an attempt at escape, but, on the other hand, to betray the confidence of others, when accepted even in a bad cause, is worthy of the severest condemnation.

It would not be out of place in this connection to mention the constant thieving that is being carried on. Indeed, a man's only safety lies in a good strong padlock. "A thief is a thief the world over," and he who will steal on the outside of a prison will be very likely to steal on the inside. Men's underclothes often mysteriously disappear from the line and are sometimes discovered on the person of a boon companion. My revered friend, Bro. Evans, in thrusting his hand into the pocket of his pants one morning recently at once detected the absence of a purse, containing two half sovereigns. During my first night behind the bar, I lost a good handkerchief, which, however, was afterwards recovered; the guilty party now wears a ball and chain on the right leg and also a gloomy aspect on his countenance. He is the same party by the way who robbed my residence last summer of abt. fifty dollars worth of jewelry, for which offence he is now serving a term of twelve months. The jewelry was also recovered. That he should rob me in the city and afterwards in the penitentiary is a curious incident; but, after all, life is full of strange coincidences. In looking for a towel belonging to me this morning, I discovered that it had silently disappeared, had perhaps taken a trip on attorney [Charles S.] Varian's underground railway. My reputation, I fear, will next be stolen away, and then I shall indeed be undone. Already, in the estimation of a great many of my companions, I am a thoroughly bad man, but those who have passed judgment upon me, failed to first apply to themselves that passage of scripture which speaks of the mote and beam [Matthew 7:3].

Many are the ways in which the convicts endeavor to break away from prison life; as for instance, a short time since four desperados conferred together and proceeded to execute with boldness the following plan of escape. Repairing to the dining room, which has already been described, they immediately detached from the ceiling two long rafters and with short cross pieces soon manufactured a ladder. While this was going on and to guard against betrayal, every man who came into the room unsuspectingly was compelled to remain, being threatened, if he attempted to withdraw, with instant death. Everything finally being in readiness, the four men passed out of the room, glided swiftly across the yard, placed the ladder against the wall and in the twinkling of an eye disappeared. The guard on the wall, being far advanced in life and not very active at the best, gazed upon the proceedings in wild excitement, and called after the men several times, but failed to fire. The sequel may be summed up in a few brief words:

one of the four, in dropping from the wall on the outside, sprained an ankle and was consequently unable to continue the flight; the other three rushed with great precipitation into the arms of a guard who happened at the time to be out in the garden.

Thus were they all captured. Finale: the unhappy four are now heavily ironed and are sadder if not wiser men. A little forethought would teach a man, it seems to me, that these hair-breadth escapes from death and fierce struggles with guards, &c., might all be avoided by leading a correct and proper life and thus being independent of the law. But human nature presents many singular phases to the gaze of the curious observer. Why cannot men see that it does not pay to violate the just laws both of God and the land, and thus throw them-selves open to a loss of liberty and severe punishment. There is not a man in this prison, however hardened, who does not feel the disgrace of it, and when taken out to work will draw his hat over his eyes, if a stranger chance to pass by, to escape possible recognition. A convict, whose term is two or three years, remarked this very day (Dec. 1, 1884) that rather than his aged mother should know the whereabouts of her son, he would willingly serve a sentence of ten years. Two thirds of all the men in this prison came under assumed names. This leads me to the conclusion that Satan has great hold on the hearts of the children of men, many of whom willfully do wrong, realizing the terrible con-sequences, but stifling the still small voice of conscience.

Every few months the prisoners are subjected to a thorough search, and any article being found that would aid in an attempt to escape is, of course, confiscated. When this proceeding takes place, the men are all driven like a herd of cattle into one corner of the yard, and closely watched by a guard on the wall. They are then called out, two and two, and repair to the dining room, where they are compelled to strip in the presence of two guards, who examine their clothes with the keenest scrutiny, after which they proceed to another corner of the yard, and so on until all have been inspected. The dining room and dungeon next receive the attention of the guards, who peer into every box and turn the beds upside down; the yard is also closely examined for instruments of danger buried beneath the surface. The last great search was very complete, and resulted in the capture of a number of pocket knives and other less dangerous articles.

It now becomes my unpleasant duty to record the first fight that has occurred since my incarceration. We were all busily engaged, a few mornings since, in disposing of our regulation breakfast, when with all the suddenness of an earthquake a mad rush was made for the east end of the room, where a fierce and desperate struggle ensued. The excitement became intense, when it was discovered that two of the men were pummeling each other with "intent to do bodily harm." By standing on a chair I succeeded in catching a glimpse of the struggling combatants, who appeared to derive great encouragement from such expressions by the crowd, as "let them alone," "go it, boys," "stand back," "that's it, strike him hard," "bravo! bravo!" As nearly as I could afterwards learn both men were pretty severely beaten up, but neither yielded the victory. This vicious encounter was occasioned, it appears, by a very trifling circumstance: one party politely asked the other for some pepper, which was insultingly refused. High words arose, followed by the fight. During the progress of the row, I noticed several persons quickly leave, and, upon enquiry, learned that this movement was caused by fear of possible injury to themselves; injury that might arise from coming in contact with stray bullets. On such occasions, it sometimes happens that the guards shoot indiscriminately down through the roof, thereby endangering the lives of both combatants and spectators. By way of punishment both the guilty parties were together thrust into the sweatbox, and there passed a night and day without food or drink. At this writing they present a subdued and repentant appearance, having doubtless profited by sad experience. For myself I can see no good resulting from these promiscuous fights. The satisfaction derived from vanquishing an opponent is very often swallowed up in the punishment awarded by the prison authorities. In any light which the subject may be viewed, it will readily be seen, that fighting in the penitentiary is a poor business.

Every morning in emerging from the dank and dingy dungeon at daybreak, the prisoners may be seen to pair off, two and two, and then proceed to take their usual exercise. The scene that is now presented to the eye is both singular and impressive. Thirty or forty couples may be observed to pass back and forth at a brisk pace, intermingling, separating, advancing, and receding, the clanking of chains all the while filling the air with noises harsh and offensive to the sensitive ear.

Among many other strange things that constantly happen here are religious services on the Sabbath day. The various ministers of Salt Lake City, barring the Latter-day Saints, share the honors. These services are very impressive in their way, and while in progress appear to hold the convicts spellbound; but if any good has resulted from them, I am free to say, with all due respect to the ministers, after the keenest scrutiny that it is not apparent to the eye. Although the prisoners at these meetings are quiet and attentive, manifesting sincere penitence, I have learned that it is simply a lull before the storm, for no sooner does the minister withdraw from view than all is disorder and confusion. The ear is greeted with the usual profanity, and those who a moment before were so quiet and passive, often rush out and engage in a spirited game of ball.

Our last service (Nov. 27, [18]84) was conducted by the Rev. Mr. [Nathaniel F.] Putnam, Church of England, who brought with him some papers for general distribution, and a basket of apples intended for Fred Welcome as a Thanksgiving offering, and carelessly placed them on a side table. No sooner were the services ended, than a tremendous rush was made for the papers and apples, which to speak the truth, vanished like a dream. Unfortunately for me, I sat close at hand and was considerably jostled up by the crowd in the struggle that took place. The Rev. preacher stood back in dismay, apparently much grieved at beholding such rudeness, and if he is not by this time considerably discouraged in his labors at this place, I willingly put him down as a man of no little nerve and perseverance.

If any young man, living within the confines of Utah, who is pursuing a course that might eventually lead him here, could but spend a week in the penitentiary, speedy and permanent reform would, I think, be almost certain to follow. Intemperance is perhaps the foundation of two thirds of the crimes committed in this great nation; consequently, liquor is man['s] deadliest foe. Those who desire the love and respect of all good men and women would do well to adopt the motto: "Touch not, taste not."

APPENDIX 3

Mormon Polygamists at the Utah Penitentiary

This list is based upon Rosa Mae M. Evans, "Judicial Prosecution of Prisoners for LDS Plural Marriage: Prison Sentences, 1884–1895" (M.A. thesis, Brigham Young University, 1986), 117–32. However, the names of Joseph Hale, Isaac Jackson, and Charles D. Smith were eliminated because they were non-Mormons convicted of adultery, and James W. Burton, Myron W. Butler, Thomas Butler, William R. Butler, Arthur H. Campbell, and Hiram H. Webb were added to her listing.

Concurrent imprisonment of one person for two convictions is given on one line. Successive imprisonments of the same individual are listed on separate lines. When it is known that individuals with the same name are really different, an abbreviation of the hometown is added in capitals surrounded by parentheses. The abbreviations used in the "Charge" column are as follows: A = adultery; B = bigamy; I = incest; P = polygamy; and UC = unlawful cohabitation.

Name	Charge	Imprisonment	Release	Fine
Niels Aagaard	UC	23 Mar. 1889	11 May 1889	
Hugh Adams	UC	3 Jan. 1887	5 July 1887	100
John Adams	UC	21 Feb. 1887	22 Aug. 1887	300
Joshua Adams	UC	24 Mar. 1888	24 Aug. 1888	100
Peter Ahlstrom	UC	24 Sep. 1889	7 Dec. 1889	
John Aird	UC	30 Apr. 1885	29 May 1885	300
Jacob P. Albertson	UC	7 Nov. 1892	7 Jan. 1893	
Charles A. Allen	UC	20 Dec. 1893	14 Mar. 1894	
Ira Allen	UC	13 Feb. 1888	13 July 1888	300
Ira Allen	UC	6 Jan. 1891	16 Jan. 1891	
John M. Allen	UC	24 May 1894	8 July 1894	

continued

Name	Charge	Imprisonment	Release	Fine
James M. Allred	A	14 Oct. 1891	14 Dec. 1891	
Reddick N. Allred	UC	24 Sep. 1888	22 Dec. 1888	50
Samuel Allred	UC	6 Mar. 1888	6 Aug. 1888	
Stephen H. Allred	UC	28 Sep. 1889	23 Dec. 1889	
Wilson M. Allred	UC	6 Mar. 1888	6 Sep. 1888	100
Thomas Allsop	UC	14 Dec. 1886	13 May 1887	50
Thomas Allsop	UC	13 Mar. 1888	29 May 1888	50
Andrew Amundsen	UC	19 Dec. 1888	8 Mar. 1889	65
Oluf A. Andelin	UC	9 Nov. 1889	17 Mar. 1890	300
Charles A. Andersen	UC	12 Feb. 1888	3 Apr. 1888	
Christian Andersen	A	23 Sep. 1889	15 Nov. 1890	
John L. Andersen	UC	23 Dec. 1887	8 Mar. 1888	
Peter C. Andersen	UC	3 Jan. 1887	6 June 1887	100
Peter C. Andersen	A	13 Dec. 1888	28 Feb. 1890	
Samuel Andersen	UC	12 Oct. 1887	12 Apr. 1888	50
Andrew Anderson	UC	19 Dec. 1888	17 June 1889	300
Andrew O. Anderson	UC	7 Mar. 1890	7 Aug. 1890	300
Andrew R. Anderson	UC	9 Oct. 1888	1 Feb. 1889	50
Christian Anderson	A	12 Oct. 1891	12 Mar. 1892	
Gustav Anderson	UC	21 June 1887	20 Nov. 1887	100
James Anderson	UC	10 Oct. 1889	22 Jan. 1890	50
James Anderson	UC	7 Nov. 1892	6 Jan. 1893	50
Jens Anderson	UC	13 Oct. 1888	28 Jan. 1889	50
Mons Anderson	A	23 Mar. 1889	23 Jan. 1890	
Neils Anderson	UC	24 Sep. 1889	7 Dec. 1889	
Neils C. Anderson	UC	28 May 1888	28 Nov. 1888	300
Neils C. Anderson	UC	18 May 1891	18 June 1891	50
Oluf J. Anderson	UC	19 Nov. 1888	27 Mar. 1889	50
Peter Anderson	UC	27 Feb. 1889	26 Aug. 1889	
Nelson Arave	UC	6 Mar. 1893	5 May 1893	
John Archibald	UC	29 Dec. 1890	29 Mar. 1891	
William Archibald	UC	30 Jan. 1890	14 May 1890	50
Lorenzo D. Argyle	UC	29 Sep. 1888	30 Mar. 1889	150
Orson P. Arnold	UC	21 Oct. 1886	20 Mar. 1887	450
J. T. Arrowsmith	UC	12 Apr. 1887	11 Sep. 1887	100
Christopher Arthur	UC	18 May 1889	24 Oct. 1889	300
John Ash, Sr.	UC	24 Dec. 1888	24 May 1889	
William Ashworth	UC	26 Feb. 1894	17 Apr. 1894	
Lars J. Augustson	UC	22 Sep. 1892	19 Nov. 1892	
Rodney C. Badger	UC	21 Nov. 1887	21 Apr. 1888	100
Charles R. Bailey	UC	24 Nov. 1888	4 Mar. 1889	100
George B. Bailey	UC	10 May 1886	10 Nov. 1886	300
George B. Bailey	UC	26 Nov. 1888	26 Apr. 1889	

continued

Name	Charge	Imprisonment	Release	Fine
Alexander Baird	UC	23 June 1888	23 Dec. 1888	50
John Baird	A	11 May 1892	20 Aug. 1892	
Albert M. Baker	UC	10 Jan. 1890	10 Feb. 1890	
John P. Ball	UC	27 Feb. 1886	2 Sep. 1886	300
Samuel F. Ball	UC	1 Mar. 1886	4 Sep. 1886	300
William Ball	UC	23 Mar. 1889	15 June 1889	
Henry Ballard	UC	8 Feb. 1889	8 Apr. 1889	38.50
Peter S. Barkdull	UC	21 Feb. 1887	22 Aug. 1887	300
John R. Barnes	UC	30 Apr. 1888	22 June 1888	300
Benjamin Barney	UC	20 Sep. 1889	13 Dec. 1889	
Joseph S. Barney	UC	23 Dec. 1888	21 June 1889	300
Thomas Barrett	UC	22 Sep. 1888	2 Jan. 1889	
Peter S. Barson	UC	21 Nov. 1887	4 Apr. 1888	100
Hyrum Barton	UC	15 Feb. 1889	30 Apr. 1889	100
Joseph P. Barton	UC	25 May 1887	25 Nov. 1887	300
Joseph P. Barton	UC	14 Dec. 1889	7 Feb. 1890	300
Joseph P. Barton	A	19 Sep. 1893	25 Dec. 1893	
Peter D. Barton	A	6 Feb. 1889	20 July 1889	
Stephen S. Barton	UC	23 Dec. 1887	22 June 1888	300
Stephen S. Barton	A	19 Sep. 1893	25 Dec. 1893	
Jacob Bastian	UC	2 June 1888	1 Dec. 1888	300
Samuel Bateman	UC	19 Dec. 1888	13 Mar. 1889	75
Nephi J. Bates	UC	14 Apr. 1886	29 June 1886	1
Henry Beal	UC	24 Oct. 1887	8 Jan. 1888	200
Thomas Beard	UC	17 Feb. 1891	18 Mar. 1891	75
Christian Beauregard	UC	29 Sep. 1888	27 Dec. 1888	50
John F. Beck	UC	10 Oct. 1889	13 Feb. 1890	200
Henry Beckstead	UC	26 Sep. 1887	26 Feb. 1888	100
Elias A. Beckstrand	UC	24 Sep. 1889	16 Jan. 1890	
William Beeston	UC	29 Sep. 1888	8 Feb. 1889	200
M. S. Bell	UC	27 Feb. 1889	27 July 1889	
William Bench	A	27 Nov. 1891	17 Dec. 1891	
H. B. Bennett	A	20 Sep. 1890	23 Dec. 1890	
Josiah Bennett	UC	23 Sep. 1891	3 Oct. 1891	50
Peter Benson	UC	23 Dec. 1887	24 May 1888	100
Ludwig Berg	UC	1 June 1886	2 Dec. 1886	300
John Bergen	UC	17 Apr. 1886	24 Mar. 1887	1200
John Bergen, Sr.	P	23 Dec. 1887	23 Mar. 1890	
Andrew C. Berlin	UC	25 Oct. 1887	25 Apr. 1888	300
Charles H. Berrett	UC	6 Dec. 1888	19 Feb. 1889	
Alfred Best	UC	5 Oct. 1885	8 Mar. 1886	300
William G. Bickley	UC	27 May 1886	29 Nov. 1886	300
David Bigelow	UC	22 Nov. 1894	10 Jan. 1895	146.68

continued

Name	Charge	Imprisonment	Release	Fine
Alexander Bills	UC	20 Sep. 1887	20 Feb. 1888	100
Sanford Bingham	UC	7 Jan. 1889	6 Apr. 1889	100
Thomas Bingham	UC	23 Sep. 1892	5 Dec. 1892	
Willard Bingham	UC	28 May 1887	27 Oct. 1887	
Kelsey Bird	UC	22 Oct. 1889	21 Apr. 1890	300
Mahonri M. Bishop	UC	19 Sep. 1890	17 Feb. 1891	
Joseph S. Black	UC	10 Oct. 1889	23 Dec. 1889	
William Blood	UC	30 Sep. 1887	29 Feb. 1888	150
Joseph Blunt	UC	21 Feb. 1887	22 Aug. 1887	300
Ole P. Borg	A	29 Sep. 1888	16 May 1889	
Carl M. Borgstrom	UC	13 Feb. 1888	25 June 1888	100
Niels H. Borrenson	UC	13 Oct. 1888	11 Dec. 1888	
Niels H. Borrenson	UC	19 Sep. 1890	17 Feb. 1891	
John Henry Bott	UC	23 June 1888	23 Dec. 1888	100
Elijah Bourne	UC	22 Sep. 1888	28 Jan. 1889	
John Bowen	UC	17 Feb. 1886	20 Aug. 1886	300
Robert Bowman	UC	15 Oct. 1891	15 Dec. 1891	100
Elijah Box	UC	24 Dec. 1888	24 May 1889	300
Francis C. Boyer	UC	19 Sep. 1888	19 Nov. 1888	200
Henry G. Boyle	UC	24 Mar. 1888	24 Sep. 1888	100
Sylvester Bradford	UC	20 Apr. 1889	11 July 1889	25
Edward Brain	UC	2 Oct. 1885	5 Mar. 1886	300
Jens C. L. Breinholt	UC	24 Oct. 1888	5 Feb. 1889	
Ephraim Briggs	UC	15 Mar. 1888	15 Aug. 1888	25
William Bringhurst	UC	25 Mar. 1888	24 Sep. 1888	300
Thomas Broadbent	UC	14 Oct. 1889	29 Jan. 1890	100
Isaac Brockbank	UC	15 Feb. 1887	14 July 1887	300
William M. Bromley	UC	3 Aug. 1886	9 Feb. 1887	300
Alexander Brown	A	20 June 1888	20 July 1888	
Francis A. Brown	UC	11 July 1885	13 Jan. 1886	300
James H. Brown	UC	1 Dec. 1888	11 Apr. 1889	200
James S. Brown	UC	12 Mar. 1888	28 May 1888	100
Jens Larson Brown	A	24 Sep. 1889	20 Mar. 1890	
Jens Larson Brown	UC	19 Dec. 1893	18 Jan. 1894	
Moroni Brown	UC	11 July 1885	13 Jan. 1886	300
Casper Bryner	UC	2 June 1888	1 Dec. 1888	300
William Bullard	UC	11 Mar. 1893	7 Aug. 1893	
Isaac Bullock	UC	12 Nov. 1887	1 Jan. 1888	300
Thomas H. Bullock	UC	1 Dec. 1886	30 Apr. 1887	
Thomas H. Bullock	UC	11 May 1889	21 Sep. 1889	100
Thomas H. Bullock	A	5 Dec. 1891	20 Feb. 1893	
Charles Burgess	UC	11 Oct. 1887	11 Mar. 1888	25
Mark Burgess	UC	2 June 1888	1 Dec. 1888	300

continued

Name	Charge	Imprisonment	Release	Fine
Thomas Burningham	UC	17 Feb. 1886	20 Aug. 1886	300
John A. Burr	A	25 Mar. 1890	25 Apr. 1890	
Alexander Burt	UC	26 Mar. 1888	27 Aug. 1888	
James W. Burton	UC	21 May 1887	21 Nov. 1887	
Myron W. Butler	UC	1 Dec. 1886	30 Apr. 1887	100
Thomas Butler	UC	28 Feb. 1887	29 Aug. 1887	300
William Butler	UC	21 June 1887	21 Dec. 1887	300
William R. Butler	UC	23 Dec. 1888	21 June 1889	300
David B. Bybee	UC	25 Oct. 1887	25 Apr. 1888	50
James Bywater	UC	28 May 1888	28 Nov. 1888	50
James Bywater	UC	9 July 1889	28 Nov. 1889	150
James Bywater	UC, A	28 Nov. 1891	1 Dec. 1892	
Arthur H. Campbell	A	6 Oct. 1890	13 Oct. 1891	
Elisha Campbell	UC	21 June 1887	20 Nov. 1887	50
Abraham H. Cannon	UC	17 Mar. 1886	17 Aug. 1886	300
Angus M. Cannon	UC	9 May 1885	14 Dec. 1885	300
George Q. Cannon	UC	17 Sep. 1888	21 Feb. 1889	450
Joseph Carlisle	UC	2 Mar. 1889	25 May 1889	100
Carl F. Carlson	UC	28 Sep. 1889	27 July 1890	
Samuel Carter	UC	21 June 1887	30 Sep. 1887	100
Sidney R. Carter	A	20 Oct. 1888	20 Mar. 1889	
William Carter	UC	2 June 1888	1 Dec. 1888	300
William H. Casady	A	13 Feb. 1893	13 July 1893	
Abraham Chadwick	UC	8 Jan. 1887	8 July 1887	300
Thomas Chamberlain	UC	19 Dec. 1888	18 May 1889	300
George Chandler	UC	7 Dec. 1886	7 June 1887	100
Jonathan Chatterton	UC	8 Feb. 1886	25 May 1886	150
David Chidester	UC	23 Dec. 1887	22 June 1888	300
Axel Christensen	UC	23 June 1888	3 Nov. 1888	100
Chris L. Christensen	UC	10 Dec. 1889	9 June 1890	300
Frands Christensen	UC	14 Mar. 1889	26 June 1889	
Hans Christensen	A	5 Mar. 1889	5 Apr. 1890	
Hans Christensen	UC	14 Oct. 1893	14 Dec. 1893	
James Christensen	UC	23 Dec. 1887	23 June 1888	300
Jens Christensen	UC	26 May 1888	26 Nov. 1888	50
Jens C. Christensen	A	24 May 1890	7 June 1890	
Lars P. Christensen	UC	5 Mar. 1889	27 June 1889	50
Mads Christensen	A	13 Feb. 1888	3 Sep. 1888	
Niels P. Christensen	A	2 May 1891	2 Mar. 1892	
Peter C. Christensen	UC	18 Feb. 1889	3 May 1889	
Soren C. Christensen	UC	2 Oct. 1888	30 Nov. 1888	
C. P. Christiansen	UC	7 Mar. 1887	6 Aug. 1887	
Fred J. Christiansen	UC	9 Oct. 1888	29 Jan. 1889	50

continued

Name	Charge	Imprisonment	Release	Fine
William Christiansen	UC	19 Nov. 1888	6 Mar. 1889	
John Christopherson	UC	12 Dec. 1889	24 Feb. 1890	
William Chugg	UC	17 Dec. 1887	18 June 1888	200
Hyrum S. Church	UC	25 Mar. 1888	24 Sep. 1888	300
Ezra T. Clark	UC	21 Feb. 1887	20 July 1887	300
Joseph Clark	UC	21 Sep. 1887	21 Mar. 1888	300
Joseph Clark	UC, A	23 Mar. 1889	30 Nov. 1889	300
Hiram B. Clawson	UC	29 Sep. 1885	2 Mar. 1886	300
Rudger Clawson	UC, P	3 Nov. 1884	12 Dec. 1887	800
Edward Cliff	UC	14 Oct. 1887	14 Apr. 1888	200
Thomas P. Cloward	UC	9 Mar. 1889	27 Apr. 1889	
Harvey H. Cluff	UC	14 Apr. 1888	14 Sep. 1888	300
Samuel S. Cluff	UC	19 Nov. 1888	27 Feb. 1889	50
Richard Collett	UC	30 Apr. 1887	29 Sep. 1887	100
Gibson Condy	UC	9 Oct. 1888	20 Jan. 1889	200
John Connelly	UC	6 Oct. 1885	12 Apr. 1886	300
Phineas W. Cook	UC	1 Dec. 1888	1 Jan. 1889	
Andrew W. Cooley	UC	5 Oct. 1885	8 Apr. 1886	300
Andrew W. Cooley	UC	1 Mar. 1887	31 July 1887	25
Frederick A. Cooper	UC	8 Mar. 1886	11 Sep. 1886	300
John Cottam	UC	29 Sep. 1887	29 Mar. 1888	50
John T. Covington	UC	19 Dec. 1888	17 June 1889	300
Edward Cox	UC	27 Feb. 1888	27 July 1888	50
Fred W. Cox	A	24 Oct. 1891	13 Nov. 1891	
William J. Cox	UC	28 May 1886	29 Nov. 1886	300
George E. Cozier	A	22 May 1892	3 Oct. 1892	
Charles Crabtree	UC	29 May 1890	14 Aug. 1890	
G. M. Crawford	UC	14 Sep. 1890	12 Mar. 1891	300
Robert Crawshaw	UC	24 Dec. 1888	8 Apr. 1889	
George Crismon	UC	7 Mar. 1887	6 Aug. 1887	150
Alvin Crockett	UC	13 Feb. 1888	24 May 1888	
George H. Crosby	A	9 Dec. 1890	23 Feb. 1891	
Edwin D. Crowther	UC	19 Apr. 1890	19 Sep. 1890	
Richard Crowther	A	21 Sep. 1894	5 Dec. 1894	
George Curtis	UC	10 Oct. 1889	8 Dec. 1889	
Levi Curtis	UC	24 Mar. 1888	29 Aug. 1888	100
Morton B. Cutler	UC	22 May 1889	22 Oct. 1889	300
Thomas R. Cutler	UC	19 Oct. 1888	19 Mar. 1889	300
James Dalley	UC	22 Mar. 1887	21 Sep. 1887	300
Robert B. Dalley	A	19 Sep. 1893	8 May 1894	
William Dalley	UC	22 Mar. 1887	21 Sep. 1887	300
Luther A. Dalrymple	A	5 Mar. 1892	15 June 1892	
Robert Davidson	UC	5 Dec. 1888	15 Apr. 1889	100

continued

Name	Charge	Imprisonment	Release	Fine
David E. Davis	UC	5 Oct. 1885	8 Apr. 1886	300
Edwin L. Davis	UC	18 Sep. 1888	1 Dec. 1888	70
George Davis	UC	1 Dec. 1888	12 Mar. 1889	
Eli A. Day	UC	19 Nov. 1888	24 Apr. 1889	150
Eli A. Day	A	21 Dec. 1892	20 Jan. 1893	
Joseph Dean	UC	24 May 1889	21 Sep. 1889	200
Joseph H. Dean	UC	27 Sep. 1886	28 Mar. 1887	300
Theodore Dedrickson	UC	12 Mar. 1889	14 June 1889	
Charles Denney	UC	1 June 1886	1 Dec. 1886	300
Joseph Dilworth	A	2 Mar. 1892	1 Apr. 1892	
Henry Dinwoodey	UC	23 Feb. 1886	26 July 1886	300
William H. Dopp	A	1 June 1892	10 Sep. 1892	
Carl C. N. Dorius	UC	10 Mar. 1888	10 Aug. 1888	100
John F. F. Dorius	UC	19 Nov. 1888	29 Mar. 1889	50
Ralph Douglas	UC	28 May 1887	27 Oct. 1887	
William Douglas	UC	21 June 1887	20 Nov. 1887	100
Appolos Driggs	UC	19 Feb. 1887	18 July 1887	300
Benjamin W. Driggs	A	10 Apr. 1891	20 July 1891	
Thomas Duce	UC	9 Nov. 1888	25 Jan. 1889	100
Oluf F. Due	UC	1 Mar. 1886	6 Sep. 1886	300
George Dunford	UC	24 Nov. 1886	23 Apr. 1887	150
Levi S. Dunham	A	10 Oct. 1889	22 Nov. 1891	
Charles O. Dunn	UC	10 Dec. 1887	11 June 1888	150
James Dunn	UC	23 Sep. 1886	23 Mar. 1887	300
John J. Dunn	UC	28 May 1887	28 Nov. 1887	100
John M. Dunning	UC	26 Sep. 1888	23 Mar. 1889	300
Francillo Durfey	UC	23 Dec. 1887	23 June 1888	300
John Durrant	UC	21 Oct. 1886	20 Mar. 1887	100
John Durrant	A	29 Sep. 1888	14 Dec. 1889	
Bedson Eardley	UC	21 Feb. 1887	22 Aug. 1887	300
Bedson Eardley	A	4 Oct. 1889	19 Dec. 1890	
Alexander Edwards	UC	30 Apr. 1887	29 Sep. 1887	100
Fred W. Ellis	UC	13 Dec. 1886	17 May 1887	100
Fred W. Ellis	A	13 Dec. 1890	11 Feb. 1891	
German Ellsworth	UC	17 Nov. 1887	17 Apr. 1888	100
German Ellsworth	UC	7 Nov. 1892	7 Dec. 1892	
Kanute Emmertsen	UC	21 June 1887	21 Dec. 1887	200
Kanute Emmertsen	UC	25 May 1889	25 Nov. 1889	
Gottlieb Ence	UC	5 Mar. 1889	27 June 1889	50
John England	UC	21 Mar. 1887	21 Sep. 1887	150
Niels C. Erickson	A	1 June 1892	1 Apr. 1893	
Hyrum H. Evans	UC	3 Oct. 1887	3 Mar. 1888	50
Joseph H. Evans	P	8 Nov. 1884	15 Mar. 1887	250

continued

Name	Charge	Imprisonment	Release	Fine
W. P. Evans	A	16 July 1889	9 Aug. 1890	
George Facer	UC	21 Mar. 1889	1 July 1889	150
Isaac Farley	UC	9 Nov. 1887	9 May 1888	300
Winslow Farr	UC	26 May 1888	26 Nov. 1888	300
James Farrer	UC	26 Sep. 1886	26 Mar. 1887	300
Thomas Featherstone	UC	18 Mar. 1891	18 Apr. 1891	50
William Felsted	UC, P	14 Sep. 1886	23 Nov. 1887	300
James M. Fisher	UC	29 Sep. 1887	29 Feb. 1888	100
Hyrum P. Folsom	UC	25 Sep. 1886	24 Feb. 1887	300
Joseph B. Forbes	UC	22 Sep. 1888	1 Feb. 1889	100
Peter A. Forsgren	UC	13 Dec. 1888	28 Mar. 1889	
William H. Foster	UC	21 Feb. 1887	20 July 1887	300
William Fotheringham	UC	23 May 1885	9 Aug. 1885	300
Herbert J. Foulger	UC	26 Feb. 1886	2 Sep. 1886	300
Isaac H. Fox	UC	23 Mar. 1889	26 Apr. 1889	
Jens Frandsen	UC	21 June 1887	21 Dec. 1887	100
Jens Frandsen	UC	27 May 1891	27 June 1891	100
John Frandsen	A	5 Mar. 1889	25 Jan. 1890	
Charles Frank	UC	8 Jan. 1887	7 June 1887	100
Charles Frank	A	7 Dec. 1889	23 June 1890	
Robert G. Fraser	UC	3 Nov. 1888	3 Dec. 1888	100
Richard Fry	UC	19 Nov. 1887	19 Oct. 1888	300
Jacob Fuhriman	UC	10 Dec. 1888	23 Feb. 1889	50
Sanford Fuller	UC	12 Apr. 1887	11 Sep. 1887	100
Hans Funk	UC	19 Nov. 1887	19 May 1888	300
Marcus Funk	UC	25 Mar. 1888	24 Sep. 1888	300
John B. Furster	UC	1 Oct. 1886	1 Apr. 1887	300
William W. Galbraith	UC	22 Sep. 1886	21 Feb. 1887	300
Henry Gale	UC	17 Dec. 1885	21 June 1886	300
William Gallup	UC	19 Nov. 1888	1 Feb. 1889	
Jessie Gardiner	UC	19 Sep. 1888	4 Jan. 1889	
John W. Gardiner	UC	29 Sep. 1888	3 Feb. 1889	
Martin Garn	UC	19 Feb. 1889	30 May 1889	200
William Geddes	UC	6 Dec. 1886	5 May 1887	100
William Gee	UC	18 Dec. 1889	18 May 1890	
Peter C. Geertsen	UC	22 Jan. 1889	22 June 1889	
John T. Gerber	UC	11 Oct. 1887	11 Apr. 1888	100
John L. Gibbs	UC	12 Apr. 1887	11 Sep. 1887	100
John Gillespie	UC	30 Sep. 1886	31 Mar. 1887	300
George Godfrey	A	17 Oct. 1892	3 May 1893	
Thomas Godfrey	UC	1 June 1889	10 Oct. 1889	100
Hyrum Goff	UC	3 Mar. 1886	9 Sep. 1886	300
Peter T. Goss	UC	20 Feb. 1889	15 May 1889	75

continued

Name	Charge	Imprisonment	Release	Fine
Josiah Gough	A	10 Apr. 1893	7 Aug. 1893	
Hugh S. Gowans	UC	26 Feb. 1886	30 Aug. 1886	300
George L. Graehl	UC	25 May 1888	25 June 1888	10
John Graham	A	27 May 1890	27 Mar. 1891	
Walter Granger	UC	2 June 1888	1 Dec. 1888	300
William Grant	UC	14 Apr. 1886	24 July 1886	
William Grant	A	20 Apr. 1889	20 Aug. 1890	
John C. Gray	UC	30 Oct. 1886	29 Mar. 1887	50
Ambrose Greenwell	UC	26 May 1886	9 Feb. 1887	300
Charles H. Greenwell	UC	26 Feb. 1886	29 July 1886	300
Frank Greenwell	UC	30 June 1888	5 Nov. 1888	
Frank Greenwell	A	17 Feb. 1894	13 May 1894	
Herman Grether	UC	21 Feb. 1887	22 Aug. 1887	300
Thomas Griffin	UC	1 June 1889	2 Dec. 1889	100
William H. Griffin	UC, P	13 Feb. 1888	13 June 1890	300
Duckworth Grimshaw	A	13 Oct. 1891	13 Aug. 1892	
Nicholas Groesbeck	UC	2 Aug. 1886	8 Feb. 1887	450
Nicholas Groesbeck	A	1 Dec. 1890	2 Apr. 1891	
Nicholas Groesbeck	A	26 May 1892	26 Mar. 1893	
Isaac Groo	UC	5 Oct. 1885	8 Apr. 1886	300
John Groves	UC	15 Mar. 1889	27 June 1889	75
Henry Grow	UC	19 Mar. 1887	24 July 1887	50
Thomas Gunderson	UC	21 Jan. 1889	10 May 1889	100
William Gurney	UC	23 Mar. 1889	15 June 1889	
Reuben Gurr	A	5 Mar. 1889	4 Feb. 1890	
Henry B. Gwilliam	UC	13 Dec. 1886	13 June 1887	100
Nils G. Gyllenskog	UC	10 Dec. 1887	31 Jan. 1888	
Franklin P. Hadlock	UC	20 June 1892	20 Feb. 1893	
Jacob Hafen	UC	9 Mar. 1889	1 July 1889	50
George Hales	UC	26 Sep. 1886	26 Mar. 1887	300
John Halgreen	UC	30 Nov. 1888	29 Dec. 1888	
John Halgreen	UC	6 Jan. 1891	20 Feb. 1891	
Charles S. Hall	UC, A	8 Jan. 1889	16 Oct. 1889	
Charles S. Hall	UC	27 May 1891	26 June 1891	
George Halliday	UC	27 Oct. 1888	9 Jan. 1889	
Samuel Hamer	UC	26 Mar. 1890	23 June 1890	
Henry Hamilton	UC	24 Mar. 1888	24 Sep. 1888	100
James C. Hamilton	UC	12 Oct. 1888	25 Dec. 1888	150
Charles Hampshire	UC	13 Mar. 1889	30 July 1889	50
Andrew Hansen (WJOR)	UC	27 Sep. 1886	28 Mar. 1887	300
Andrew Hansen (NWTN)	UC	8 Dec. 1888	8 May 1889	
August Hansen	A	19 Feb. 1891	19 July 1891	
Christian Hansen	UC	27 Oct. 1887	27 Apr. 1888	300

continued

Name	Charge	Imprisonment	Release	Fine
Ferdinand Hansen	UC	22 Dec. 1887	2 Apr. 1888	100
Hans Hansen (GUNSN)	UC	3 Nov. 1887	17 Jan. 1888	
Hans Hansen (LOGAN)	UC	23 June 1888	23 Dec. 1888	100
Hans P. Hansen	UC	13 Feb. 1888	13 July 1888	200
James Hansen	UC	13 Feb. 1888	13 Aug. 1888	100
James P. Hansen	UC	5 Mar. 1889	23 May 1889	
Jens Hansen (MLCRK)	UC	2 June 1886	2 Dec. 1886	300
Jens Hansen (BRGCY)	UC	10 Dec. 1887	11 June 1888	150
Jens Hansen (GUNSN)	UC	19 Nov. 1888	6 Mar. 1889	50
Jens Hansen (NEWTON)	UC	25 May 1889	24 Aug. 1889	
Oluf Hansen	UC	19 Nov. 1887	25 Apr. 1888	100
Peter C. Hansen	UC	24 Oct. 1887	13 Dec. 1887	
Willard Hansen	UC	24 Nov. 1888	4 Mar. 1889	200
Frederick H. Hanson	UC	5 Nov. 1885	10 May 1886	300
Nathan Hanson	UC	12 Oct. 1887	12 Mar. 1888	100
Nels Hanson	UC	20 Jan. 1890	20 Mar. 1890	
Thomas Harding	UC	24 Mar. 1888	24 Aug. 1888	
Aaron Hardy	UC	14 Oct. 1887	14 Mar. 1888	
Aaron Hardy	UC	6 Oct. 1890	5 Apr. 1891	300
Warren Hardy	UC	2 June 1888	1 Dec. 1888	300
Loren Harmer	UC	19 Nov. 1888	27 Feb. 1889	100
George Harmon	UC	14 Sep. 1887	13 Oct. 1887	100
John C. Harper	UC	20 Apr. 1889	26 Sep. 1889	200
Thomas Harper	UC	28 May 1888	28 Nov. 1888	300
Charles Harris	UC	12 May 1893	18 July 1893	
John Harris	UC	28 Feb. 1888	23 Apr. 1888	50
William Harrison	UC	21 Mar. 1887	20 Aug. 1887	100
John Hart	A	23 Mar. 1889	7 June 1890	
Daniel Harvey	UC	29 Sep. 1887	4 Apr. 1888	150
Charles Hawkins	UC	9 Oct. 1888	19 Feb. 1889	100
Eli B. Hawkins	UC	3 Nov. 1888	8 Apr. 1889	200
Albert Haws	UC	26 Nov. 1888	14 Mar. 1889	50
Hans C. Hegsted	UC	28 May 1887	28 Nov. 1887	100
Anthony Heiner	UC	1 Apr. 1889	16 June 1889	200
Thomas B. Helm	UC	13 Dec. 1886	13 June 1887	100
Thomas B. Helm	UC	2 June 1888	2 Dec. 1888	300
Robert Henderson	UC	3 Jan. 1887	5 July 1887	100
Thomas Henderson	UC	14 Nov. 1887	13 Feb. 1888	100
Rasmus Henningson	UC	9 Oct. 1888	22 Dec. 1888	

continued

Name	Charge	Imprisonment	Release	Fine
Orlando F. Herrin	UC	27 Oct. 1887	27 Mar. 1888	50
Orlando F. Herrin	A	19 Nov. 1888	17 Jan. 1889	
Orlando F. Herrin	A	28 Mar. 1891	8 July 1891	
John F. R. Hicks	UC	6 Nov. 1889	6 May 1890	300
James Higgins	UC	30 Sep. 1886	28 Feb. 1887	400
Silas G. Higgins	UC	25 Mar. 1888	24 Sep. 1888	300
James G. Higginson	UC	24 Mar. 1888	24 Aug. 1888	
Thomas S. Higham	UC	30 Sep. 1889	31 Mar. 1890	300
Archibald N. Hill	UC	17 Sep. 1888	5 Nov. 1888	50
Daniel Hill	UC	9 Nov. 1888	9 Apr. 1889	100
Samuel H. Hill	UC	17 Sep. 1888	15 Nov. 1888	75
William H. Hill	UC	10 Dec. 1888	22 Feb. 1889	100
Rudolf Hochstrasser	UC	22 Nov. 1887	22 Apr. 1888	100
Goudy Hogan	UC	25 Nov. 1889	25 Dec. 1889	
Joseph Hogan	UC	21 Feb. 1887	20 July 1887	300
George Holyoak	UC	23 Dec. 1887	22 June 1888	300
Andrew Homer	UC	14 Oct. 1887	18 Feb. 1888	50
William J. Hooper	UC	23 Feb. 1887	23 Aug. 1887	300
John Hopkins	UC	13 Nov. 1893	28 Jan. 1894	300
Joseph S. Horne	A	5 Mar. 1889	20 May 1890	
Oliver C. Hoskins	UC	25 Jan. 1889	10 Apr. 1889	100
James Howard	UC	11 Feb. 1889	26 Apr. 1889	100
John R. Howard	A	13 Nov. 1891	13 Sep. 1892	
Henry Hughes	UC	26 Nov. 1887	26 Apr. 1888	100
Lorenzo Huish	UC	25 Feb. 1895	27 Mar. 1895	
Richard Humphreys	UC	31 Oct. 1889	12 Feb. 1890	300
Allen Hunsaker	UC	21 May 1887	20 Oct. 1887	300
Ebenezer Hunter	UC	22 Sep. 1888	22 Nov. 1888	
William Hutchings	A	23 Mar. 1889	28 Dec. 1889	
James K. Ingall	UC	11 Oct. 1891	10 Nov. 1891	50
John Irving	UC	18 Oct. 1888	10 Feb. 1889	250
Hans P. Iversen	UC	16 Mar. 1890	15 Sep. 1890	300
John W. Jackson	A	1 Oct. 1889	11 June 1890	
Thomas R. Jackson	A	20 Apr. 1889	21 Feb. 1890	
John Jacobs	A	23 Mar. 1889	3 Dec. 1889	
Lars Jacobsen	UC	13 Oct. 1887	13 Mar. 1888	50
Soren Jacobsen	UC	23 Feb. 1889	17 June 1889	75
Anton A. Janson	UC	24 Dec. 1889	8 Mar. 1890	
Carl Janson	UC	30 Sep. 1886	7 Mar. 1887	300
John Jardine	UC	2 June 1888	3 Dec. 1888	300
William Y. Jeffs	UC	22 Sep. 1886	21 Feb. 1887	400
James H. Jenkins	A	4 Oct. 1890	11 Feb. 1891	
John Jenkins	UC	19 Nov. 1887	19 Apr. 1888	300

continued

Name	Charge	Imprisonment	Release	Fine
Richard Jenkins	UC	19 Nov. 1888	28 Mar. 1889	50
Richard Jenkins	UC	18 Mar. 1891	3 June 1891	50
William J. Jenkins	UC	3 Mar. 1886	7 Sep. 1886	300
William J. Jenkins	UC	21 Apr. 1888	22 Oct. 1888	50
Andrew Jensen	UC	10 May 1886	10 Nov. 1886	300
Charles Jensen	UC	24 Sep. 1889	1 Mar. 1890	200
Christian Jensen	UC	1 Dec. 1888	1 Feb. 1889	150
Fred Jensen	UC	10 Dec. 1887	11 June 1888	100
Fred Jensen	UC	26 Nov. 1889	26 May 1890	100
Hans Jensen (GOSHEN)	UC	21 Oct. 1886	20 Mar. 1887	100
Hans Jensen (HYRUM)	UC	21 June 1887	21 Dec. 1887	100
Hans Jensen (MANTI)	UC	27 Sep. 1888	2 Feb. 1889	
Hans Jensen (GOSHEN)	A	30 Sep. 1889	30 Apr. 1891	
Jens L. Jensen	UC	30 Sep. 1889	30 Dec. 1889	
Jens P. Jensen	UC	4 June 1887	5 Dec. 1887	200
Jens P. Jensen	A	24 Dec. 1889	11 Mar. 1891	
Ole A. Jensen	UC	30 Nov. 1888	31 May 1889	100
Peter C. Jensen	UC	13 Dec. 1888	13 May 1889	100
Soren C. Jensen	UC	19 Nov. 1888	29 Mar. 1889	50
Jeppe Jeppson	UC	13 Dec. 1888	26 Feb. 1889	
Hans Jesperson	A, P	10 Oct. 1889	27 July 1891	
Richard Jessop	UC	27 May 1889	27 July 1889	
David John	UC	7 Mar. 1887	6 Aug. 1887	300
A. Johnson	A	25 Sep. 1892	1 Jan. 1893	
John B. Johnson	UC	24 Feb. 1888	5 Mar. 1888	150
John P. R. Johnson	UC	9 Oct. 1888	20 Jan. 1889	200
Lars P. Johnson	A	13 Dec. 1890	11 Feb. 1891	
Olaus Johnson	UC	29 Feb. 1888	29 Aug. 1888	50
Thomas Johnson	A	24 Sep. 1889	24 Feb. 1890	
Joseph L. Jolley	UC	10 Oct. 1889	31 Dec. 1889	50
Albert Jones	UC, A	19 Nov. 1888	8 Nov. 1889	200
Daniel Jones	UC	11 Apr. 1888	11 Sep. 1888	300
John Lee Jones	UC	28 Dec. 1886	27 June 1887	300
John Lewis Jones	UC	10 Dec. 1887	11 June 1888	150
John P. Jones	UC	28 Dec. 1886	27 June 1887	300
Joseph S. Jones	UC	10 Mar. 1888	10 Aug. 1888	100
Sylvester F. Jones	UC	23 Dec. 1888	21 June 1889	300
Thomas C. Jones	UC	27 Feb. 1886	30 Aug. 1886	300
Thomas J. Jones	UC	15 Dec. 1889	13 June 1890	300
William E. Jones	UC	25 May 1887	25 Nov. 1887	300

continued

Name	Charge	Imprisonment	Release	Fine
William E. Jones	A	19 Sep. 1893	25 Dec. 1893	
Jens Jorgensen	A	29 Mar. 1889	22 Feb. 1890	
Jens C. Jorgensen	UC	24 Sep. 1889	18 Dec. 1889	
Johan G. Jorgensen	UC	14 Mar. 1889	12 Sep. 1889	300
John G. Jorgensen	UC	8 Nov. 1892	7 Jan. 1893	
Mads Jorgensen	UC	25 Mar. 1890	25 Aug. 1890	
Peter Jorgensen	UC	13 Dec. 1888	28 Mar. 1889	
Rasmus Justeson	A	6 Oct. 1890	6 Aug. 1891	
John W. Keddington	UC	21 Nov. 1885	25 May 1886	300
James Kellar	UC	13 Dec. 1888	13 May 1889	
James Kemp	UC	13 Dec. 1887	13 June 1888	200
Sydney Kent	UC	2 Dec. 1889	2 Feb. 1890	
Andrew J. Kershaw	A	25 Oct. 1888	9 Jan. 1890	
Abraham A. Kimball	A	3 Nov. 1888	27 Dec. 1888	
Byron W. King	UC	22 Oct. 1887	23 Apr. 1888	50
Culbert King	UC	25 Dec. 1885	28 June 1886	300
Daniel King	UC	24 Sep. 1888	22 Dec. 1888	50
Robert T. King	UC	24 Mar. 1888	24 Aug. 1888	
Thomas W. Kirby	UC	8 Jan. 1887	8 July 1887	100
George Kirkham	UC	21 Mar. 1887	20 Aug. 1887	50
James Kirkham	UC	21 Mar. 1887	20 Aug. 1887	50
Robert C. Kirkwood	UC	7 Mar. 1887	6 Aug. 1887	300
Peter Knudsen	A	14 Feb. 1892	1 Aug. 1892	
Thomas Labrum	UC	5 Oct. 1887	20 Dec. 1887	25
George C. Lambert	UC	11 May 1886	11 Nov. 1886	300
John T. Lambert	UC	14 Oct. 1887	14 Mar. 1888	
Edwin Lamborn	UC	28 Nov. 1891	27 Dec. 1891	
Peter J. Lammers	UC	21 June 1887	21 Dec. 1887	100
John Lang	UC	5 Oct. 1885	21 Jan. 1886	300
James H. Langford	UC	19 Dec. 1888	17 June 1889	300
Bendt Larsen	UC	16 Mar. 1888	16 Sep. 1888	50
Bendt Larsen	UC	7 Nov. 1892	7 Dec. 1892	
Lars C. Larsen	UC	13 Oct. 1888	20 Jan. 1889	
Lars C. Larsen	UC	23 Dec. 1887	23 May 1888	50
Lars Larson	UC	24 Sep. 1888	9 Jan. 1889	100
Lars James Larson	A	11 Oct. 1889	11 May 1891	
Lewis Larson	UC	20 Oct. 1888	7 Dec. 1888	100
Oluf C. Larson	A	19 Nov. 1888	24 Apr. 1889	
James Latimer	UC	24 Mar. 1888	24 Aug. 1888	300
David W. Leaker	UC	6 Oct. 1886	6 Apr. 1887	300
James Leatham	UC	14 Apr. 1890	14 Sep. 1890	
Severn N. Lee	UC	23 May 1889	9 Aug. 1889	100

continued

Name	Charge	Imprisonment	Release	Fine
Wm. H. Lee (TOOELE)	UC	26 Feb. 1886	2 Sep. 1886	300
Wm. H. Lee (WDRUFF)	UC	24 Dec. 1888	4 Apr. 1889	150
Benjamin M. Lewis	A	30 Sep. 1893	2 Mar. 1894	
Creston Lewis	UC	23 Feb. 1889	15 June 1889	100
Daniel Lewis	UC	18 Sep. 1888	17 Dec. 1888	60
William J. Lewis	UC	22 Sep. 1888	27 Feb. 1889	100
Jonas Lindberg	UC	20 Sep. 1886	22 Mar. 1887	300
Samuel Linton	UC	19 Mar. 1891	4 June 1891	
Charles Livingston	UC	14 Oct. 1887	15 Dec. 1887	100
James W. Loveless	UC	21 Oct. 1886	20 Mar. 1887	300
Ledru Loveridge	UC	24 Mar. 1888	24 Aug. 1888	50
James Loynd	UC	12 Oct. 1887	12 Mar. 1888	50
Joseph Lunceford	UC	24 Mar. 1888	24 Sep. 1888	50
John H. Lutz	A	7 Dec. 1893	21 Apr. 1894	
Francis M. Lyman	UC	14 Jan. 1889	8 Apr. 1889	
Joseph W. McAllister	UC	22 Dec. 1889	19 June 1890	300
Charles McCarty	UC	13 Oct. 1887	13 Apr. 1888	200
Archibald McFarland	A	6 Jan. 1891	22 Mar. 1891	
Daniel L. MacFarlane	UC	23 Dec. 1887	22 June 1888	300
John McKellar	A	15 Oct. 1894	4 May 1895	
William McKellar	A	10 Oct. 1889	10 Aug. 1890	
Robert McKendrick	UC	18 Mar. 1886	18 Sep. 1886	300
Archibald McKinnon	UC	24 Dec. 1888	9 Mar. 1889	
Joseph McMurrin	UC	23 Feb. 1886	26 Aug. 1886	300
Thomas McNeil	UC	3 Jan. 1887	5 July 1887	100
William McNeil	UC	17 June 1889	2 Oct. 1889	100
Cornelius McReavey	UC	19 Dec. 1888	17 June 1889	300
Andrew Madsen	UC	17 Dec. 1887	17 May 1888	100
Andrew Madsen	A	26 Dec. 1889	17 July 1890	
Niels P. Madsen	UC	14 Oct. 1887	30 Jan. 1888	200
Peter Madson	UC	4 June 1887	4 Nov. 1887	100
Charles W. Mann	A	18 Feb. 1889	24 Feb. 1890	
Henry W. Manning	UC	23 June 1888	3 Oct. 1888	300
George Manwaring	UC	2 Mar. 1889	12 June 1889	
John F. Manwell	A	22 May 1889	22 Oct. 1889	
Gilbert J. Marchant	UC	8 Oct. 1892	23 Dec. 1892	
John A. Marchant	UC	30 Sep. 1887	29 Feb. 1888	100
Erasmus Marquardson	UC	23 Sep. 1889	1 Jan. 1890	
John Marriott	UC	8 Jan. 1887	7 June 1887	100
Jesse B. Martin	UC	10 Oct. 1889	29 Nov. 1889	
William H. Maughn	UC, A	3 Jan. 1889	16 Oct. 1889	200

continued

Name	Charge	Imprisonment	Release	Fine
James May	UC	13 Dec. 1886	12 May 1887	100
Amos Maycock	UC	24 Feb. 1886	1 Dec. 1886	100
James Mellor	UC	3 Nov. 1888	9 Mar. 1889	
M. W. Merrill, Jr.	UC	13 Feb. 1888	18 June 1888	
Edwin R. Miles	UC	12 May 1888	12 Oct. 1888	50
Jacob Miller	UC	17 Dec. 1887	6 Feb. 1888	
Lowritz B. Miller	UC	4 Oct. 1890	4 Apr. 1891	50
Aurelius Miner	UC	17 Oct. 1885	20 Mar. 1886	300
Levi Minnerly	UC	25 May 1886	29 Sep. 1886	
Charles Monk	UC	14 Apr. 1888	25 July 1888	100
Christian H. Monson	UC	23 June 1888	23 Dec. 1888	200
Robert Morris	UC	15 Feb. 1886	18 July 1886	150
Thomas H. Morrison	UC	1 Mar. 1887	31 July 1887	25
Jens Mortensen	UC	16 Feb. 1889	28 May 1889	
John P. Mortensen	UC	19 Feb. 1887	18 July 1887	300
M. P. Mortensen	UC	17 Dec. 1887	28 Apr. 1888	100
Niels C. Mortensen	UC	8 Jan. 1887	10 June 1887	300
Niels C. Mortensen	A	12 Dec. 1891	12 Oct. 1892	
Lars Mortenson	UC	17 Dec. 1887	28 Apr. 1888	150
Thomas F. H. Morton	UC	1 Oct. 1886	28 Feb. 1887	300
Steven Mott	UC	23 Mar. 1889	5 June 1889	
Lewis H. Mousley	UC	19 Feb. 1887	18 July 1887	300
Henry Mower	UC	10 Oct. 1889	24 Nov. 1889	
John A. Mower	A	3 Mar. 1891	19 May 1891	
John A. Mower	UC	17 Mar. 1892	26 Mar. 1892	
James Moyle	UC	1 Mar. 1886	4 Aug. 1886	300
Nicholas Muhlestein	UC	9 Apr. 1890	9 June 1890	
William S. Muir	UC	12 Oct. 1887	12 Apr. 1888	100
Harvey Murdock	P	3 Jan. 1887	2 June 1890	500
John M. Murdock	UC	21 Apr. 1891	21 May 1891	
Joseph S. Murdock	UC	20 Apr. 1889	24 May 1889	
A. Milton Musser	UC	9 May 1885	12 Oct. 1885	300
Jacob I. Naef	UC	13 Apr. 1889	1 July 1889	
Henry W. Naisbitt	UC	11 May 1886	11 Nov. 1886	300
Henry W. Naisbitt	UC	12 May 1890	12 Oct. 1890	
George Naylor	UC	3 Dec. 1886	2 May 1887	300
Henry Nebeker	A	27 Oct. 1888	27 Mar. 1889	
Amos H. Neff	UC	11 Oct. 1886	13 Apr. 1887	600
Mons Neilson	UC	26 Sep. 1888	5 Feb. 1889	200
Anton Nelson	A	7 Nov. 1892	22 Jan. 1893	
James H. Nelson	UC	16 Jan. 1886	20 July 1886	300
Fred A. Newberger	UC	10 Dec. 1888	10 June 1889	100
Henry J. Newman	UC	18 Dec. 1890	18 Apr. 1891	300

continued

Name	Charge	Imprisonment	Release	Fine
L. H. Newman	UC	10 Oct. 1889	7 Jan. 1890	
William D. Newsom	P	17 Oct. 1885	4 Apr. 1888	800
William D. Newsom	UC	16 May 1890	15 Nov. 1890	300
John Nicholson	UC	13 Oct. 1885	13 Mar. 1886	300
Andrew Nielsen	UC	5 Mar. 1889	3 June 1889	
Christian Nielsen	UC	14 Mar. 1889	12 Sep. 1889	300
Christian P. Nielsen	UC	22 Sep. 1888	7 Jan. 1889	
Hans Nielsen	UC	19 Nov. 1888	6 Mar. 1889	100
Hans Nielsen	A	12 Mar. 1889	15 May 1889	
Hans C. Nielsen	UC	24 Sep. 1889	1 Mar. 1890	200
Lars Nielsen	UC	21 June 1887	20 Nov. 1887	100
Lars Nielsen	A	1 Dec. 1890	21 Dec. 1890	
Niels Nielsen	UC	9 Oct. 1888	2 Mar. 1889	
Niels P. Nielsen	UC	20 Nov. 1888	28 Feb. 1889	
Niels P. Nielsen	UC	5 Mar. 1889	21 June 1889	50
Peter Nielsen	UC	28 Nov. 1891	28 Apr. 1892	
Rasmus Nielsen (HNT)	UC	19 Feb. 1887	19 Aug. 1887	300
Rasmus Nielsen (SPF)	UC	9 Oct. 1888	20 Jan. 1889	200
Charles Mormon Nokes	UC	18 Oct. 1888	9 Feb. 1889	150
Hyrum B. North	UC	24 Feb. 1887	24 Aug. 1887	300
Levi North	UC	23 Feb. 1887	23 Aug. 1887	300
Alonzo Norton	UC	24 Dec. 1888	26 Mar. 1889	50
Stephen Nye	UC	24 Dec. 1888	8 Apr. 1889	
John Oberg	UC	5 Mar. 1889	26 June 1889	50
John Oberg	A	7 Nov. 1892	7 Apr. 1893	
Ferdinand Oberhansli	UC	17 Nov. 1887	17 Apr. 1888	50
John Oborn	UC	7 Oct. 1887	7 Mar. 1888	50
Thomas L. Obray	UC	24 May 1890	9 Aug. 1890	
Thomas W. Obray	UC	26 Nov. 1888	1 Apr. 1889	
Thomas W. Obray	A	1 June 1892	10 Sep. 1892	
Charles R. Ockey	UC	4 Feb. 1889	16 May 1889	
Thomas Ogden	A	5 Mar. 1889	18 June 1890	
Thomas Ogden	UC	9 Oct. 1894	31 Dec. 1894	
Peter Okelberry	UC	25 Mar. 1890	25 Aug. 1890	
Samuel Oldham	UC	26 Apr. 1889	26 Oct. 1889	100
Archibald Oldroyd	UC	13 Oct. 1888	24 Jan. 1889	50
Archibald Oldroyd	A	21 Sep. 1892	20 Oct. 1892	
Carl Olsen	UC	5 Mar. 1889	17 June 1889	50
Emil Olsen	UC	13 Oct. 1885	16 Apr. 1886	300
Lewis Olsen	UC	24 Sep. 1888	4 Feb. 1889	200
William J. Orchard	UC	11 Dec. 1893	20 Feb. 1894	100

continued

Name	Charge	Imprisonment	Release	Fine
Oliver C. Ormsby	UC	18 Oct. 1888	31 Dec. 1888	200
Alex Orton	UC	25 May 1887	25 Nov. 1887	300
Christian Otteson	UC	22 Sep. 1890	22 Oct. 1890	
William B. Pace	A	14 Sep. 1890	13 Apr. 1891	
Wilson D. Pace	UC	14 Sep. 1890	11 Feb. 1891	300
Hiram S. Palmer	UC	25 Mar. 1890	25 Apr. 1890	
William Palmer	UC	3 Jan. 1887	2 June 1887	100
Joseph F. Parker	UC	5 Dec. 1893	16 Mar. 1894	
William J. Parkin	UC	17 Sep. 1888	5 Nov. 1888	50
Timothy Parkinson	UC	23 Nov. 1886	22 Apr. 1887	100
Joseph Parry	UC	8 Jan. 1887	7 June 1887	300
James M. Paxton	A	21 Sep. 1889	1 June 1890	
Harry M. Payne	UC	7 Mar. 1890	6 Sep. 1890	300
Edward Peay	UC	7 Mar. 1887	6 Aug. 1887	
George T. Peay	UC	30 Apr. 1887	29 Sep. 1887	100
John Penman	P	10 Feb. 1886	13 Nov. 1887	25
John Penman	UC	13 Nov. 1887	6 Mar. 1888	25
Benjamin Perkin	UC	19 Dec. 1888	17 June 1889	300
Joseph C. Perry	UC	30 Sep. 1887	30 Mar. 1888	50
Christian Petersen	UC	25 Oct. 1887	25 Apr. 1888	300
Fred A. Petersen	A	5 Nov. 1887	25 Jan. 1889	
Frederick Petersen	UC	4 Oct. 1887	4 Apr. 1888	100
Jens Petersen	UC	10 Dec. 1887	11 June 1888	300
Peter Petersen	UC	30 Dec. 1886	29 May 1887	100
Peter Petersen	UC	24 Oct. 1887	8 Jan. 1888	
Peter Petersen	UC	24 Sep. 1892	19 Nov. 1892	
Hans J. Peterson	UC	21 June 1887	22 Dec. 1887	200
Hans Johan Peterson	UC	24 Nov. 1888	4 Mar. 1889	
Hans Peter Peterson	UC	20 Oct. 1888	2 Mar. 1889	100
Lars C. Peterson	UC	21 June 1887	20 Nov. 1887	50
Niels L. Peterson	UC	21 Sep. 1888	27 Jan. 1889	
Soren C. Peterson	UC	7 Mar. 1887	6 Aug. 1887	
Ishmael Phillips	UC	14 Feb. 1887	14 Aug. 1887	300
Matthew Pickett	UC	23 Feb. 1887	23 Aug. 1887	300
William Pidcock	UC	30 June 1886	9 Feb. 1887	
Isaac Pierce	UC	9 Oct. 1886	9 Feb. 1887	100
Thomas Pierpont	UC	1 Mar. 1888	1 Aug. 1888	100
Job Pingree	UC	13 July 1885	17 Nov. 1885	300
William Poppleton	UC	6 Jan. 1891	20 Feb. 1891	
Thomas Porcher	UC	21 Nov. 1885	25 May 1886	300
Engebredt Poulsen	UC	9 Oct. 1888	12 Feb. 1889	
James O. Poulsen	UC	1 Mar. 1886	7 Sep. 1886	300
Paul Poulsen	UC	24 Sep. 1888	4 Feb. 1889	200

continued

Name	Charge	Imprisonment	Release	Fine
Paul Poulson	A	22 Nov. 1888	8 July 1889	
Paul Poulson	UC	12 Oct. 1894	10 Nov. 1894	
John Powell	UC	20 Sep. 1889	2 Jan. 1890	
John A. Powell	A	4 Oct. 1890	27 Mar. 1891	
Parley P. Pratt, Jr.	UC	2 May 1885	14 Oct. 1885	300
Teancum Pratt	UC	25 Feb. 1890	25 Aug. 1890	100
William C. Prouse	UC	5 Mar. 1889	7 June 1889	
Savannah C. Putnam	UC	28 Nov. 1891	28 Dec. 1891	
John Quarnberg	A	24 Sep. 1889	24 Feb. 1890	
Peter L. Quist	UC	26 Sep. 1889	5 Feb. 1890	100
Frederick G. Ralph	UC	8 Jan. 1889	20 May 1889	
Henry Rampton	UC	16 Feb. 1889	1 May 1889	100
Andrew Rasmussen	UC	16 Mar. 1889	3 June 1889	
Neal P. Rasmussen	UC	24 Dec. 1888	24 June 1889	100
Edwin Rawlins	UC	24 Sep. 1888	7 Dec. 1888	75
Charles W. Rawlinson	UC	6 Oct. 1890	5 Dec. 1890	25
Daniel B. Rawson	UC	28 May 1887	27 Oct. 1887	100
Wm. T. Reed (WDRF)	UC	1 June 1889	10 Sep. 1889	100
Wm. T. Reid (MANTI)	UC	10 Mar. 1888	26 May 1888	300
Henry Reiser	UC	14 Feb. 1887	13 July 1887	300
George Reynolds	B	14 June 1879	20 Jan. 1881	500
Joseph B. Reynolds	UC	4 Mar. 1889	17 May 1889	50
Warren F. Reynolds	UC	23 Feb. 1889	13 Apr. 1889	50
Isaac Riddle	UC	30 Sep. 1887	29 Feb. 1888	300
Joseph H. Ridges	UC	26 Sep. 1887	26 Mar. 1888	25
William F. Rigby	UC	23 Dec. 1887	23 May 1888	
James Ritchie	UC	28 Feb. 1889	8 June 1889	200
Brigham H. Roberts	UC	1 May 1889	10 Sep. 1889	200
William Robinson	UC	26 Sep. 1886	26 Mar. 1887	300
William Robinson	A	14 Dec. 1889	14 Oct. 1890	
R. M. Rogers	UC	21 Mar. 1887	6 June 1887	
George Romney	UC	10 Oct. 1885	13 Mar. 1886	300
Mons Rosenlund	UC	5 Mar. 1889	27 June 1889	50
William A. Rossiter	UC	10 Oct. 1885	13 Mar. 1886	300
William C. Rounds	UC	14 Feb. 1889	26 May 1889	
Edwin Rushton	UC	3 Oct. 1887	12 Jan. 1888	50
William T. Sampson	UC	3 Apr. 1890	18 June 1890	
William T. Sampson	UC	26 Feb. 1894	11 May 1894	
Daniel A. Sanders	UC	23 Feb. 1889	15 June 1889	150
Henry W. Sanderson	UC	4 Mar. 1889	26 June 1889	100
Victor Sandgren	UC	13 Oct. 1887	13 Apr. 1888	100
William G. Saunders	UC	18 Feb. 1886	22 Jan. 1887	25

continued

Name	Charge	Imprisonment	Release	Fine
Levi Savage, Jr.	UC	30 Sep. 1887	29 Mar. 1888	300
Bernhard Schettler	UC	29 Feb. 1888	25 Apr. 1888	300
Edward Schoenfeld	UC	1 Mar. 1887	31 July 1887	50
Thomas Schofield	UC	26 Sep. 1886	26 Mar. 1887	300
Andrew P. Schow	UC	18 May 1890	13 Nov. 1890	300
Charles Seal	UC	5 Oct. 1885	8 Apr. 1886	300
Elijah Seamons	UC	25 May 1888	26 Nov. 1888	50
James Sellers	A	5 Mar. 1889	20 May 1890	
Elijah F. Sheets	UC	13 Oct. 1888	31 Dec. 1888	150
Marcus L. Shepherd	UC	28 May 1886	27 Oct. 1886	300
Luke Sherwood	A	24 Nov. 1890	24 Jan. 1891	
Milford B. Shipp	UC	18 Sep. 1888	1 Dec. 1888	65
Albert Singleton	UC	21 Mar. 1887	20 Aug. 1887	300
Joseph H. Sisam	UC	18 Feb. 1886	20 Mar. 1886	200
Anthon L. Skanchy	UC	7 Dec. 1889	18 Mar. 1890	100
Albert G. Slater	UC	21 June 1887	21 Dec. 1887	50
Albert G. Slater	A	31 May 1890	31 July 1891	
Thomas H. Smart	UC	19 Sep. 1887	19 Mar. 1888	300
Andrew Smith	UC	13 Oct. 1885	16 Apr. 1886	300
James Smith	UC	22 Sep. 1887	22 Mar. 1888	300
James A. Smith	UC	24 May 1894	8 Aug. 1894	
John Y. Smith	UC	27 Feb. 1886	30 Aug. 1886	300
Lewis Smith	A	22 Oct. 1892	22 Nov. 1892	
Ralph Smith	UC	21 Nov. 1887	21 Apr. 1888	100
Reuben Smith	UC	25 May 1886	24 Oct. 1886	
Samuel H. B. Smith	UC	20 Feb. 1886	23 July 1886	300
Warren B. Smith	UC	20 Oct. 1890	20 Apr. 1891	200
William R. Smith	UC	31 Mar. 1888	21 July 1888	300
James Smuin	UC	20 Apr. 1889	12 Aug. 1889	50
George D. Snell	UC	12 Apr. 1887	11 Sep. 1887	200
John W. Snell	UC	9 Mar. 1886	23 Nov. 1886	300
Don C. Snow	UC	12 Apr. 1887	11 Sep. 1887	50
Lorenzo Snow	UC	12 Mar. 1886	8 Feb. 1887	900
Willard L. Snow	UC	1 Oct. 1886	28 Feb. 1887	300
Hans Sorensen	A	30 Sep. 1889	1 Mar. 1890	
Soren N. Sorensen	UC	29 Feb. 1888	9 June 1888	50
Christian Sorenson	UC	29 Sep. 1888	14 Dec. 1888	
James L. Sorenson	UC	16 May 1889	2 Aug. 1889	
Jens Sorenson	UC	28 Nov. 1888	13 Feb. 1889	50
Lars C. Sorenson	UC	21 Nov. 1888	20 Dec. 1888	
John Spencer	UC	19 Nov. 1888	27 Feb. 1889	
Orson J. Spencer	UC	12 Feb. 1890	27 Apr. 1890	100
Harrison Sperry	UC	28 Feb. 1887	27 July 1887	300

continued

Name	Charge	Imprisonment	Release	Fine
John P. Squires	UC	31 May 1888	5 Oct. 1888	300
Henry Stander	A	26 Nov. 1888	26 Apr. 1889	
Henry Stander	A	26 May 1893	5 Sep. 1893	
Michael Standley	A	15 Mar. 1890	30 May 1891	
Edwin Standring	UC	12 Apr. 1887	11 Sep. 1887	200
Ulrich Stauffer	UC	13 Feb. 1888	13 July 1888	
James I. Steele	UC	14 Oct. 1886	14 Apr. 1887	600
Elijah Steers	UC	23 Dec. 1887	22 June 1888	300
Thomas C. Stephenson	UC	28 Oct. 1889	26 Mar. 1890	
James M. Stewart	UC	19 Sep. 1890	17 Feb. 1891	
Randolph H. Stewart	A	19 Nov. 1888	16 May 1889	
William A. Stewart	UC	7 Mar. 1890	17 June 1890	50
William A. Stewart	UC	24 Nov. 1893	8 Feb. 1894	
Joseph C. Stickney	A	20 Apr. 1889	20 Sep. 1889	
William Stimpson	UC	5 June 1886	20 Dec. 1886	300
Thomas Stirland	A	17 Jan. 1891	17 Nov. 1891	
John Stoddard	UC	29 Nov. 1886	31 May 1887	300
Andrew W. Stratford	UC	23 Dec. 1887	23 June 1888	100
Andrew W. Stratford	UC	25 June 1889	25 Nov. 1889	
James A. Stratton	A	20 Sep. 1894	28 Nov. 1895	
Andrew Stromberg	UC	27 Oct. 1887	27 Apr. 1888	100
Andrew Stromberg	A	27 Apr. 1888	27 Sep. 1888	
David M. Stuart	UC	4 Jan. 1886	8 July 1886	300
Traugott Stumpf	P	17 Dec. 1887	17 July 1889	
Lorenzo Stutz	UC	29 Nov. 1886	31 May 1887	100
Henry Sudweeks	I	14 May 1890	27 June 1891	
Richard H. Sudweeks	UC	26 Sep. 1886	26 Mar. 1887	600
Robert Swain	UC	2 Nov. 1885	6 May 1886	300
Peter Swansen	UC	31 Oct. 1893	8 Feb. 1894	
August Swensen	UC	4 Mar. 1889	17 May 1889	50
August Swensen	A	7 Nov. 1892	11 June 1893	
Lars Swensen	UC	9 Oct. 1888	21 Jan. 1889	50
Peter Swensen	UC	24 Dec. 1888	4 May 1889	100
John Tanner	UC	25 Mar. 1888	24 Sep. 1888	300
George H. Taylor	UC	1 Mar. 1886	4 Aug. 1886	300
Levi J. Taylor	UC	28 May 1887	27 Oct. 1887	100
Levi J. Taylor	UC	3 Oct. 1892	18 Dec. 1892	
Pleasant G. Taylor	UC	12 Oct. 1888	28 Dec. 1888	300
Samuel Taylor	UC	28 May 1888	13 Aug. 1888	
Stanley Taylor	UC	10 May 1886	10 Nov. 1886	300
Zachariah Taylor	UC	4 Oct. 1890	5 Mar. 1891	50
Henry Teeples	A	25 Feb. 1890	1 May 1891	

continued

Name	Charge	Imprisonment	Release	Fine
Charles A. Terry	A	20 Sep. 1890	27 July 1891	
Otis L. Terry	A	4 Oct. 1889	20 May 1890	
Daniel F. Thomas	UC	31 May 1888	16 Aug. 1888	300
Ed Thomas	UC	23 Sep. 1892	4 Dec. 1892	
John Thomas	A	18 May 1891	17 July 1891	
Gustav Thomasson	UC	17 Dec. 1887	18 June 1888	100
Richard Thorn	UC	1 Dec. 1888	12 Mar. 1889	100
Christian L. Thorpe	UC	29 Feb. 1888	12 June 1888	100
John Thorpe	UC	1 Dec. 1888	30 May 1889	100
Herman F. F. Thorup	UC	14 Mar. 1887	13 Aug. 1887	25
Herman F. F. Thorup	UC	8 Sep. 1890	8 Dec. 1890	
Joseph H. Thurber	UC, P	27 Dec. 1886	27 Feb. 1889	500
Hans Thurgeson	UC	15 Dec. 1889	13 Jan. 1890	50
Soren C. Thygerson	A	27 Oct. 1888	12 June 1889	
James H. Tidwell	UC	20 Apr. 1889	18 July 1889	
Henry Tingey	UC	13 Dec. 1888	23 Apr. 1889	200
Simon T. Topham	UC	23 Dec. 1888	21 June 1889	300
William H. Tovey	UC	1 Mar. 1887	2 Aug. 1887	25
William H. Tovey	UC	21 Apr. 1888	22 Oct. 1888	50
Helon H. Tracy	UC	26 Feb. 1886	29 Dec. 1886	
Amasa Tucker	A	24 Oct. 1891	13 Nov. 1891	
Henry Tuckett	UC	25 Apr. 1892	25 Oct. 1892	300
Gustave Turnberg	A	3 Nov. 1888	29 Apr. 1889	
Alfred Turner	UC	19 Nov. 1888	17 Jan. 1889	50
James Turner	UC	18 Sep. 1888	6 Nov. 1888	50
Joseph H. Turner	A	29 Mar. 1889	28 Oct. 1890	
Jesse R. Turpin	UC	14 Oct. 1887	14 Apr. 1888	100
James E. Twitchell	UC	25 Dec. 1885	28 June 1886	300
William Tyrell	A	27 Oct. 1893	14 Feb. 1894	
William Unthank	UC	22 Mar. 1887	21 Sep. 1887	300
Newman Van Leuven	UC	10 Oct. 1889	17 Jan. 1890	
Michel Vaughn	A	23 Mar. 1889	8 Nov. 1889	
James M. Wade	UC	13 Dec. 1888	24 Mar. 1889	
Joseph W. Wadsworth	UC	28 May 1887	27 Oct. 1887	
Samuel Wagstaff	UC	24 Sep. 1888	22 Dec. 1888	50
Niels O. Wahlstrom	UC	29 Nov. 1891	28 Dec. 1891	
Lorenzo Waldram	UC	26 May 1888	26 Nov. 1888	300
Joseph Walls	UC	29 Sep. 1892	7 Oct. 1892	200
John J. Walser	UC	10 Mar. 1888	10 Aug. 1888	100
William L. Walters	UC	4 June 1887	12 Dec. 1887	300
John Walton	UC	9 Oct. 1888	19 Feb. 1889	50
Richard Warburton	UC	20 Sep. 1886	21 Mar. 1887	300
John Warwood	UC	3 Nov. 1887	3 Apr. 1888	

continued

Name	Charge	Imprisonment	Release	Fine
John Warwood	A	24 Oct. 1891	13 Nov. 1891	
John B. Wasden	A	28 Mar. 1891	27 July 1891	
James C. Watson	UC	9 May 1885	12 Dec. 1885	300
James C. Watson	UC	11 Oct. 1887	11 Mar. 1887	300
Lorenzo D. Watson	UC	27 Mar. 1886	29 Sep. 1886	300
Lorenzo D. Watson	UC	23 Dec. 1888	21 June 1889	300
William H. Watson	UC	21 Feb. 1887	22 Aug. 1887	300
William H. Watson	UC	8 Mar. 1893	18 June 1893	
William Watterson	UC	8 Feb. 1889	23 Apr. 1889	300
Baldwin H. Watts	A	26 Sep. 1888	26 July 1889	
George C. Watts	UC	21 Apr. 1888	6 Aug. 1888	50
Gilbert Webb	A	20 Sep. 1892	19 Feb. 1893	
Hiram H. Webb	A	19 Mar. 1890	18 Aug. 1890	
Simon Webb	UC	11 May 1888	11 Oct. 1888	50
William R. Webb	UC	7 Mar. 1887	7 Sep. 1887	300
William R. Webb	A	10 Nov. 1888	25 Jan. 1890	
Francis Webster	UC	23 Dec. 1888	21 June 1889	300
Jens C. A. Weibye	UC	25 Feb. 1890	25 July 1890	
John Welch	UC	8 Feb. 1889	20 May 1889	
James Welsh	UC	15 Oct. 1887	16 Apr. 1888	50
Peter Westenschow	UC	9 Oct. 1888	20 Jan. 1889	
Levi L. Wheeler	UC	20 Nov. 1890	10 Dec. 1890	
M. B. Wheelwright	UC	24 Dec. 1888	4 Apr. 1889	
Isaac Whicker	UC	20 Sep. 1890	18 Feb. 1891	
Charles L. White	UC	6 Oct. 1885	7 Apr. 1886	300
Charles L. White	UC	2 Dec. 1889	2 May 1890	
Charles L. White	A	6 May 1891	15 Aug. 1891	
Hyrum G. White	A	13 Oct. 1894	13 Mar. 1895	
Frank Whitehead	UC	17 June 1889	2 Sep. 1889	
Edwin L. Whiting	UC	12 Apr. 1887	11 Sep. 1887	50
Henry Whittaker	UC	19 Feb. 1887	19 Aug. 1887	300
George Wilding	UC	21 Sep. 1887	21 Mar. 1888	100
Moses Wilkinson	UC	23 May 1890	4 Dec. 1890	150
Walter E. Willcox	UC	2 Oct. 1889	2 Mar. 1890	
William W. Willey	UC	10 Feb. 1886	19 July 1887	200
William Williams	UC	13 Feb. 1888	13 Aug. 1888	100
William Willie	UC	10 Dec. 1887	10 May 1888	150
Peter Wimmer	UC	28 May 1886	29 Nov. 1886	300
Peter Wimmer	A	25 Mar. 1890	25 Apr. 1890	
Anders W. Winberg	UC	28 Feb. 1887	29 Aug. 1887	300
Christopher S. Winge	UC	25 May 1888	26 Nov. 1888	50
Christopher S. Winge	UC, A	28 Nov. 1891	5 Mar. 1892	33.60
Jens P. C. Winter	UC	21 June 1887	21 Dec. 1887	300

continued

Name	Charge	Imprisonment	Release	Fine
Solomon A. Wixom	UC	28 Apr. 1887	28 Oct. 1887	300
George C. Wood	UC, P	29 May 1886	5 Nov. 1889	800
George H. Wood	A	14 Sep. 1890	11 Feb. 1891	
James A. Woods	UC	19 Sep. 1887	19 Mar. 1888	100
Samuel W. Woolley	UC	19 Dec. 1888	3 Mar. 1889	80
Thomas Woolley	UC	17 Feb. 1891	16 Mar. 1891	200
James Woolstenhulme	UC	24 Sep. 1888	27 Nov. 1888	65
Samuel Worthen	UC	25 May 1887	25 Nov. 1887	300
Hiram S. Wright	UC	3 Jan. 1893	3 June 1893	
John P. Wright	UC	30 Sep. 1887	30 Mar. 1888	50
Henry Yates	A	20 Nov. 1891	5 Feb. 1892	
Thomas Yates	A	21 Sep. 1889	1 June 1890	
William Yates	UC	13 Oct. 1887	13 Mar. 1888	50
Fred Yeates	UC	18 May 1888	19 Nov. 1888	100
Fred Yeates	UC	6 Jan. 1891	20 Feb. 1891	
Franklin W. Young	UC	18 May 1889	7 Dec. 1889	300
Parley R. Young	UC	27 Sep. 1888	29 Mar. 1889	150
Parley R. Young	UC	26 Feb. 1894	25 Apr. 1894	
Royal B. Young	UC	1 June 1886	10 Feb. 1887	900
Thomas Young	UC	9 Dec. 1887	9 June 1888	150
Isaac E. D. Zundel	UC	17 June 1889	28 Sep. 1889	100

APPENDIX 4

Selected Diaries, Journals, and Autobiographies of Mormon Polygamists at the Utah Penitentiary

This appendix gives the more important first-hand accounts written by Mormon cohabs that are located at major repositories; no attempt has been made to list all such accounts. The number of pages in the account provides an indication of the depth of coverage. Full information on the published accounts is given in the bibliography. Libraries are referred to by the standardized National Union Catalog abbreviations: CSmH = Henry E. Huntington Library; UHi = Utah State Historical Society; ULA = Utah State University; UPB = Brigham Young University; USlC = Historical Department, Church of Jesus Christ of Latter-day Saints; and UU = University of Utah.

Name	Pages of Coverage	Location and/or Publication
John Adams	31	UU
Reddick N. Allred	2	Carter, *TPH*, vol. 5
Christopher Arthur	18	UPB, ULA, CSmH
William Ashworth	5	UU, UPB, USlC, UHi
Charles R. Bailey	12	ULA
Henry Ballard	3	USlC, CSmH
John R. Barnes	7	USlC
Thomas Bingham	2	UPB, UHi
Joseph S. Black	13	UPB, CSmH, Carter, *OPH*, vol. 10
William Blood	8	USlC
William M. Bromley	46	USlC
James S. Brown	1	USlC, Brown, *Life of a Pioneer*
James Bywater	27	CSmH, Valentine, *Trio's Pilgrimage*
Abraham H. Cannon	192	UPB, USlC, UHi, ULA, UU

continued

Name	Pages of Coverage	Location and/or Publication
Angus M. Cannon	204	UPB, USlC
George Q. Cannon	14	UU, Cannon, *PHR*, vol. 16, USlC, but copy is restricted
Rudger Clawson	217	UU, UHi, USlC
Harvey H. Cluff	4	USlC, CSmH
Morton B. Cutler	2	UPB
Joseph H. Dean	348	USlC
Henry Dinwoodey	45	USlC, UU
Carl C. N. Dorius	1	USlC, Carter, *OPH*, vol. 2
George Dunford	24	USlC
Gottlieb Ence	3	UU, UHi
William Fotheringham	4	UU, CSmH
Herbert J. Foulger	128	USlC, UU
John T. Gerber	82	USlC
William Grant	27	UPB, UU, USlC
Duckworth Grimshaw	5	UU, USlC, Carter, *Pioneer Heritage*
Henry Hamilton	34	USlC
Joseph S. Horne	26	USlC
William Y. Jeffs	36	USlC, UU
Ole A. Jensen	3	UPB
David John	165	UPB
John Lee Jones	10	UPB
Abraham A. Kimball	19	USlC, UPB, UHi
Thomas W. Kirby	99	USlC, UPB
George Kirkham	49	USlC
James Kirkham	64	USlC
George C. Lambert	304	USlC, Carter, *Heart Throbs*, vol. 9
Francis M. Lyman	?	USlC, but papers are restricted
James May	1	USlC, UU
Thomas F. H. Morton	18	USlC
James Moyle	49	USlC
James H. Nelson	26	*Autobio. of James H. Nelson*
James M. Paxton	53	USlC
John Penman	2	USlC
Teancum Pratt	4	USlC
Henry Reiser	50	USlC, ULA
George Reynolds	46	USlC, but papers are restricted
Brigham H. Roberts	6	UU, USlC is restricted
William Robinson	43	USlC, UU
Levi Savage, Jr.	68	UPB, UHi, UU, ULA, Hilton, *Levi Savage*
Elijah F. Sheets	2	USlC

continued

Name	Pages of Coverage	Location and/or Publication
Ralph Smith	9	USlC
Lorenzo Snow	?	USlC, but papers are restricted
Harrison Sperry	3	USlC
John P. Squires	11	USlC
George H. Taylor	55	UHi
Levi J. Taylor	169	USlC
Pleasant G. Taylor	2	USlC
Charles A. Terry	17	UPB
John Thomas	10	UPB
Helon H. Tracy	74	UU
Jens C. A. Weibye	13	USlC
George C. Wood	302	USlC
William Yates	7	USlC
Franklin W. Young	12	USlC

SELECTED BIBLIOGRAPHY

Alexander, Thomas G. "Charles S. Zane, Apostle of the New Era." *Utah Historical Quarterly* 34 (Fall 1966): 290–314.
———. *Things in Heaven and Earth: The Life and Times of Wilford Woodruff, a Mormon Prophet.* Salt Lake City: Signature Books, 1991.
Allen, James B. " 'Good Guys' vs. 'Good Guys': Rudger Clawson, John Sharp, and Civil Disobedience in Nineteenth-Century Utah." *Utah Historical Quarterly* 48 (Spring 1980): 148–74.
Anderson, Nephi. "Rudger Clawson." *Juvenile Instructor* 35 (1 Dec. 1900): 772–76.
Baird, Russell N. *The Penal Press.* Evanston, Ill.: Northwestern University Press, 1967.
Bashore, Melvin. "Life behind Bars: Mormon Cohabs of the 1880s." *Utah Historical Quarterly* 47 (Winter 1979): 22–41.
Brown, James S. *Life of a Pioneer, Being the Autobiography of James S. Brown.* Salt Lake City: G. Q. Cannon, 1900.
Brown, Vernal A. "The United States Marshals in Utah Territory to 1896." M.S. thesis, Utah State University, 1970.
Cannon, Abraham H. "Mormons in Prison." In *Voices from the Past: Diaries, Journals, and Autobiographies,* comp. Campus Education Week Program, Education Week Department, Division of Continuing Education, Brigham Young University. Provo, Utah: Brigham Young University Press, 1980.
Cannon, Kenneth L., II. "After the Manifesto: Mormon Polygamy 1890–1906." *Sunstone* 8 (Jan.–Apr. 1983): 27–35.
———. "Beyond the Manifesto: Polygamous Cohabitation among LDS General Authorities after 1890." *Utah Historical Quarterly* 46 (Winter 1978): 24–36.
Cannon, M. Hamlin, ed. "The Prison Diary of a Mormon Apostle [George Q. Cannon]." *Pacific Historical Review* 16 (Nov. 1947): 393–409.
Carter, Kate B., comp. "The Diary of Reddick N. Allred." In *Treasures of Pioneer History,* 5:297–373. Salt Lake City: Daughters of Utah Pioneers, 1956.
———. "The Dorius Family." In *Our Pioneer Heritage,* 2:253–64. Salt Lake City: Daughters of Utah Pioneers, 1959.
———. "The Journal of George Cannon Lambert." In *Heart Throbs of the West,* 9:269–384. Salt Lake City: Daughters of Utah Pioneers, 1948.
———. "The Journal of Joseph Smith Black." In *Our Pioneer Heritage,* 10:257–320. Salt Lake City: Daughters of Utah Pioneers, 1967.

Clawson, Rudger. Journal, [Nov.–Dec. 1884]. Rudger Clawson Collection, Manuscript 481, Bx 2, Fd 1, Special Collections, Marriott Library, University of Utah, Salt Lake City.

———. Letters to Lydia Spencer Clawson, 3 Nov. 1884–7 Sep. 1887. Rudger Clawson Collection, Manuscript 481, Bx 16, Fds 4–6, Marriott Library, University of Utah, Salt Lake City.

———. [MS I] "Personal Experiences in the Utah State Penitentiary." Rudger Clawson Collection, Manuscript 481, Bx 2, Fds 2–7 and Bx 26, Fd 1, Marriott Library, University of Utah, Salt Lake City.

———. [MS II] "Personal Experience in the Utah State Penitentiary." Rudger Clawson Collection, Manuscript 481, Bx 2, Fds 8–11 and Bx 26, Fds 2–3, Marriott Library, University of Utah, Salt Lake City.

———. [MS III] "Personal Experience in the Utah State Penitentiary." Rudger Clawson Collection, Manuscript 481, Bx 26, Fds 4–9, Marriott Library, University of Utah, Salt Lake City.

———. [MS IV] "Memoirs of the Life of Rudger Clawson Written by Himself." Rudger Clawson Collection, Manuscript B-21, Utah State Historical Society, Salt Lake City. Microfilm (Manuscript 8912), Archives, Historical Department, Church of Jesus Christ of Latter-day Saints, Salt Lake City.

———. [MS V] "Memoirs of the Life of Rudger Clawson Written by Himself." Rudger Clawson Collection, Manuscript 481, Bx 1, Fds 1-13, Marriott Library, University of Utah, Salt Lake City.

———. [MS VI] "Personal Experience in the Utah State Penitentiary of Rudger Clawson." Manuscript 2690, Archives, Historical Department, Church of Jesus Christ of Latter-day Saints, Salt Lake City.

Day, Robert B. "Eli Azariah Day: Pioneer Schoolteacher and 'Prisoner for Conscience Sake.' " *Utah Historical Quarterly* 35 (Winter 1967): 322–41.

Driggs, Ken. "The Prosecutions Begin: Defining Cohabitation in 1885." *Dialogue: A Journal of Mormon Thought* 21 (Spring 1988): 109–25.

Embry, Jessie L. *Mormon Polygamous Families: Life in the Principle.* Salt Lake City: University of Utah Press, 1987.

———. "Ultimate Taboos: Incest and Mormon Polygamy." *Journal of Mormon History* 18 (1992): 125–45.

Evans, Rosa Mae M. "Judicial Prosecution of Prisoners for LDS Plural Marriage: Prison Sentences, 1884–1895." M.A. thesis, Brigham Young University, 1986.

Firmage, Edwin Brown, and Richard Collin Mangrum. *Zion in the Courts: A Legal History of the Church of Jesus Christ of Latter-day Saints, 1830–1900.* Urbana: University of Illinois Press, 1988.

Foster, Lawrence. *Religion and Sexuality: The Shakers, the Mormons, and the Oneida Community.* Urbana: University of Illinois Press, 1984.

Gillespie, L. Kay. *The Unforgiven: Utah's Executed Men.* Salt Lake City: Signature Books, 1991.

Grow, Stewart L. "A Study of the Utah Commission: 1882–96." Ph.D. diss., University of Utah, 1954.

Guynn, Randall D., and Gene C. Schaerr. "The Mormon Polygamy Cases: Politics, Religion, and Morality in the Court of Last Resort." *Sunstone* 11 (Sept. 1987): 8–17.

Hardy, B. Carmon. "Self-blame and the Manifesto." *Dialogue: A Journal of Mormon Thought* 24 (Fall 1991): 43–57.

———. *Solemn Covenant: The Mormon Polygamous Passage.* Urbana: University of Illinois Press, 1991.

Hill, James B. "History of Utah State Prison, 1850–1952." M.S. thesis, Brigham Young University, 1952.

Hilton, Jerold A. "Polygamy in Utah and Surrounding Area since the Manifesto of 1890." M.A. thesis, Brigham Young University, 1965.

Hilton, Lynn M., ed. *Levi Savage Jr. Journal.* [Salt Lake City:] John Savage Family Organization, 1966.

Hoopes, David S., and Roy Hoopes. *The Making of a Mormon Apostle: The Story of Rudger Clawson.* Lanham, Md.: Madison Books, 1990.

Hoopes, Roy. "My Grandfather, the Mormon Apostle: Discovering a Giant in the Family." *American Heritage* 41 (Feb. 1990): 82–92.

Hopper, Columbus B. *Sex in Prison: The Mississippi Experiment with Conjugal Visiting.* Baton Rouge: Louisiana State University Press, 1969.

James, Kimberly J. " 'Between Two Fires': Women on the 'Underground' of Mormon Polygamy." *Journal of Mormon History* 8 (1981): 49–61.

Jenson, Andrew. "Prisoners for Conscience Sake." Manuscript 2690, Archives, Historical Department, Church of Jesus Christ of Latter-day Saints, Salt Lake City. MS copy, Accession 381, Marriott Library, University of Utah, Salt Lake City.

Jorgensen, Victor W., and B. Carmon Hardy. "The Taylor-Cowley Affair and the Watershed of Mormon History." *Utah Historical Quarterly* 48 (Winter 1980): 4–36.

Kirby, Dale Z. "From the Pen of a Cohab." *Sunstone* 6 (May–June 1981): 36–39.

Larson, Gustive O. *The "Americanization" of Utah for Statehood.* San Marino, Calif.: Huntington Library, 1971.

Larson, Stan. *A Ministry of Meetings: The Apostolic Diaries of Rudger Clawson, 1898–1904.* Salt Lake City: Signature Books, 1993.

———. "Rudger Clawson: A Prisoner of Polygamy before and after the Manifesto." Paper presented at the Sunstone Symposium, 24 Aug. 1990, Salt Lake City.

Linford, Orma. "The Mormons and the Law: The Polygamy Cases." *Utah Law Review* 9 (Winter 1964): 308–70; 9 (Summer 1965): 543–49.

Lyman, Edward Leo. *Political Deliverance: The Mormon Quest for Utah Statehood.* Urbana: University of Illinois Press, 1986.

Mandell, James E. *History of the Utah State Prison, 1850 to 1935.* [Salt Lake City, 1935].

Mulder, William. "Prisoners for Conscience' Sake." In *Lore of Faith and Folly,* ed. Thomas E. Cheney, 135–44. Salt Lake City: University of Utah Press, 1971.

238 / *Selected Bibliography*

Nelson, Horace J., ed. *Autobiography of James Horace Nelson, Senior.* Portland, Ore.: Press of Kilham Stationery and Printing, 1944.

Nicholson, John. *The Martyrdom of Joseph Standing; or, The Murder of a "Mormon" Missionary—A True Story. Also an Appendix, Giving a Succinct Description of the Utah Penitentiary.* Salt Lake City: Deseret News, 1886.

O. W. W. T. [John Nicholson]. "Sketches and Reminiscences of Prison Life." *The Contributor* 8 (Dec. 1886): 75–79.

Paxton, James M. *The Cotter and the Prisoner or Whisperings from the "Pen".* Salt Lake City, 1889.

Quinn, D. Michael. "LDS Church Authority and New Plural Marriages, 1890–1904." *Dialogue: A Journal of Mormon Thought* 18 (Spring 1985): 9–105.

Seifrit, William C. "The Prison Experience of Abraham H. Cannon." *Utah Historical Quarterly* 53 (Summer 1985): 223–36.

Tompkins, Dorothy Campbell, comp. *The Prison and the Prisoner.* Berkeley: Institute of Governmental Studies, University of California, 1972.

Utah State Prison Admission Records. Series 80388, Utah State Archives, Salt Lake City.

Valentine, Rose Ellen Bywater, comp. *The Trio's Pilgrimage: Autobiography of James Bywater, including Brief Life Sketches of His Wives Maria Thomas [and] Hanna Maria Jensen.* [Salt Lake City,] 1947.

Van Orden, Richard D. "A Brief History of Corrections in Utah, 1853–1978." MS, dated 6 June 1978, Accession 612, Marriott Library, University of Utah, Salt Lake City.

———. "A History of the Utah State Prison, 1950–1980." M.A. thesis, University of Utah, 1981.

Van Wagoner, Richard S. *Mormon Polygamy: A History.* 2d ed. Salt Lake City: Signature Books, 1989.

Walters, Jean Ann. *A Study of Executions in Utah.* N.p., 1973.

Whitney, Orson F. *History of Utah.* 4 vols. Salt Lake City: George Q. Cannon and Sons, 1892–1904.

INDEX

Utah Territorial Penitentiary. *See* Prison

Van Leuven, Newman, 229
Varian, Charles S., 205
Varnell's Station, Georgia, 1
Vaughn, Michel, 229
Venereal disease, 145

Wade, James M., 229
Wadsworth, Joseph W., 164, 229
Wagstaff, Samuel, 229
Wahlstrom, Niels O., 229
Waldram, Lorenzo, 229
Walls, Joseph, 229
Walser, John J., 229
Walters, William L., 164, 229
Walton, John, 229
Warburton, Richard, 126, 131, 229
Warwood, John, 164, 229–30
Wasatch Literary Association, 1
Wasatch Mountains, 195
Wasden, John B., 230
Washington, D.C., 119, 156, 159
Washington, George, 64, 104
Watkins, J., 132
Watron, John, 124–25
Watson, Hugh, 173
Watson, James C., 60, 77, 85, 90, 122, 155, 158, 164, 173–74, 230
Watson, Lorenzo D., 102, 118–19, 121, 230
Watson, William H., 140, 145, 230
Watterson, Edward, 86, 132
Watterson, William, 230
Watts, Baldwin H., 230
Watts, D. C., 132
Watts, George C., 230
Watts, Gilbert, 230
Webb, Hiram H., 209, 230
Webb, Simon, 230
Webb, William R., 140, 230
Webster, Francis, 230
Weibye, Jens C. A., 230, 234
Welch, John, 230
Welcome, Fred. *See* Hopt, Fred
Welsh, James, 155, 164, 230
West, Caleb W., 110–19, 137, 163
Westenschow, Peter, 230
West Jordan, Utah, 139
West Weber, Utah, 136

Wheeler, Hank, 65, 147
Wheeler, Levi L., 230
Wheelwright, M. B., 230
Whicker, Isaac, 230
White, Charles L., 26, 83, 230
White, Hyrum G., 230
White, Nellie, 198
Whitehead, Frank, 230
Whiting, Edwin L., 141, 230
Whittaker, Henry, 140, 230
Wilding, George, Sr., 155, 230
Wilkinson, Moses, 230
Willcox, Walter E., 230
Willey, William W., 101, 118–19, 121, 230
Williams, William, 230
Williamson, Ernest, 125, 132
Willie, William, 164, 230
Wimmer, Peter, 107, 131, 162, 230
Winberg, Anders W., 140, 146, 230
Winge, Christopher S., 230
Winter, Jens P. C., 164, 230
Wixom, Solomon A., 141, 231
Wood, George C., 30, 92, 107, 132, 135, 152, 165, 231, 234
Wood, George H., 231
Woodruff, Abraham Owen: exhorted to post-Manifesto polygamy, 18
Woodruff, Wilford: offered dedicatory prayer at grave of Brigham Young, 1; issued Manifesto, 6, 17, 22; approved Clawson to receive second anointing, 15; forbad discussion of polygamy at conference, 15–16; possible post-Manifesto marriage of, 31; described two kinds of polygamists, 139; mentioned, 8, 129, 133, 139
Woods, James A., 155, 231
Woolley, Samuel W., 231
Woolley, Thomas, 231
Woolley, Young, and Hardy Co., 122
Woolstenhulme, James, 231
Word of Wisdom, 9
Worthen, Samuel, 164, 231
Wright, Hiram S., 231
Wright, John P., 155, 231
Wright, Leander, 132

Yates, Henry, 231
Yates, Thomas, 231

STAN LARSON received his B.A., M.A., and M.L.I.S. degrees from Brigham Young University and his Ph.D. from the University of Birmingham in Birmingham, England. Previously he has published *Unitarianism in Utah: A Gentile Religion in Salt Lake City* (coauthored with Lorille Miller) and *A Ministry of Meetings: The Apostolic Diaries of Rudger Clawson, 1898–1904.* He has also published articles on Mormonism in *Dialogue, Journal of Mormon History, Sunstone, BYU Studies, Ensign,* and *Trinity Journal.* Presently he is in charge of the Utah History, Philosophy, and Religion Archives of the Marriott Library at the University of Utah. He is married to Patricia Margaret Rowsell, and they have five children (Timothy, James, Daniel, Deborah, and Melissa) and three grandchildren (Andrew, Brittany, and Caitlin).